CHILDREN GOING

dartington social research series

Making Residential Care Work: Structure and culture in children's homes
Elizabeth Brown, Roger Bullock, Caroline Hobson and Michael Little

Secure Treatment Outcomes: The care careers of difficult adolescents
Roger Bullock, Michael Little and Spencer Millham

Research in Practice: Experiments in Development and Information Design
Roger Bullock, Daniel Gooch, Michael Little and Kevin Mount

Children Going Home: The re-unification of families
Roger Bullock, Daniel Gooch and Michael Little

The Children Act 1989: Putting it into practice (2nd edition)
Mary Ryan

Children Going Home

THE RE-UNIFICATION OF FAMILIES

Roger Bullock
Daniel Gooch
Michael Little
Dartington Social Research Unit

Aldershot • Brookfield USA • Singapore • Sydney

Published by
Ashgate Publishing Limited
Gower House
Croft Road
Aldershot
Hants GU11 3HR
England

Ashgate Publishing Company
Old Post Road
Brookfield
Vermont 05036
USA

British Library Cataloguing in Publication Data
Bullock, Roger
    Children going home : the re-unification of families.
    (Dartington social research series)
    1.Social work with children 2.Separation anxiety in
    children
    Research
    I.Title II.Good, Daniel III.Little, Michael, 1958-
    362.7

Library of Congress Cataloging-in-Publication Data
Bullock, Roger.
    Children going home : the re-unification of families / Roger
    Bullock, Daniel Gooch, Michael Little.
        p.   cm.
    Includes bibliographical references and index.
    ISBN 1-84014-494-7. – ISBN 1-84014-496-3 (pbk. : alk. paper)
    1. Children–Deinstitutionalization–Great Britain. 2. Problem
children–Great Britain–Family relationships. 3. Foster children-
-Great Britain–Family relationships. 4. Family reunions–Great
Britain. I. Gooch, Daniel. II. Little, Michael, 1958-
III. Title.
HV866.G7B84   1998
362.7–dc21   98-34053
                                                         CIP

ISBN 1 84014 494 7 (Hbk)
ISBN 1 84014 496 3 (Pbk)

Printed and bound in Great Britain by
Biddles Ltd, Guildford and King's Lynn

Contents

Index of tables and figures

Figures

Checklists

Acknowledgements

This study has been prepared by members of the Dartington Social Research Unit, Roger Bullock, Daniel Gooch and Michael Little. It would not have been possible without the active support of their colleagues at the Research Unit and the help of several local authorities and voluntary and independent organisations. We are extremely grateful, too, to the social workers, families and children who helped us with our task: we were made welcome, often at moments of uncertainty and anxiety, and it is only through their perseverance with our tedious requests that we were able to learn about issue of return.

The research was funded by the Department of Health and we would like to thank the Directors of Research and Development, Professor Sir Michael Peckham and Professor John Swales. The study would not have been possible without the assistance of the Social Care Division and the Social Services Inspectorate and we are grateful for their help. We have also benefited greatly from the research management undertaken by Dr Carolyn Davies.

Finally, we wish to thank colleagues in universities, local authorities and voluntary agencies who have advised, assisted and commented on our work. Particular thanks go to David Gordon for his statistical advice and to Michael Kelly for his typesetting skills.

Preface

This book brings up to date and extends the description of research first published by Dartmouth in 1993 as *Going Home: The Return of Children Separated from their Families*. The account of much of the earlier work is repeated here, but it is more than an ordinary revision of an old text: it reports on the extensive testing of a predictive model described in the closing chapters of the earlier book and, as a result, reaches rather different conclusions. It was felt that the new work deserved a new title; we hope we will not be accused of window dressing.

1 Introduction

Since the Second World War, one of the most cogent issues to preoccupy those concerned with the care of children has been the best way to manage involuntary rifts between parents and children. Many previous studies have charted the effects of separation on children and the difficulties parents and wider family have in maintaining contact, particularly when the absence is long and stressful. Yet, despite this knowledge, there has been relatively little interest in the corollary of separation: return. As is so often the case with social systems, more emphasis has been given to entry than to exit.

Nonetheless, despite the paucity of research interest in return, getting children back home has long been an integral part of child-care. Fifty years ago, the evacuation of children from cities during the Blitz aroused great anxiety. The maintenance of links between families and absent loved-ones was very difficult. Telephones were few, letters often went astray and visits were almost impossible. Separation was also difficult to manage at an administrative level. Many of those who were subsequently to take key roles in the children's departments of local authorities, created in 1948 as a consequence of the Curtis Report (HMSO, 1946), began their child-care careers coping with the tearful city children who arrived brown-labelled in the shire counties, Welsh valleys and sleepy West Country. These experts, along with a posse of wireless gurus whose broadcast chats enlivened many a damp evening in the Anderson shelter, all shared the pervading gloom that children evacuated to the countryside would soon lose touch with home and become rootless. Winnicott, Priestley and the Brains' Trust joined with Lord Haw-Haw in a chorus of doom. For example, Winnicott (1984) warned mothers in a broadcast talk in 1945 that returning evacuees would be extremely difficult to manage.

1

What I want to say now is that when children come home they are not necessarily going to fall into and fit nicely into the holes that they made when they went away, for the simple reason that the hole has disappeared. Mother and child will have become able to manage without each other and when they meet they will have to start from scratch to get to know each other. This process must take time and time must be allowed. It's no use mother rushing up to the child and throwing her arms around his neck without looking to see whether he is going to be able to respond sincerely.

In a subsequent talk he emphasised that,

their return means that your life will be richer, but less your own. There will be few immediate rewards. At times, you will wish all of them back again in billets. Indeed, some children will have been so hurt by evacuation that it is beyond the power of parents to manage them.

This can hardly have been a welcome prospect for mothers also awaiting the return of husbands.

But like the maelstrom from which the children were rescued, so the consequences of evacuation seemed at first to be different from those first feared. Return was achieved by the vast majority. The widespread unease generated by separation was dismissed with official hindsight as an over-dramatisation from the well publicised behaviour of a few children entering Winnicott's clinic. Indeed, in the euphoria of peace it was emphasised that some children had the time of their lives and were much better cared for. Neither was there a catalogue of abuse and neglect inflicted by their frequently grudging hosts.

It is possible that the effects of the evacuation upon the children involved were mitigated because both separation and return were group experiences. Both were undertaken with school friends and supervised and organised by teachers who themselves were sharing the pains of upheaval. The Jewish experience at the 'return' to Israel of children surviving the holocaust likewise suggests that the pains of separation and loss were reduced because it was a group experience and because a shared ideology gave it purpose and direction. Yitzhak Kashti, a survivor of the holocaust, described to us how,

normality was confirmed by the group, particularly for young children, in that they found it difficult to envisage any alternative and were swallowed up by the daily demands of coping. I cannot remember being acutely distressed at being separated, I was just numb and busy keeping afloat.

These may be among the reasons why the return of evacuated children caused fewer administrative problems than expected and why the apprehensions that many children would find themselves abandoned or the victims of dual loyalties were not borne out. Thus, the problems of separation remained seared into the administrative memory, mainly because it was very difficult to organise, while return, which was, after all, going back to normal, caused little lasting concern (Titmuss, 1976). Separation also touched a sad chord in group consciousness, amply orchestrated by Vera Lynn, Gracie Fields and other hardy annuals, while the difficulties of return did not. Coming home was obviously a rapturous experience, the stuff of which made many 'B' movies. The fact that return might contain as many private griefs as separation had to wait for returning servicemen, prisoners of war and residual evacuees to highlight the issues (Johnson, 1968).

In the past decade, interest in the return of children from long separations and the problems faced by families on reunion has been revived, due to a variety of pressures. First, there has been increasing exploration of the outcomes of welfare interventions. Profound questions have been raised concerning the State's ability to parent. Particularly influential in raising the issue of return has been the emphasis on the need for hard criteria to evaluate the success or otherwise of various aspects of child welfare. Sadly, numerous studies of children in state care have revealed the drift and insecurity many experience while away from home. In addition, there has been a growing awareness that the majority of children and adolescents return home after separation in spite of lengthy absences and cogent reasons for the initial rift. Whether professionals like it or not, good substitute care is difficult to provide and most children's families shoulder the burden of support for their offspring when the State's interventions falter. The *Children Act* 1989 rightly emphasises that an attitude towards planning of 'let's wait and see' is unlikely to be compatible with the best interests of children looked after.

A second reason for the increased interest in return has been an awareness that not only do children eventually go home but that both children and families also find the process extremely stressful. For example, Pill (1979) highlights how difficult children coming home from hospital are likely to be.

> Return is likely to be stressful for the whole family not only for the returning child and the degree of upset is not necessarily related to the length of time spent away.

The stress that return places on children and families has once more become of interest to social workers because much work demonstrates not only that return is difficult but that the problems generated by reunion can also be sufficient to cause breakdown and further separations. In Little's study of Young Men in Prison (1990) a young man comments

> banged up in here is bad enough but going home isn't likely to be a bed of roses either.

A third explanation for an increased concern about the return of children looked after has been the gathering emphasis on the need for family participation in welfare processes in order to ensure the continuities of care essential for satisfactory child development. This means that return as well as separation have to be managed and going home no longer represents the close of the episode. Indeed, the multi-disciplinary teams now obligatory in the approach to child abuse and delinquency are constant reminders that the difficulties families face are usually complex and of long standing. Problems may be inter-generational and have long careers of their own in which the children's current difficulties play but a small part. Thus, return and separation are again being viewed as part of a process in which roles, territory and family relationships are continuously under negotiation.

These theoretical and practical concerns should excite more than academic curiosity. Research findings now consistently stress the complicated careers of children looked after and the potentially adverse consequences of many apparently benign interventions. However, in contrast to other groups of separated children, such as those in hospital or boarding schools, the returns of children looked after are difficult to predict. Sometimes the child's natural family will have dissolved and reconstituted during the child's absence and, as a consequence, key family members will be scattered across different households, the memberships of which may be fluid and volatile. In addition to these changes in personnel, families may relocate geographically while the child is away. When these probabilities are linked to the changes of placement and social worker experienced by many children whilst looked after, the potential complexity surrounding the child's return home becomes apparent. Return for many a child looked after is more than just fitting back into a niche previously left; it is re-negotiating a set of roles, adapting to new faces and re-mastering unfamiliar school and community territories. All of these occur in a context where family structures and memberships may have changed and where the links between children and families may also have become tenuous. Return home is by no means the end of the story. Moreover, as will be seen, re-admission to substitute care after return is not uncommon.

Nonetheless, for most children looked after, a swift, enduring rehabilitation to their family is the central goal of care planning during separation. The successful management of a child's return home and his or her subsequent adjustment to family, neighbourhood and school should, therefore, be among the indicators of a satisfactory social services' intervention and the willingness or ability of the family to change. Unfortunately, not only is there a dearth of information both in terms of established concepts and research explanation but there are also few practical guide-lines for social workers faced with the management of a child's reunion with his or her family. The need to scrutinise the cluster of decisions surrounding a child's return home from substitute care and to suggest ways in which reunion might be effectively managed should be seen against this background. The aim has been to gather insights into the social work process and to develop an understanding of the adaptations of individual family members during the return period. In addition, attempts have been made to develop clear guide-lines for social workers faced with return decisions and considerable care has been taken in defining when a reunion can be said to be successful. How, then, has this scrutiny of return been approached?

Fashioning a research design

Return as a process

The study *Lost in Care* (Millham et al., 1986) focused on the child-care process, exploring the decisions made by social workers about separated children over time. Two other child-care studies subsequently confirmed the benefits of this perspective and the importance of return as a research issue. Rowe, Hundleby and Garnett's (1989) study of child-care placement patterns and outcomes, for example, indicated that the large majority of children who cease to be looked after, go home. However, Farmer and Parker (1991) showed that returns did not always endure, and nor were children's needs always met once back at home. The social work profession has long been anxious for more information on and guides to good practice in returning children home. However, child-care practitioners also thought that it would be helpful in viewing children's return to weigh the implications of particular factors, such as family reconstitution or elements of 'risk', in the social work management of individual cases.

Thus, a broad view of return was encouraged. For example, could return be viewed as the state re-investing or sharing parenting duties with the child's natural family? As will be seen, it is noticeable that whereas the divesting of parental power on a child's separation is marked by elaborate symbols and rituals, the reinvestment of parental power appears to have fewer rites of passage, legal safeguards or accountability. Indeed, if parents were able to give up parenting responsibilities as easily as the State, they would probably be viewed as deficient. On the other hand, few parents of looked after children would qualify as suitable foster parents, although many have their children living with them.

It was decided, therefore, that the research should cover a wide range of looked after children, including those separated under voluntary arrangements and in emergencies. Scrutiny has also fallen upon oscillators or 'yo-yo' children as they were previously known, that is, children who frequently move in and out of substitute care. However, it should be stressed that return should not be equated with the legal process of ceasing to be looked after nor necessarily be viewed as a successful resolution to a child's difficulties. Return home should be perceived as a placement, which like others, has positive and negative aspects and should be viewed in the context of children's longer term looked after 'careers'. Indeed, a child may experience a number of reunions and have to manage return to a wider variety of situations, of which the family is only one.

Children's looked after careers

Several previous studies have highlighted the difficulties experienced by children and adolescents in making transitions. Many of these moves involve not only changes of role and status but also geographical separation and subsequent return home. These issues have been explored in follow-up studies of young offenders, those leaving residential care and children moving from school to employment. It was found that at each transition, the options open to children were often limited by what had gone before. These inter-connections were best understood by using the concept of a care 'career' as this incorporated a developmental perspective on children's experiences.

Naturally, the ways that different children and parents cope with return will vary but it seems from these previous studies that leaving any situation that is alternative to their home will engender difficulty, even for those children whose separation has been short. Children's subsequent careers can also be complex. It will be noted later that many older adolescents moving to live in the community stay intermittently with relatives. Although existing theoretical perspectives on children's careers concern the experiences of individual children, many children return home from care or accommodation accompanied by siblings and have to re-negotiate entry into households radically changed in membership and location.

Definitions of return

Although going home after an absence may appear straightforward, return is a concept requiring considerable clarification. For example, at what point does frequent access between parents, family and child become return? When does lengthy absence from the home, as is common amongst adolescents, cease to be family membership? At what point do children cease to view their households as home? What level of structural change in the natural family renders the transition not a return but a move to a completely new ambience? Is the family to which the child returns a site or a set of relationships? It has been necessary in this study to clarify these issues, particularly as answers to these questions will differ according to the age, gender, social class, ethnicity and culture of participants.

In view of these difficulties in defining return, it was decided that the research should be concerned with all children looked after who go *home* to *live*. By *home* is meant the house of a parent or other relative but not necessarily the parent or other relative from whom the child was separated. Going home to *live* necessarily involves an extended stay. As such, children returning for weekend leaves or for preparatory visits prior to eventual reunion would not be considered to have returned, although these restorations have been scrutinised as possible indicators of a successful return subsequently.

Outcomes

A further concern has been the development of appropriate outcome measures, the complexities of which have been explored for child-care by Parker (1990), Ward (1995) and colleagues. Clearly, any child-care outcome emanates from the outcomes of earlier interventions. Hence, an understanding of a child's return to home and family is incomplete without a consideration of the reasons behind the initial separation. Any measurement of the outcomes of reunion must look at features of the return itself, such as whether it endures and what it provides for the child; it must also consider participants' perceptions of return, such as whether the families' and children's expectations are met, agreements upheld and stresses mitigated; finally, it must assess the consequences of the child's return for social services and other agencies, such as whether the child is looked after again, what problems arise and how effectively agencies co-operate in their resolution. Because of the complexity of child-care cases, as the following pages reveal, the returns experienced by children can seldom be viewed as entirely successful or as catastrophic. As in most human relationships, credits have to be weighed against debits.

Aims of the research

It was against this background that the studies were undertaken. The aims are as follows:

i.   To clarify the concept of return through an exploration of child-care law and relevant literature.

ii.   To scrutinise the return process as experienced by looked after children, concentrating particularly on the sequence of events that precede and follow reunion.

iii. To chart the processes and return avenues experienced by all looked after children.

iv. From this data to identify groups of children particularly vulnerable to return difficulties, such as re-abuse, placement breakdown, behaviour problems and family rejection.

v. To highlight factors significantly associated with the likelihood of return and its success.

As it was intended that the study would assist social work practice, an additional aim was:

vi. To inform social workers about the most effective ways of preparing and managing children's returns.

In the pages that follow, the issue of return is explored in several complementary studies. Firstly, there is a scrutiny of reunion in child-care law and research in a variety of contexts. Secondly, the progress of 24 families and their 31 children who were selected by social services as highly likely return candidates is followed in considerable detail. This analysis reveals something of the problems faced by individual families welcoming home a son or daughter from a substitute care placement. Finally, the results of a major study of children looked after are presented. This study involved over a thousand children, over a period of more than a decade. Initially, the care careers of 875 children looked after in the 1980s were re-analysed and hypotheses drawn from the emerging data. These hypotheses were then tested prospectively on a sample of 463 children separated from parents in 1993 in order to identify the factors that best predict the likelihood of a child's reunion and its success.

How to read this book

With a complicated research design, it is inevitable that readers will find some aspects of the study more relevant to their work than others. To help clarify the contribution that each part of the research makes to an understanding of the return process, the book is divided into four sections, each dealing with a particular issue.

Part I (Chapters 1-5) looks at return in child-care law, policy and research.

Part II (Chapters 6-12) presents findings from an in-depth study of the return process.

Part III (Chapters 13-15) explores who out of all looked after children goes home.

Part IV (Chapters 16-17) examines how social workers can predict which looked after children return home and whether the reunion is successful.

The study begins with a look at return in child-care policy and law.

Summary points

1. The impact of the Second World War on the relationship between the state and the family was considerable. Since that time, the rights of parents and children have been increasingly recognised and the need for parents to remain in contact and to share in the welfare and happiness of their separated children has been clearly demonstrated.

2. As most children return home after separation it would seem wise to know more about reunion and to manage the reconciliation sufficiently well to minimise subsequent breakdown and repeated severance of family bonds.

3. There is a need to know how many children and adolescents go home, in what ways groups of young people differ and the reunion problems each group presents. How long do they remain looked after and in what ways do aspects of separation affect the likelihood and success of reunion?

4. There has been an increase in interest in the outcomes of welfare interventions, particularly in the success or failure of social work to solve the problems of separated children and their families.

   a) This investigation of children and families experiencing reunion has three strategies:

b) an intensive look at the experiences of 31 children from 24 families likely to experience reunion;

c) an extensive scrutiny of 875 children and adolescents as they return home; and

d) testing hypotheses derived from the two previous studies prospectively on a sample of 463 children separated from their families in 1993.

2 Return in child-care policy and law

The half-century since the Second World War has seen a shift in child-care policy, away from child rescue and the exclusion of the natural family towards encouraging parental participation in the care task; 'shared care'. There has been growing recognition of the heterogeneity of family and children's needs and the strategies necessary to meet them. Here the legislation and accompanying guidance concerning the issue of reunion are explored.

The last two decades have seen considerable changes in the situation of parents and separated children. For example, the recommendations of the Warnock Report (Department of Education and Science 1978) led, via subsequent education acts, to the greater integration of children with special educational needs into ordinary day schools. The growth of residential schools serving the difficult or less able child has thus been checked (Parker 1988, Gooch 1996). Within both ordinary and special education, greater rights to consultation and powers of appeal have been granted to parents.

Likewise, not only has separation been discouraged within child-care policy but, as will be shortly noted, the *Children Act* 1989 gave parents considerable power *vis-à-vis* social services and enjoined co-operation from all parties. An emphasis is given to parental participation in the rearing of children even if they are unable or reluctant to provide nurture themselves. Far from being excluded from the care of separated children, parents are expected to take a key role.

Unfortunately, resistance to change among professionals in bureaucratic organisations is well documented and there remains the perennial problem of just how effective legal arrangements prove to be.

Several studies have demonstrated that improvements in social work practice are difficult to engineer (Ward 1995). The reluctance of social workers to share with parents the care of their separated children has a healthy pedigree and a philosophy of child rescue may still influence policy and practice unnecessarily.

Certainly the rights of parents who, for a variety of reasons, failed or were unable to look after their children did not haunt the conscience of those who administered the Poor Laws and it is not difficult to understand why. Today it is fashionable to criticise 19th century welfare approaches to children at risk but any guided holiday tour of downtown Cairo or Mexico City would encourage us to entertain more charitable attitudes towards the efforts of Lord Shaftesbury, Dr. Barnardo, Thomas Coram and others. The sprawling inner cities of the Third World mirror the problems of Victorian England. Even the gaunt walls and closed gates of the industrial and reformatory schools might excite a more sympathetic understanding, springing, as they did, from a context where anarchy seemed constantly to threaten and half the population was under twenty-five.

The number of children living in desperate circumstances was very considerable and through vagrancy, disease and prostitution, the 'street Arabs' represented an ever present threat to the respectable; and, quite as potent, a constant reproach to the religious. Certainly the doors of the workhouse were unwelcoming but destitute children represented an almost overwhelming burden. As Parker (1990) points out, for more than a century, a third of those receiving indoor relief were children and, if separation from impoverished parents gave these waifs access to better conditions, allowed them to be educated and receive vocational skills, then isolation from families and neighbourhood seemed a small price to pay.

There were also other constraints on the Poor Law besides discouraging the poor able-bodied and their children from seeking relief. As today, economy suggested that the fewer children and families for whom the state assumed responsibility, the lower would be the cost. Frequently severance from children occurred as a by-product of efforts to get parents back to work and off relief. There was universal concern at the cycles of deprivation and of pauperisation; that poverty and dependence in one generation of a family were invariably repeated in the next. If poor children could be rescued swiftly and early enough and placed far from contaminating influences, among which natural families and inner city neighbourhoods were deemed as particularly potent, then cyclical misery could be broken; particularly when youthful independence, resilience and orthodoxy were cemented and strengthened by strong religious faith.

In practice, however, not all child-care organisations worked with such vigour to separate and rescue the luckless, impoverished and delinquent children of the 19th Century. In Aberdeen, for instance, Sheriff Watson and Alexander Thomson established the Industrial Feeding Schools and proudly stated that the

> family is the place prepared and ordained by God for the training and upbringing of children, and this is an ordinance which men can never infringe with impunity. (Smeaton, 1869)

Mor enduring concern of the voluntary organisations, highly influenced by the severance lobby, that training would be rendered ineffective when parents reclaimed their children at 16, many separated children did, in fact, go home. Ward (1990) found that over a quarter (27%) of children coming under the aegis of the Waifs and Strays Society between 1887 and 1894 were reunited with parents or other relatives.

But it was not surprising in such a welfare climate that the return of children after a long separation was not a practice priority. Those children who did return went home more by default than through active encouragement. Indeed, when parents requested the return of older children who had been long separated, particularly when their offspring's earning might cancel out the insupportable burden that they had previously posed, official eyes usually viewed parental desire for reunion as evidence of cupidity. While the late 19th and early 20th century legislators repeatedly anguished over curtailing the common law rights of fathers in relation to the custody of their children and legitimating the State's power to intervene, there was in the legislation almost no mention of return. Not until 1948, when a duty was placed on local authorities to ensure that children and parents were reunited as soon as possible, if appropriate, did the law face up to the problems of access and reunion.

During the Second World War a marked shift in policy can be detected, although practice, in some areas, had already outstripped policy. The prevailing ideology in the 1940s and 1950s was to increase the role of public services in the care of children, to extend foster care and to get separated children back home as quickly as possible. There were several reasons for these policy changes. As was seen earlier, the evacuation of children from the inner cities exposed to an ignorant public the deprivations and needs of the poor. In addition, many residential institutions for children and young people were taken over by the military and were never subsequently re-opened. Most evacuees were successfully placed in private family homes, that is fostered by default, and at the end of the war, much to everyone's surprise, all but a very few children were reclaimed by their parents, so contradicting popular and professional expectations cited by Parker (1990) that a quarter of a million children would be left abandoned. Such parental devotion, in spite of the many difficulties facing inner-city families as the war ended, challenged assumptions about fecklessness and indifference among poor parents.

Furthermore, the increased scrutiny of child-care provision revealed low standards in much of child-care and in residential institutions in particular. These deficiencies were highlighted in the Curtis Report of 1946. There were other problems after the war: the high costs of capital renewal and a strict quota on building materials deterred welfare agencies from renewing or expanding institutional provision. The changing employment patterns among women also added to the difficulties of providing substitute care. Finally, of course, the growing acceptance of psychological theories which stressed the damage wrought by separation also led to a re-assessment of the importance of family and the wisdom of maintaining bonds with parents.

All of these trends were reflected and implemented in the new legal and administrative framework brought about by the 1948 *Children Act* and the local authority children's departments which were created as a result. Nevertheless the vigorous pursuit of the swift rehabilitation of separated children has been tempered by two factors. First, there has been an increasing concern with prevention rather than treatment. Indeed in the last 20 years, the number of children looked after has fallen across the country as a result of deliberate policies; one criterion against which a successful child-care service is measured has become the low numbers in care or accommodation at any one time. The 49% drop between 1976 and 1996 has no historical precedent. Alongside this, child protection became a growing issue throughout the 1980s and has highlighted the damage done by keeping children in, or returning them to, dangerous situations. This tension and the need to balance services are accepted as intrinsic features of child welfare and have modified extreme commitments to prevention and return (Department of Health, 1995). Thus, a far more sober and 'refocused' view of children's situations is now entertained.

There is also a growing awareness of the heterogeneity of children's needs and the range of provision required to meet them. Rather than pretend that vulnerable children need never be looked after, attention has turned to improving their experiences while there. The perception of prevention as being merely one child-care approach and not the only valid policy should modify the negative view of being looked after as something harmful and worthless, a view which has been particularly influential in recent years.

The *Children Act* 1989 reduced these difficulties by establishing a range of services for children and families, some of which may involve the child's living away from home. The aim has been to reduce the stigma of welfare interventions, to provide services which encompass the family's involvement and to achieve re-unification as smoothly and speedily as possible, should it be in the best interests of the child.

Return in child-care law

The return of separated children is rarely mentioned in child-care law. Indeed, compared with the elaborate procedures surrounding the removal of a child from his or her parents and the precise delineation of those attendant duties to be assumed by others, the arrangements for a child's leaving care or accommodation and returning home seem almost cavalier. The tendency noted earlier for welfare systems to be more concerned with how children get into systems than how they get out is confirmed. In the Curtis report of 1946, return is not even discussed.

However, while the word 'return' did not appear in the legislation that followed, there was an explicit statement in the 1948 Act that children in care voluntarily should not remain there longer than is absolutely necessary for their welfare.

Nothing in this Section 2 (2) of the Act shall authorise a local authority to keep a child in their care under this Section if any parent or guardian desires to take over the care of the child, and the local authority shall, in cases, where it appears to them consistent with the welfare of the child to do so, endeavour to secure that the care of the child is taken over either (a) by a parent or guardian of his or (b) by a relative or friend of his.

This expectation was made explicit because, for a long period, considerable benefit could accrue to those sheltering children and adolescents, particularly those in residential care. However, the historical antecedents of child-care law are also reflected in the only condition attached to reunion, namely that the relative or friend should be 'where possible, a person of the same religious persuasion as the child'.

For children on care orders under the *Children and Young Persons Act* 1969, there was a similar requirement constantly to review the need for the child to remain in care. The local authority had a duty under Section 27.4 of this legislation to review after six months had elapsed whether to make an application for the discharge of the care order, although this did not apply to children committed to care in family proceedings or in parental rights resolutions. Several other well established legal principles had implications for a child's return from care. For example, Section One of the *Child-Care Act* 1980 required local authorities generally to seek to obviate the need to keep children in care.

A further concern with the welfare of children once they have left care was re-emphasised in the 1983/84 report on children in care by the House of Commons Social Services Committee, chaired by Renée Short, although their recommendations reflected a long-standing disquiet about children's long-term welfare. For example, the 1927 report of the Departmental Committee on the Treatment of Young Offenders concluded that the value of training can be thrown away if support is not afforded after release.

The Short report recommended that legislation, which had 'become the conglomerate of centuries', should be rationalised. This was taken up by the 1985 *Review of Child-Care Law*. In its report, the Review Committee accepted the principles of returning children home as soon as the need for absence diminished and proposed that the requirement to return children to their families swiftly should become an overall duty, irrespective of the child's legal status, and subject to safeguarding the child's welfare. The Committee's recommendation also dropped the religious requirements previously noted and added some safeguards for natural parents when their children returned elsewhere. The review suggests that

> local authorities should seek to return any child in their care to the care of a parent or guardian or, failing this, a relative or friend, unless this is contrary to the child's best interest. In the latter two cases, the parent should be informed and consulted.

The report of the Child-Care Law Review was the first occasion that return as part of a child's care career received special attention. Naturally, as this review informed the *Children Act* 1989, it followed that the need for successfully managing the return of children and adolescents separated from their families was emphasised in this legislation, particularly by giving local authorities a clear duty to return looked after children. In fact, the Act went further than this by also including principles and requirements to facilitate their successful reunion. For example, the welfare principle requires that return be constantly viewed as an option and a checklist is provided to ensure consistency when decisions are made. Similarly, the careful management of children's separations and looked after careers encouraged by the legislation reduces the risk of subsequent return problems. The benefits of continuity have been emphasised in subsequent judgements, for example on the need to consider the dangers of disrupting the *status quo* when separation is a possibility (Humberside County Council v B (1993) 1FLR 257). They are also manifest in the requirement for regular reviews, the need to consider the child's wishes and the support given to children and families after reunion. Particularly significant is the emphasis on promoting contact between separated children and parents, relatives and friends, the elimination of all informal barriers to contact and the requirement in care proceedings (Section 34) for access arrangements to be a part of care order conditions.

The principles espoused in legislation were expanded in accompanying regulations and guide-lines. These consider the issues of return or 'reunification'. For example, *The Guidance and Regulations on Family Placements* provides practical advice for social workers helping children to return successfully and is extremely sensitive to the stresses associated with reunion. Paras 4.38-4.40 specify:

> The aim should be to achieve a planned ending to a placement with careful preparation and transition, whether to their family, another placement or adoptive placement.

A child's return to his family may need equally careful preparation, and a child and family may need support over the settling-in period until the child is re-integrated into the family. A period of gradual re-introduction may be needed, depending on the length of time the child has been away from home and the extent of changes in the family. The need for continuity is equally critical at the end of a placement as at the beginning. Children often return to different addresses, new babies in the family, new step-parents and step-brothers and sisters. Sometimes a child must change schools and leave behind friends and interests acquired during foster placement. Parents too, need to be prepared for changes in the child's habits, interests and routines; and for the possibility of disturbed behaviour while the child is settling in.

It is sometimes appropriate for contact between a former foster parent and child to continue for a time through visits, telephone calls or letters. In most cases it is helpful to foster parents to be given news of how the child has settled into his new life. Feedback of this kind can contribute to their development in the fostering role.

The regulations concerning children who return to live with parents while remaining on care orders are even more extensive, mostly because of the risks associated with the return home of abused children. Following the recommendation of inquiries into the deaths of Jasmine Beckford and other children at risk, *Charge and Control Regulations* were implemented in 1989. At first, they caused some confusion, as the new arrangements seemed over-elaborate. As a result, weekly access of adolescents to their families in some CHEs was checked by zealous local authorities until references and family situations had been verified. However, the judgement in Regina v Newham, ex parte B, 1989 ruled that the new requirements need only apply when the permanent return of a child to the care of a relative, guardian or friend was envisaged and not to holiday or extended visits.

The regulations accompanying the *Children Act* 1989 on the ¬lacement of children in care with relatives introduced further changes to the conditions for returning children home. For example, short stays are included, provided they are longer than 24 hours and parents retain some parental responsibility under care orders but the placement of children with their relatives and friends is excluded, provided no previous residence order is in force, such arrangements being subject to the *Foster Placement Regulations* 1991. Considerable control has to be exercised over the return of children from compulsory care to their parents, to those with parental responsibility or those with residence order rights. Before the placement, for example, written views on the proposed move must be sought from a wide variety of sources and carefully considered. The child, the parent, others with parental responsibility and agencies such as the district health authority, the child's doctor, the authority in the new area to which a child might move and all those currently and potentially likely to be involved in the child's welfare have to be consulted. Indeed, enquiries have to be made about all the factors necessary to provide 'a general picture of the carers, their households and life style'.

In the same way, the child's return must be discussed by the new household, hopefully clarifying the roles, relationships and care responsibilities that will be adopted. A placement agreement then has to be drawn up and the local authority must visit the child regularly, see him or her alone and ascertain the views of both the child and the sheltering household. Interactions between the child and family must also be observed and information should be gathered from schools and other contexts in which the child may have manifested behaviours and feelings independently. Similarly, the arrangements for the emergency protection of children and after-care duties are designed to promote effective rehabilitation. In the former, there is a duty on the applicant who gained the order to return the child once it is safe to do so and, in the latter, external guide-lines are provided on the support of young people up to the age of 21. Thus, return issues are implicit in many of the decisions and procedures now in operation.

Such guidance is sensitive to children's return problems and the perspective adopted in this research, namely *return as a process*. However, practice can still be somewhat limited for some groups. The approach to after-care, for example, can be rather child-focused if it is predominantly concerned with linking a range of services to individual cases. There can also be complications if a local authority and parents are in dispute. The courts have no power as such to order a phased return home or to require the local authority to provide the necessary support once the child has returned, even if it is in his or her best interests.

The point underlying all these discussions is that return is a process which faces all children separated from home, whatever their age and length of stay, and the adaptations that children and their families need to make if reunion is to be successful are considerable. There is a risk that the human and spiritual needs of children and their families can get lost in preoccupations with services and case management. Neither is there much evidence that the passage of time and its impact on families receives sufficient consideration. Putting legal guidance into operation requires knowledge about the return experiences of children and families, both at a macro level, such as who goes home and when, and at a micro level, such as the stresses and strains faced by individuals.

Conclusion

This chapter has charted changes in child-care policies and law with regard to the departure and return of separated children. Prior to the *Children Act* 1948, the severance of children 'at risk' from their families was common practice, such policies being reinforced by a variety of political and religious ideologies and moralistic attitudes as well as by practical requirements and economic opportunities. Yet, even in such inauspicious situations, more children returned to their families than might have been expected.

Ideas on children's separation from and return to families were further influenced by the events surrounding the Second World War. The evacuation of children had highlighted the deleterious effects of insensitively handled departures and an increased scrutiny of child-care provision had revealed poor standards. Also, the successful returns of most evacuees questioned assumptions about the fecklessness of poor families. The 1948 Act that reorganised child-care services, emphasised the need to avoid the unnecessary separation of children from their parents and the benefits of swift rehabilitation, whenever possible. This policy still prevails, although it has since been tempered somewhat in the light of developments in child protection and preventative strategies.

The *Children Act* 1989 and its accompanying guidance and regulations, all reflected a growing awareness of the careers of children looked after and the need to maintain continuities in children's lives, both features highlighted in recent child-care research. They also perceived return as an important part of that career. It is a process in itself and is an outcome of earlier decisions and separations. Thus, the implication in both the current legislation and regulations is that return is best managed as much by reducing the problems of traumatic separation, drift, isolation and poor after-care as by handling it effectively when it occurs. This policy is pithily stated in para 2.33 of Volume 2:

> The Act requires local authorities to promote contact between a child who is being looked after and all those who are connected with the child unless it is not reasonably practicable or consistent with the child's welfare. The Act also firmly addresses the re-unification of a child with his family. These are linked issues. If contact is not maintained, re-unification becomes less likely and recognition of this has to underpin all considerations in planning for a child.

Summary Points

1. The *Children Act* 1989, in seeking to simplify and give coherence to the legislation regarding children and families, particularly by seeking parental co-operation and in stressing voluntary arrangements, discourages separation and increases the sharing of care between local authorities and families.

2. A swift return is envisaged for the majority of those children who have to be separated from their families. Not only is separation of children from parents discouraged by the legislation but, at reunion, support is an obligation on social services.

3. For those children who remain vulnerable while at home there is a duty on the local authority to advise and 'befriend' and to assist those in need up to the age of 21 years.

4. The *Children Act* 1989, in its requirement for regular reviews, the need to consider the child's wishes, the freedom of access accorded

to most parents and the support given to families after reunion, thrusts the management of return into the forefront of social work practice.

3 The return experience identified in child-care research

This chapter explores the research material on looked after children returning home or moving to live in the community. Although few recent research studies have focused on the problems children and families face in managing reunion, the research offers considerable evidence on the numbers leaving care or accommodation, their destinations and the duration of their reunions. In addition, groups of children vulnerable to problems on return can be identified. Consumer studies and evidence from abroad are also useful.

Return in literature

Returns are liable to be emotional affairs. The excitements, tensions and problems surrounding separation and return touch people's innermost feelings, as much through perceptions of home and everything associated with it as through a sense of belonging and identity. Such aspects of the human condition are almost 'too deep for tears', to borrow Wordsworth's words, let alone amenable to simple and objective analysis. It is not surprising, therefore, that return home has long exerted a hold over the imagination of writers and poets. The heroes cut off for one reason or another from their home and the problems they encounter on their return to what has become for them an alien environment have provided the stuff of legends such as the Odyssey. It has also proven a rich source of both comedy and tragedy, farce and family drama, not to mention being a rich source of narrative in the Bible.

Some literary descriptions of return are simply sentimental;

24

Browning's 'Oh to be in England' and Payne's 'There's no place like home' spring instantly to mind. Other, more subtle texts succeed better in capturing the emotions, negotiations and adjustment difficulties explored in this study. MacNeice, for example, imagines Ulysses recollecting home whilst far away; 'Here could never be home, No more than the sea around it. And even the sea is a different sea round Ithaca'. Memories of home, on the other hand, may be more satisfactory than the real thing. Fanny Price, for example, found Portsmouth 'men all coarse, the women all pert, everybody underbred' on a visit home from Mansfield Park. Some literary figures echo the experiences of children looked after when they return to changed families and new home situations. Hamlet, for instance, returned from school in Wittenberg to find not only his beloved father dead but his mother married to his father's murderer. This is perhaps an extreme example: Wordsworth found awkwardness and lack of cordiality among former friends due to something as simple as preferring different clothes. Odysseus was unrecognised on arrival, and even then it was his nanny who was first to understand, while Jane Eyre's similar dismay was compensated for by the greetings of the dog, Pilot.

Return is clearly an ambivalent event. Whether it is resolved in tears of joy, as for Ulysses, or tears of grief, as for Hamlet, will depend largely upon its subjects' ability to readjust. War poets describe the difficulties of fitting in once back from fighting. Paul in *All Quiet on the Western Front* wistfully concludes, 'A sense of strangeness will not leave me; I cannot feel at home among these things'. Reunion implies making fresh sense of a world once understood and, as such, is a painful business. Those who are separated seem driven to return, either to resume things at the point at which they left off or to incorporate separation into their identity and give meaning to the rift.

But while numerous poets and authors have fathomed the deep emotions of those who return, the event usually has some wider function, such as to dramatise tragedy or comedy. Interestingly, few literary studies look at the return experiences of children. Thus literary comparisons with children's return from care, the focus of interest, cannot be taken too far. What, then, does recent child-care research tell us about the return of separated children?

Return in child-care research

The child-care research literature on return can be divided into two groups. The first group - longitudinal studies of children looked after - is potentially highly relevant, but small. Such studies have drawbacks for the purposes of this book. Since they focus on children looked after, few studies examine in any great detail what happens to the children following return. The exceptions tend to be from the United States or Canada (Simard et al., 1991; Maluccio et al., 1993b; Fuchs, 1993) but caution must be taken when translating research findings from one national context to another. There is in addition the body of work that underpinned the *Children Act*, 1989. The Dartington Unit's *Lost in Care* (Millham et al., 1986), Vernon and Fruin's (1986) *In Care; A Study of Social Work Decision Making*, Farmer and Parker's (1991) *Trials and Tribulations* and Rowe and colleagues' (1989) *Child Care Now* are authoritative works, but all investigated practice prior to the 1989 legislation. More recent research (Packman and Hall, 1998) and the evidence accumulating from this study suggest some changes but whatever their drawbacks, these longitudinal studies offer a wealth of insight and data and provide a context for the present study.

A second group of 'return literature' is much larger, but can be somewhat tangential. This comprises studies of specific and often specialised interventions and institutions for children and young people, such as hospitals and prisons. Here, return home is usually incidental to the main research focus. Events following return are scrutinised for the light they shed on the effects of interventions, rather than for the exploration of return itself. These studies focus on very specific, usually institutional, populations separated from their families for specific reasons. In the context of return from psychiatric hospital, for example, Pilling (1991) warns against,

> the critical approach which assumes that all that is wrong with most, if not all the patients, is that they have spent too long in a large mental hospital. Such an assumption is a denial of the disability and suffering that long-term mental illness brings for many people. A danger of this assumption, particularly as it is generally unspoken, is that it will lead to inadequate preparation and support for people leaving hospital. Unfortunately, when things do not work out the blame will usually be laid at the hospital's door.

It would be naive to assume that what applies to return in one context - from boarding school, say - can be applied uncritically to another, such as return from prison. Neither, however, must one lose sight of what all these returning children and young adults have in common. It was Bowlby's insight that separation could be considered a phenomenon irrespective of its context. This review of the literature, examines how far this is also true of return.

The first group of literature - general cohort studies of children in care or accommodation - is considered in this chapter, and the second - studies of specific, usually institutional, populations - in the next.

Studies of children's care careers

The National Children's Bureau report *Caring for Separated Children* (Parker, 1980) was one of the first to provide specific guidance on the return of children to their parents. Pointing out that return to parents fell from 77 to 71% of all discharges during the 1970s, it concluded that

> it is hard to know.....how much more rehabilitation could be achieved (or achieved more quickly) given regular contact with parents and the mobilisation of help and support.....what might enable parents to keep their children in the face of adversity is likely to be similar to what is needed to help them resume their care.....the mode of discharge blends into preventive measures to avoid further admissions to care.

The early 1980s saw widespread concern about the ballooning numbers of children in state care and the consequent 'drift' they experienced. In response, the then Department of Health and Social Security commissioned a number of studies, several of which covered the whole spectrum of children involved. The Dartington contribution considered the problems of maintaining links between children in care and their families and was published as *Lost in Care*. This study, which followed 450 children looked after for two years after separation, highlighted the fact that nearly nine in ten of these children eventually returned home. The evidence also suggested that the return process was fraught. Moreover, difficulties were likely to be compounded by several factors, including changes in the membership, structure and location of the child's family while he or she was away and the tendency for links between child and family to wither during the separation. Such problems affected even short-stay cases, a third of whom returned to households where there had been a change in membership or location and nearly two thirds of whom experienced difficulties in maintaining contact with their families while looked after.

For those children long separated, family links frequently withered. Although families and separated children rarely lost their sense of belonging, many found it increasingly difficult to maintain regular contact. In addition to formal barriers erected to safeguard children's welfare, there were various informal impediments in place. A third of the children, for example, were placed more than 20 miles from home. Routines and attitudes amongst foster-parents and residential staff often made parents feel unwelcome. Frequent change of placement led, amongst other things, to the splitting of sibling groups. Whilst such developments called for a redoubling of social work efforts to maintain contact, the reality was more likely to be a gradual loss of professional interest. In the second year of separation, nearly half the children were visited by parents less than once a month and social workers had lost touch with one mother in three. These findings were disquieting on their own; with the knowledge that many of these children were destined to return home they became doubly so.

A second study in the DHSS research programme, Vernon and Fruin's *In Care: A Study of Social Work Decision Making*, reiterates many of the points just made. Although concerned mainly with factors affecting the duration of separations, this research produced one additional finding significant for a study of return. Whilst many social workers are ideologically opposed to placing children in State care and have considerable scope to influence children's care careers once there, they nevertheless rarely work towards children's return. Hence, factors other than social work actions tend to determine what happens to children and the social work influence on case histories is more by default than design. The returns of many children, therefore, are unlikely to be either planned or purposefully pursued by social workers. Indeed, return may only become an issue when raised by parents or children or when precipitated by extraneous event, such as the child absconding or a foster home breakdown. The authors write, since at the time of entry to care social workers demonstrated a basically negative attitude to care, it is surprising, if not a matter of some concern, that the balance of factors contributing to children leaving care should be so heavily weighted towards factors other than social work involvement.

In a third study in the DHSS programme, Packman and colleagues looked at 361 children seriously considered for admission to state care. Of these, 161 were actually looked after and the remaining 200 stayed at home, although at least 45 of these were separated later on. Six months after the initial scrutiny, 26 (16%) of the 161 admissions had returned home but had been looked after again, so suggesting a failed return. Packman's study is particularly pertinent to an understanding of this latter group, a category of children that has received little research attention, and her follow-up study is discussed below.

Packman and colleagues' findings were confirmed in Rowe, Hundleby and Garnett's (1989) analysis of the patterns and outcomes of child-care placements. They looked over a two year period at all admissions, discharges and moves among children looked after in six English local authorities; 5,688 children were studied and more than 10,000 placements charted. The majority of children discharged went home to family or their local community. Only 2% were adopted. Nevertheless, as many as seven per cent of all departures involved young people reaching the age of 18 years whose return was necessitated by legal requirements rather than welfare considerations. Moreover, 18% of all those children who returned home during the two years were re-admitted within the study period and 7% of them twice. Such figures mirrored those of Packman and colleagues, and the 22% and 6% found in the *Lost in Care* study.

Research since the implementation of the Children Act, 1989

Much of the research described above contributed to the changes in child care policy and practice that were incorporated in the *Children Act*, 1989. The legislation was implemented in 1991 and one important source of longitudinal evidence to emerge has been Packman and Hall's (1998) exploration of the use of Section 20 of the Act, which allows children to be looked after under voluntary arrangements between parents and the local authority. They studied 153 children looked after in eight social work teams in the two cities first studied in Packman's 1986 study *Who Needs Care?*.

The new research shows that six months after separation nearly half (46%) the children had returned home and were still there. Only one in five (20%) of the 153 children had remained looked after during the entire six month period. On the other hand, nearly a quarter (24%) had returned home but unsuccessfully at least insofar as they were once again being looked after six months after separation. Moreover, one in ten had returned twice during the six months. When Packman and Hall returned to these 153 children 18 months later, the pattern of oscillation was even more exaggerated. The majority (52%) of children had by now gone home *and* been looked after again and nearly a quarter (24%) had experienced more than one reunion.

In some situations, such as in respite care arrangements for children with disabilities, separations from family were short and infrequent. For other children, it was the returns that proved to be temporary. Nonetheless, these rates for being looked after again following reunion with family are twice as high as those found by Millham et al. (1986), Packman et al. (1986) and Rowe et al. (1989) prior to the 1989 legislation. This tendency for oscillation to replace a single longer stay as a strategy for children who need to live away from the family home is not limited to the social services: it is similarly noticeable in health and education (Gooch, 1996). Whether these changes are desirable can be judged from the data collected for this study and reported in later chapters.

Why do some children but not others settle happily back at home? If children on programmes of regular respite care are removed, Packman and Hall's data can be re-analysed to identify risk factors for subsequent periods of being looked after following return home. In this context a 'return breakdown' is defined as any re-admission to care or accommodation following return.

The age group most likely to experience 'return breakdown' was not, as might have been expected, teenagers but children of primary school age. Aspects of the child's behaviour, particularly a tendency to violence or self-harm, were also good predictors of difficulties following return, although, interestingly, offending as such did not increase the risk of breakdown. The reasons for the initial placement were also important especially if the initial separation had been attributable to parental mental illness, alcohol or drug abuse. Tensions between siblings and concerns about child protection were also associated with further separation.

The child's experiences during separation also bore upon the chances of a successful return. Overall, the more change experienced during separation, the less likely was a successful reunion. An especially powerful predictor of difficulties following return was a change of placement during separation but changes in the composition of the child's birth family in their absence also had a disruptive effect. Where family difficulties spilled over into the school the chances of further separation were increased.

Logistic regression techniques, such as those described in Appendix A, permit the extraction of the four factors which, in combination, best predict return breakdown. It was found that children aged five to eleven separated because they were not getting on with their carer and causing difficulties at school who then experienced a breakdown in placement while away from home were many times more likely to have difficulties on reunion. These findings are summarised in Table 3.1 below. Whether factors predicting difficulties for children returning home under Section 20 of the *Children Act* will hold for all children looked after will be seen in Chapter Sixteen.

Table 3.1: Success of return by presence or absence of risk factors

	% 'return breakdown'	df	p
All children	44	-	-
Referral to SSD from school	55	1	ns
Carer/child relationship a major cause of original separation	51	1	<0.05
Child aged 5 to 11	63	2	<0.05
Placement changes during separation	61	1	<0.05
Only one factor, or no factor applies	32	3	<0.01
Any two factors	40	3	<0.01
Any three factors	65	3	<0.01
All four factors (n=4)	100	3	<0.01

Studies of children placed with parents

Prior to the implementation of the *Children Act*, 1989 it was common for a child to return to relatives yet remain legally in state care. This placement was called 'home on trial', but is now termed placement with relatives or friends. Such children are included in Rowe, Hundleby and Garnett's *Child Care Now* (1989) and Thoburn's *Captive Clients* (1980) and are the focus of Farmer and Parker's *Trials and Tribulations* (1991*)* and, in Northern Ireland, by Pinkerton's *Home on Trial in Northern Ireland* (1991).

Thoburn's study was the first to alert social workers to the large numbers of children living at home while in care and to explore the particular difficulties that 'home on trial' placements posed. In an intensive study of 34 children she found that such placements were rarely negotiated and that parents had little choice in what was offered to them - hence the title of her book, *Captive Clients*. Three influences were found to bear on the decision to let children go home. These were: the attitudes of parents and children and their reactions to the placement; the attitudes of the social workers and the nature of the practical and emotional support offered and the quality of the placement. Most important of all, however, was the determination of the parents and - when old enough - the children to stay together as a family.

Nearly a decade later, Rowe and colleagues found that of all the placement types considered, 'home on trial' was the least likely to endure for as long as social workers thought advisable. A third of such placements ended prematurely, a risk which affected all age groups. Indeed, using the criteria of whether the aim of the placement was met and whether it endured, Rowe concluded that only 36% of placements with parents were successful. The aims of placements at home were mostly associated with providing an ambience for care and upbringing. Nevertheless, there was a wide range of other situations. Nearly a third of the children under ten were returned as part of an assessment exercise and for 26% of those aged 11 or over, the placement was viewed as a 'bridge to independence'. Social workers' assessments of such placements varied considerably according to the aims behind the return, as shown in Table 3.2.

Table 3.2: Proportion of placements with parents meeting stated aims

Aim of placement	% met aims
Remand	68
Assessment	64
Temporary care	50
Roof	49
Care and upbringing	48
Treatment	45
Bridge to independence	33

Combining the two measures of success used in Rowe's study - whether the placement lasted as long as expected and met desired aims - satisfaction declined as children's ages increased. Nearly half (46%) of placements of children under the age of 5 met both criteria, compared with only a quarter (23%) of placements for over 10s. What should have been a happy event for children and families, therefore, more often than not ended in difficulties and the older the child the more likely were problems. This may indicate that placement with relatives was frequently a last ditch attempt at the rehabilitation of children with families whose caring abilities were poor, or that the placement reflected a lack of viable alternatives rather than a deliberate plan for the child. On the other hand, these disquieting results may reflect insufficient preparation and support for the family and child from social workers.

Around the same time, Farmer and Parker looked at 321 children who had returned 'home on trial'. They divided the study population into two groups: children looked after for protection or because families could not provide for them (N=172) and those separated to control behaviour (N=149). The abused and neglected children who did well after their return were distinctive in several ways.. They tended to have been looked after for shorter periods, that is less than one year; they had not changed placements while away and they returned to households where there had been no change of membership. Children who settled successfully also tended to be the only child in the household or, if they had siblings looked after, to have returned with them. In addition, they tended to be young. Other factors related to success were highlighted in interviews with children, families and social workers. Among these were: the quality of attachment to parents before separation, contact with the family prior to return and the number of other changes the return required for the child, such as school or friends.

A follow-up of these placements revealed that 42 of the 172 children were re-abused or neglected but only nine had to be removed from home. Generally, the greater the concern of supervising agencies, the more likely it was that 'home on trial' failed. Yet it was difficult to judge the quality of placements, as breakdowns often occurred well after the original return, suggesting that the 'trial' element had long been superseded. Indeed, pressure to terminate the placement came mostly from families and children (58%) rather than from the dissatisfaction or unease of social workers (33%) or courts (7%) and, in most cases, children moved to the care of another relative.

For the behaviour control group, the home placement was seldom viewed by social workers as a controversial and fraught decision, a sharp contrast to the child protection cases. Indeed, few community supports other than intermediate treatment were offered to families. The researchers found it difficult to interpret the behaviour of these young people while at home. Fifty five per cent offended, a similar number truanted and 44% of the girls got pregnant but these setbacks rarely resulted in the young person leaving home. Such figures, moreover, must be seen in context; the question is whether they would be any lower had the young people remained away from home.

Much also depended on the circumstances of the return. In some cases the move was purposeful, in others it was clearly *faute de mieux*. Certainly, a return home on trial neither greatly improved young people's behaviour nor offered social workers much control over difficult and anti-social behaviour. Indeed, social services tolerated levels of misbehaviour that would have been unacceptable in those living away in care. Thus, social workers were hardly enamoured of placement with parents for this group. Paradoxically, because difficult cases received most support, there was a correlation between poor results and high social work input. Independent of this relationship, however, difficulties in gaining access to the child and loss of contact with social workers were particularly bad omens. Social workers' interest waned, planned reviews did not take place and care orders were simply left to expire.

These studies of children 'home on trial' emphasise the wide range of situations that may be involved in a return from care or accommodation. Return occurs from a variety of settings, including penal establishments, and placements at home have a range of aims. Whatever the circumstances, most returners face difficulties and there is a high likelihood that further separations will be necessary, particularly among adolescents. Social workers have only moderate expectations of success and give variable attention to the preparation for such moves, again particularly for adolescents.

This study will show that 87% of separated children go home. A pertinent question, given this finding, is what happens to those who do not find their way back to relatives? Although it is known from adoption and permanency studies that many of these young people find stability away from their birth families, this body of research has a few words of warning.

First, less than five in every 100 looked after children are eventually adopted. This finding indicates among other things that it is not easy to find a permanent alternative to birth relatives. There are many people coming forward to adopt babies but difficult adolescents and abused and neglected children, who form the majority of children in need of permanence, are less attractive. It also takes a long time to find a permanent alternative to birth relatives. Local authorities often claim they can secure placements within six months of a court order being made but this can be over optimistic and the period of waiting can be a discontinuity for the child, threatening the viability of the adoptive placement when it eventually occurs.

It is also clear that adoptive parents require support if the placement is to succeed. Gibbons and colleagues' (1995) 10 year follow-up of children whose names had been originally been placed on the child protection register because of physical abuse showed that children who remained at home enjoyed better psychological health a decade later than those who had been fostered; and that fostered children had better outcomes than those who had been adopted. A likely interpretation of these research results is not that adoption is unworkable for these children but that they are a reflection of the support services offered in each case.

The messages from these studies for understanding children's return is that permanent alternatives to the birth family are not necessarily permanent. Fratter and colleagues (1991) followed up 1,165 special needs adoptions and long-term foster placements for an extensive period (up to six years). She found that a fifth (22%) of placements broke down. Those placed in the first three years of life seldom experience a disruption (the rate was generally less than 5% for these cases) but for those placed at 12 years of age, the breakdown rate rose to 49%. Many of these young people went back to their families. Moreover, she found that for those older children who are at high risk of adoption or fostering breakdown, the key protective factor was some form of contact with birth relatives, so indicating the complexity of the relationship between contact, permanency outside the family and return.

Consumer studies

Important insights into return as it affects children looked after are offered in several studies in which adults and children describe their experiences of care or accommodation. Triseliotis and Russell, for example, in *Hard to Place* (1983), interviewed 84 young adults who had either been adopted or placed for long periods in residential homes. Those who had stayed long in residential care were largely critical. They recalled a sense of being different from other children and a lack of family roots. Former residents felt cut off in that they knew few other young people outside care, rarely had to make decisions or establish themselves as individuals and found it difficult to revisit former institutions. They also lacked continuity of support after leaving. Hence, the demands of a return to the community came as something of a shock for those long in residence, compounding more general anxiety about jobs and accommodation.

These experiences are echoed in other consumer studies of the period, such as Kahan's (1979) *Growing Up in Care*, Festinger's (1983) *No-one Ever Asked Us* and Page's (1977) *Who Cares?* Hundelby's (1988) paper on returning children home confirms the likelihood of change in family structures while children are away and concludes that in order to effect a satisfactory reunion, social workers have to reconcile ambivalent feelings between children and their relatives. Children may not understand what has happened to them or why, they may feel guilty that they have upset or destroyed their family while at the same time feeling angry that the family has broken up. They are certain to be fearful about returning to changed situations.

The work of Wendelken (1983) and Brearley and colleagues (1982) complements Hundleby's stress on the ambivalence of children's and parents' feelings about return. Parents, they argue, are the most difficult to prepare; their children will have changed while away, their feelings are confused and, instead of being happy to be home, their offspring may be aggressive, troublesome and enuretic. Similarly the returning child has to face a new home, perhaps including a new step-parent. The family home may appear small, dull, cold and poverty stricken; food seem poor and irregular. Parents may not have much free time to spend with the child. Outside the home, local schools may strike the child as unfamiliar, for instance in terms of ethnic or racial composition. Cawson (1988) similarly emphasises the problems arising when children settled in one geographical area return home to another. She draws attention to the paradox that the more placements try to integrate the child, the greater will be the disruption caused for children by reunion.

Interestingly, studies postdating the *Children Act*, 1989 have found less evidence of such problems. In *Teenagers and the Social Work Services* (1996), for example, Triseliotis and colleagues show that the complaint amongst teenage clients is more likely to be that social workers do not do enough, rather than that their interventions are too disruptive. Residential school placements were particularly popular, suggesting that it is not residential care itself that leads to social isolation and rootlessness but particular styles of residence.

Several consumer evaluations of respite care discuss issues of separation and return. Since the implementation of the *Children Act*, 1989 respite care has been available to all 'children in need' but most research has focused on the experiences of children with disabilities and their families. Several authors call attention to possible dangers associated with frequent separation and return. A child is particularly likely to experience anxiety where he or she lacks the capacity to conceptualise the nature of a respite placement and insecurities are likely to be exacerbated where relationships are already fraught. There can be a discrepancy between the views of parents and of professionals, with the former preferring many short separations and the latter fewer, longer ones. Nonetheless, many parents report that respite care is all that stands between their coping and a family breakdown leading to long-term separation.

Thus even with something as seemingly straightforward as respite care the effects of separation and ease of return differ according to the context and professionals, parents and children offer contrasting views of the benefits and drawbacks.

Those who have themselves experienced a return home from care or accommodation offer many suggestions for the effective management of the transition. Children seem to cope best if they feel secure because they understand the past and its effect on them and if they have participated in decisions about their future and in the departure process.

Studies from North America

In the United States, Public Law 96-272 *(The Adoption Assistance and Child Welfare Act,* 1980*)* established permanency planning via reunification with the natural family as a primary goal in out of home care (Maluccio et al., 1986; Warsh et al. 1996). Goerge (1990) summarises the reasoning behind the act as follows

> First, it is believed that, in most cases, the child's well-being is enhanced by a continuous caretaking relationship... Second, it is possible that a child will be psychologically harmed in foster care... Third, the state prefers re-unification for administrative reasons because foster care is costly and adoptive families are hard to find.

Overall, the chances of reunion following separation are much the same in North America as in the United Kingdom. This inevitably varies from state to state and from one client group to another. Nationally, 40% of children return to parents within the first year of separation (Wattenberg, 1993) and half to three-quarters of the youngsters who enter care are reunited with their families in under two years (Fein et al., 1983; Fein and Staff, 1993; Walton et al., 1993; Goerge, 1990). 'Recidivism rates', that is further family breakdown following return are estimated at around 30% - again much the same as in Britain (Rzepnicki, 1987; Wulczyn, 1991; Walton et al., 1993).

Certain groups, however, remain vulnerable to an extended sojourn in state care, particularly children with multiple disabilities and children from minority groups (Wattenburg, 1993). A study by the National Black Child Development Institute (NBCDI, 1993) found that of a thousand African-American children entering foster care in six cities in 1986 only half (51%) had been discharged by the end of a 26 month follow-up. Where parental drug abuse was a major cause of separation, the figure fell to just over a quarter (28%), and even those discharged were more likely to return to the extended family than to parents.

'Despite the articulation of this goal in policy', concludes Maluccio (1995), 'agencies continue to struggle to achieve it in practice'. Pressure groups such as the NBCDI stress the paucity of basic welfare services - particularly housing - that might make a real difference to parents' abilities to resume the care of their children (NBCDI, 1989). Parental drug abuse, particularly where it involves crack cocaine, is a far more common barrier to re-unification in North America than currently in the United Kingdom (Curtis and McCullough, 1993). Other authors (Maluccio et al., 1993; Lewis and Callaghan, 1993) suggest that the attitudes of foster carers are often a barrier to return, particularly where they feel marginalised in the decision-making process. In such situations, they may encourage children to identify more with their new foster family than with the birth family (Gardner, 1996). Fein and Staff (1993) suggest that field social work staff of state agencies not only have too large caseloads for the intensive work required in reunification, but that they are also trained 'typically in the case management of the crisis situations their cases present'.

Nonetheless, over 100,000 children return to relatives after a period of out-of-home care in the United States every year (Tatara, 1989), and it is hardly surprising that such numbers should have led to some noteworthy practice innovations. For instance, the Peer Parent Project in Utah seeks to facilitate reunification by providing foster carers with payment over and above normal fostering allowances for work with the birth family. An evaluation of the project (Lewis and Callaghan, 1993) found a number of encouraging dividends from this investment;

> the procedure appeared to increase support of reunification goals on the part of foster parents, to facilitate the transition of the children from foster care to their own homes, and to strengthen the ability of biological parents to maintain their children at

home. Foster parents reported greater satisfaction with their role and status… in not being required to abruptly terminate relationships with the foster children.

Walton et al. (1993) provide an optimistic assessment of another family reunification programme in Ohio, whilst Werbach (1993) describes the use of 'family reunification role play' in the training of social workers at the University of Maine. Finally, no discussion of family reunification would be complete without mention of the work of Maluccio, Warsh and colleagues at the University of Connecticut. Basing their guidelines upon a wealth of research data and practical experience, they argue that 'reunification refers to the form of family relationships and not the place where children live' (Maluccio et al., 1994). They stress the importance of ensuring that reunification informs all planning, even prior to separation, and is not merely tacked on to the end of an intervention. Early and consistent contact between child and family is seen as an essential ingredient of a successful reunion, and the role of the extended family is emphasised. Whilst the authors are clear that services should be offered for as long as they are needed, they are also of the opinion that a degree of awareness of the impact of separation and loss on the part of professionals may be all that is needed to make a significant difference. The University and Casey Family Services, a private child welfare agency, have collaborated on a number of demonstration projects (Fein and Staff 1991; 1993).

Further North in Canada, the importance of continuity in children's care careers has also been stressed. Simard, Vachon and Moisan's (1991) Quebec studied children returning to parents after an absence in care of more than 30 days. The successful returners had fewer placements while away and received consistent help from social workers. A further auspicious factor was the child's ability to integrate with peers. The impact of these variables was reduced, however, if foster families and natural parents were in competition or if step-parents in newly reconstituted families sought to discipline the newly arrived child.

What is noticeable from this overview, is the commonality of themes in studies of return undertaken from different standpoints. This is echoed in the next chapter which broadens the focus further to consider children and young adults returning home not from state care or accommodation but from other separations, such as following a period of independence or a spell in hospital.

Summary points

1. Although many child-care studies have scrutinised returning children, the process of return has never been properly studied in its own right in Britain. This is a surprising deficiency in social work literature, considering that nearly all looked after children eventually go home.

2. Several longitudinal studies from the 1980s - particularly those focusing on children placed 'home on trial' - have yielded helpful insights into the difficulties faced by all concerned.

3. More recent studies indicate both continuity and change before and after the implementation of the *Children Act,* 1989. Consumer studies and research from Canada and the United States are other important sources.

4. There is general agreement in all studies that return cannot be understood in isolation. It is part of a process in which the difficulties and tensions surrounding the initial separation are likely to remain central.

5. It is also clear that the experience of being looked after itself can complicate plans and modify, for better or worse, expectations for rehabilitation.

4 Return in other contexts

Studies of children outside the child welfare system throw additional light on the return process. Of particular importance are investigations of children leaving hospitals and boarding schools. Further insights can be gained from a scrutiny of other groups experiencing separation and return; young offenders, psychiatric in-patients, soldiers and young people moving to independence.

The experience of return is not confined to children looked after. Indeed, many more children return home each term from boarding schools and many other young people spend time away in hospital. Moreover certain occupations, such as the armed services, require their personnel regularly to leave home. Research studies in these areas may offer findings and perspectives relevant to the family reunions of children looked after. One of the first reasonably rigorous modern studies of children returning home was Heinicke and Westheimer's study of two-year-olds placed for a few weeks in a residential nursery (Dinnage and Kellmer Pringle, 1967). The authors found little evidence of long-term 'emotional or intellectual damage' in their subjects. Other studies of children in various forms of institutional care have identified the difficulties of returning home as one of the chief drawbacks of this form of provision. According to Williams (1991), for example, the difficulty of constant re-adjustment between family and school was one of the chief reasons for the decline in residential special education during the 1970s and 80s. Others (Rowe and Lambert, 1973; Colton, 1988) have suggested that the formal atmosphere of residential care may be particularly conducive to re-unification. In an admirable summary of the evidence, Parker (1988) concluded that 'residential care could play a special part in the rehabilitation of children' but only if return was 'conceived as an explicit function and not as a coincidental result of the circumstances'.

Hospitalised children

The separation experienced by children on admission to hospital has been the focus of many psychological and psychiatric studies and much separation theory rests on this work. Bowlby (1952) was probably the first to undertake such research systematically and subsequently used his evidence to inform general theories of attachment and child development. Much of the concern about the harmful effects of separation, especially of children from mothers, stems from this work. Since Bowlby, the effects of separation have been further scrutinised and the conditions of danger clarified, for example by Rutter (1972). Also, there have been more intensive studies of children in hospital, such as those by the Robertsons (1970), and radical changes in the hospital care of children have been encouraged by official reports, such as Platt (Ministry of Health, 1959).

While many studies have concentrated on the separation of hospitalised children, few have looked at return other than in terms of a medical follow-up. One exception is *Beyond Separation* by Hall and Stacey (1979), a set of papers concerned with various aspects of the hospital care of children. This book argues that children's levels of distress reflect more than the nature and severity of the child's medical condition. An explanation of children's disturbance within hospital, they say, must concentrate on the hospital environment and that of the home and must not fragment the two. Also, the organisational aspects of the hospital are as important for understanding individual disturbance as are the insights of psychology.

Hall and Stacey attempt to integrate medical, psychological and sociological variables to explain how the behaviours and attitudes which the hospital approves can determine children's problems after leaving. However, it is important to emphasise that children looked after are usually far more seriously disadvantaged with regard to separation difficulties than are children in hospital. It has been seen that their families are usually more fragmented with key members spread across a number of households and while they are away, the children are often moved around placements, making it difficult for parents to keep in touch.

Discontinuity is, however, still a common experience for children in hospital. Not only is the child's educational and social development likely to be affected by long or repeated hospitalisation but the lives of parents or siblings are also changed. Although hospitals have made enormous strides to include families in the nursing of children and to inform them about treatment and prospects, a mother's stay with the child may still mean separation from father and siblings. Moreover, brothers and sisters may resent the attention given to the sick child, producing wider family tensions, especially when the effect on one sibling is greater than on others. Parents, too, may face frustrations arising from restricted occupational or geographical mobility.

Rutter (1975), Pill (1979) and Mrazek (1986) also raise a very important issue, highly relevant to children in care, namely the difficulties faced by children who are repeatedly admitted to hospital. They found that some young children were not only highly anxious but also fearful of pain on every occasion and did not seem to have developed coping strategies. Pill writes,

> little is known about the long-term psychological effects of repeated admissions and there is no evidence to suggest that this pattern is any less damaging to a child's health than a stay involving months. Parents are often not sure where to turn for advice concerning the management of the child and sometimes have considerable difficulty in obtaining equipment. The initiative is left entirely to them, and the hospital appears to take little interest in the patient once discharged, even though the child may be readmitted in the fairly near future.

The National Association for the Welfare of Children in Hospital has done most to co-ordinate research into hospitalised children but admits that much current practice is based on the work of writers in the 1950s, such as the Robertsons and Menzies and, later, Maureen Oswin, all of whom were alarmed about the effect on children of hospital admissions. Current research was summarised by Sylva and Stein in 1990. Whilst a number of innovative projects have helped children to adjust to the hospital environment there appears to have been none expressly concerned with helping them re-adjust to life outside. Naturally, there are children who still spend long periods in hospital but improved practice seeks to ameliorate the risks and to make the stay as family-like as possible (Audit Commission, 1993).

The Association's publication most relevant to the issue of return is Woodward's (1978) pamphlet *Has Your Child Been in Hospital?* She begins by discussing the problems of separation and shows how, for some children, these are exacerbated by the child's lack of time sense, confusion about their situation, difficulties of gaining comfort, view of hospital as a punishment and fears and fantasies about their fate. The children most at risk are under fives who stay in hospital for more than one day, particularly if admitted in an emergency (Rutter 1981) though any harm is likely to be temporary where the stay is less than a week. Temperamental factors in the child are also influential. Woodward then considers the parents' position, noting the likelihood of anger, fears of responsibility, change of role, feelings of guilt and failure, sensitivity to criticism and the difficulties and strains of visiting.

Difficulties can also arise from the ways that children and family interact as a result of mutually stressful experiences. Children's unquestioning love for their families may have been shattered, they may find it hard to trust their mother and father and may test out parents' commitment to them. Parents are often physically tired and cannot easily comprehend the changes they see in their youngster. The most common reaction is for the child to regress. Responses include thumb sucking, clinging, aggression, destructive behaviour, wetting, rocking, fear of the dark or of the unknown and, for older children, smoking. Woodward advises parents to see their children as needing reassurance rather than as simply being naughty or as having been spoiled by nurses. Children need help to relinquish the sickness role and parents need to know how to remain optimistic when talking to their child as well as to relatives, neighbours and friends. As sickness and disability among children are not restricted to disadvantaged groups, these problems have been articulated for a wide range of family situations rather than merely for those where children are looked after. However, the difficulties described probably apply with similar force whatever the circumstances.

These studies of separated children in hospitals confirm the personal difficulties posed by return for all parties but also highlight the role of family attitudes and the need for parents to feel involved. While that involvement means delegating caring tasks to nurses and doctors, the formal power of parents, as they perceive it, remains considerable. One can only contrast this with the child-care situations previously described.

Boarding schools

By far the largest group of children, over 100,000, separated for long periods from parents and family are to be found in boarding schools. The public independent schools and the preparatory schools that feed them have long been the subject of plays and novels but, while the isolation and discomforts of their regimes have often been highlighted, the problems of return home which children face have been little explored. In these boarding schools, the pains of separation experienced by pupils and parents are considerable but the context of separation acts as considerable compensations for children (Lambert and Millham, 1968; Lambert, Millham and Bullock, 1975). In situations where generations of families have gone away to school and where siblings, cousins and peers undergo the same experiences, the perceived deprivations are less, even though many children are homesick and can be anxious about their families.

A group more likely to experience return difficulties are those children in residential schools, particularly those for children with emotional and behavioural difficulties (EBDs). Research evidence on the backgrounds of these pupils suggests that many face problems at home every bit as severe and complex as those faced by children looked after (Anderson and Morgan 1987; Malek, 1993; Gemal, 1993). A significant proportion of pupils, particularly in the voluntary sector schools, will actually be looked after (Grimshaw and Berridge, 1994). On the whole, the schools do not seek to incorporate the child's family effectively into the curriculum or treatment programmes and contacts between parents and children very much follow a half-term, holidays and annual open day model (Upton, Bundy and Speed, 1986).

Nonetheless, change is afoot. Cooper (1992, 1993), for example, found the following aims (in order of priority) in two schools he studied. First, to aid pupils' social and emotional development; second, to reintegrate pupils into their home situations; third, to aid pupils' academic development; fourth equal, the reintegration of pupils into their local schools and the preparation of pupils for the world of work.

Most of these goals involve helping youngsters manage transitions, initially between home and school but subsequently extending to mainstream school and work. Whilst Grimshaw and Berridge (1994) suggest that such aspirations are likely to be honoured in the breach, they too found evidence of a strong formal commitment to reintegration. This stands in contrast to some of the pioneers of residential special education, for whom return was remarkable only as the point at which all the good work achieved by the schools was likely to be undone (Laslett, 1995; Bridgeland, 1971; Balbernie, 1966).

Thus boarding schools and therapeutic communities now find themselves facing conflicting demands. On the one hand is a therapeutic tradition that sees parents as the cause of their offspring's difficulties and seeks to exclude them from the treatment process as far as possible. On the other, changing attitudes, research evidence and legislation increasingly oblige schools to give families an active role. These tensions are examined in Little and Kelly's (1995) study of children in a therapeutic community and are illustrated by the circumstances in which children left the community. Only in a minority of cases (39%) were all interested parties agreed that departure was appropriate. A third (32%) of departures were engineered either by residents or their families against the advice of the community and a sixth were exclusions. Return to the family home was the most common destination on departure and the circumstances of return a major factor determining evaluations of the placement by parents and professionals. One leaver in ten, for example, left to attend a mainstream day school and, whilst parents and professionals invariably saw such an outcome as a success, staff at the community were often more ambivalent. The departure of others gives new meaning to the word expel. According to one mother,

> first (they) didn't want anything to do with me, next they are saying you can have him back. We never did see eye to eye and then things went from bad to worse. When I got him back he was totally out of control. I needed more help than I did before he went (away) but the staff didn't want anything to do with him. They rejected him and they rejected me.

The book *A Life Without Problems?* highlights the difficulties faced by young people, mainly boys, prematurely leaving residential school between their fourteenth and sixteenth birthday. For many, a return home was the result of an absence of alternatives rather than a positive care plan. At home, they were seen by every agency as the responsibility of another and ended up drifting through a series of increasingly controlling care settings towards custody. Frequently, return home was used as a means by which agencies could wash their hands of awkward clients. In such circumstances, one does not need a crystal ball to predict poor outcomes.

Return from secure settings

Although it affects several thousand young people each year, little is known about return from secure settings. It is known that return of adult prisoners is problematic. Roles and relationships are likely to have changed considerably during separation: for example, it is a common occurrence for the eldest son of a prisoner to become the head of the family and for this to be welcomed by the mother (Shaw, 1987). Spouses, too, may feel more ambivalence than joy at the return of a prodigal husband: Copley (1981) found that nearly a quarter reported taking a 'substitute' while their usual partner was incarcerated. One ex-prisoner describes the experience as follows,

> when I got my home leave I thought everything would be great... but it wasn't like that at all. Everything had changed. I don't mean the outside - I got used to that right away. But here at home. The kids had changed, they had grown up without me. I'd had no input to their upbringing. And she, God had she changed. I was berserk the whole time. We did nothing but yell at each other and in a bizarre way I was glad to go back (quoted in McDermott and King, 1992).

A young person's return from prison as a parent, however, is perhaps less important for our current purposes than their return to family as a dependent. A study of interest in this context, not least because many of its subjects were at the time in State care, is Dartington's follow-up of graduates from Youth Treatment Centres and other long stay secure units (Bullock et al., 1998). A scrutiny of the living situations of the 204 young people who left the Centres between 1982 and 1992 reveals instability and frequent change. While most young people eventually achieve some independence, the transition is by no means smooth, often interrupted by custody, homelessness or returns to former situations. Hence, parental relationships not only wither but also periodically tend to revive and returns home may occur long after the young person has moved out of residential care. For example, twice as many leavers lived at home at some point within two years of leaving as returned there directly.

The patterns of changing family structures and enduring tensions were found again for these leavers but an intensive follow-up scrutiny showed that the depth and significance of relationships between children and relatives were greater than levels of contact would suggest. Despite continuing stresses in family relationships, parents provided considerable support for their offspring, especially male offenders and girls. However, it is wrong to assume an uninterrupted strengthening of relationships over time, for they fluctuate, reflecting particular circumstances, such as pregnancy, employment and criminality.

The returns of many of the young people studied were seriously impaired by the consequences of offending so that remands in custody frequently disrupted living patterns, social relations and employment prospects. This situation has been emphasised by Farrington (1995) in his long-term follow-up of offenders. Poor physical and mental health, in contrast, were less common constraints on young people's lives.

Despite extensive social work efforts, a quarter of the leavers failed to resolve their difficulties and remained highly dependent on welfare agencies for accommodation and support long after their return to home and community. Generally, the more deprived and fragmented the young person's earlier family care experience, the more difficult were the post-return adjustments. Young people long bereft of any family support, for example, rarely succeeded in creating a new support network after leaving. Boys who had been long looked after found it especially difficult to cope and many quickly found themselves back in a residential setting, usually prison. The relative success of girls appears to indicate the importance of achieving an acceptable role in society, since many were coping surprisingly well as single parents. These findings are echoed by Bailey et al. (1994) in their study of admission to a secure psychiatric unit operated within the National Health Service.

Social workers' responses to the needs of these young people were more varied than for less extreme child-care cases. As the young people had posed severe behaviour problems in the past and as there is no clear philosophy of effective after-care for such cases, social workers responded to their supervisory tasks in different ways. For example, some consciously sought to discourage the dependency that can follow institutionalisation and restricted their help to instrumental areas, such as housing or jobs, while, in contrast, one local authority allocated two full-time staff to one individual. Nevertheless, despite these efforts, Garnett (1992) found that key decisions were often left to the young people themselves and emphasised that young people's requirements are equally variable and support needs to be available according to their demands.

These studies of adolescents' experiences indicate the significance not only of the return situation itself but also of people's perceptions of the reason for being in care or accommodation, the quality of the looked after experience and young people's circumstances after leaving. They also highlight, once again, the complexity of the return process, the variety of adjustments and transitions that have to be made and the problems of coping with the stigma associated with being looked after. In their emphasis that return takes place over time and involves negotiations with and re-evaluations of not only family but also friends and neighbourhood, they recall the social network that Whitaker, Archer and Hicks (1998) identify as easing the return home of children in residential care.

Return to parents from psychiatric hospital

Another context in which return has achieved salience during the past generation concerns the closure of psychiatric hospitals and the return of their patients to the care of the community (Pilling 1991). Far greater numbers, meanwhile, are discharged following a short stay as a result of recovery. Whilst it is the former who catch the public imagination, it is the latter whose experiences are most relevant to a study of children leaving care. The voluminous research literature suggests that, although their needs and problems may be very different, the experience of children looked after has many parallels.

One consistent theme of the community care research literature is the tendency for support services quickly to wither once the ex-patient returns to the family home. Return home can jettison mental patients into the isolated, helpless environment of their families of origin, who appeal in vain for further hospital admissions (even for a temporary period of respite), for counselling or support and even for basic information and advice.

Griffin Francell and colleagues (1988) surveyed the families to which ex-patients returned and found a general dissatisfaction with follow-up services, including a tendency for professionals to pass the buck when crises occurred, a lack of material support such as day provision and transport, very little advice on the management of difficult behaviour and a lack of family involvement in planning treatment (though families were responsible for carrying out much of that treatment). Relatives also experienced unwelcome pressure to attend family therapy sessions, the purposes of which were not always made clear to them. In general, carers wanted rather less therapeutic and rather more material support, a frustration echoed by the parents of many children returning from care and accommodation. The stress on relatives is considerable: McCarthy (1988) estimates that almost a third of carers experienced serious psychiatric problems themselves as a result of caring for a mentally disabled relative.

Perhaps the most revealing study of return home from psychiatric care in the present context is Norris's (1984) study of patients discharged from Broadmoor, which found that 44% of men left to hostels but that 28% returned to parents. A further 11% returned to wives, 6% to siblings and 3% to friends. Despite very long separations, men were as likely to be living with parents at discharge (28%) as at admission (35%). Returns could and did succeed even in the most inauspicious contexts;

> problems of accommodation did result in the return of some matricides, patricides, fratricides and infanticides to their families, if not at discharge then quite soon afterwards. Only one such case in the study was totally unsuccessful...contrary to expectations...schizophrenics were not less well integrated than other patients.

Norris is in no doubt, however, that, where such returns were successful, it was despite, rather than because of, the policies and practices of the special hospitals. It is worth quoting her conclusions at length;

> A patient discharged to parents may be in a more favourable environment than if he were given a hostel placement. However,...parents were often discouraged from taking too active

an interest in their son whilst he was in Broadmoor; letters to doctors remained unanswered for long periods and requests for interviews were refused or ignored. Some parents were undoubtedly a great nuisance to hospital staff...Not all were helpful to their son after discharge. Nevertheless, parents were a major source of support for many patients in the immediate post-discharge period and sometimes for years afterwards; this was despite the parents' age, illness and incapacity and also sometimes the illness and incapacity of the patient.

Return and independence

Jones (1995) scrutinised the National Child Development Study, a longitudinal follow-up of all children born in one week in March 1958, and found that although nearly half (47%) of men and a quarter (25%) of women were living with parents at the age of 23, a third of them (30% of the men, 38% of the women) had previously left home for a period of six months or more. Of all those who had left home by age 23, nearly a third (29%) had subsequently returned. She suggests that such returns remain a feature of young people's lives into their mid-twenties.

One finding particularly relevant to a study of children looked after was that return is particularly likely for those who originally left home because of domestic problems rather than because of marriage or employment. Jones suggests that return must not always be seen as evidence of failure

> it may be because it is convenient for them to do so, because they have missed their families, because the reason they left has passed, or because they decide the time is not yet right to make the final break from the parental home.

It should be noted however that return often followed exposure to the difficulties of independent living; financial problems, arguments with flatmates, the collapse of relationships, unemployment, loneliness and frustration.

Patterns of leaving and returning home are highly class and culture dependent but the patterns described have many parallels with the recorded experience of those leaving care and accommodation in their mid to late teens. Each year, several thousand young people cease to be looked after simply because they reach the age of 18. Stein (1986) and Biehal and colleagues (1995) have explored the problems experienced by young people who leave care and accommodation. Although special leaving care schemes helped, it was abundantly clear that many faced a miserable time. Happiness, warm relationships, security, relief and help were left behind and young people's low job aspirations led them into continual financial difficulties. Simple survival was a challenge; to eat sufficiently and launder clothes cheaply became priorities. Loneliness was also a problem, counteracted by sad wanderings round cafes, cinemas and pubs. Enduring petty delinquency also meant that many young men were in continual trouble with the police. Movement between living situations was, therefore, common, either to survive or to relieve depression. In other instances, it was thrust upon them by circumstances.

Bonnerjea (1990) emphasises the mobility of such young people. Only 20% stayed in the same place for two years. Most hated living alone and had all kinds of difficulties, from rows with neighbours to poor sleep or extreme fears. They left the lonely situations of flats or bedsits and moved quickly to group or shared situations. None undertook further education and all were fitful in employment. Former care-givers occasionally proved important sources of support, especially foster parents who were often seen as 'family'. Many young people, however, continued to be dependent on welfare agencies and viewed the decisions made about them as being largely out of their hands.

Biehal and colleague's (1995) estimates of young leavers' chances of finding any lasting solutions back at home are, therefore, hardly surprising

> Some of these young people attempted to renew contact with parents after many years, only to have their advances met again with outright rejection...a few had brief reconciliations with parents they had not seen for a long time which rapidly fizzled out due to lack of parental commitment.

Even where they were unable to return to live, however, those young people who had experienced regular contact with their parents whilst looked after were often able to go home for other purposes; to borrow money, for example, or even just for its own sake,

> even though regular access did not lead to reunification with parents, in these cases it at least allowed the child and family to

keep in touch. It enabled them to maintain and, in a few cases, improve their relationship.

Military families

Before drawing final conclusions about the return process, it is important to consider whether return studies of other social situations have anything to offer child-care research. Several occupational groups, such as the armed forces, merchant navy, trawlermen and light-house keepers, experience regular separation from and return to their families and it is interesting to explore how people in these situations cope.

Jolly (1987) emphasises in particular the changing role of fathers in recent years and shows how the military machine fails to acknowledge these by continuing to make demands, such as sudden and prolonged absences, that seriously hinder parenting opportunities. She writes,

> the resentment which many fathers feel in missing continuous contact with their children often surprises them. The young military father, like any other, has absorbed the ideal of 'involved fatherhood' and then seems to be frustrated at every turn when he tries to put this ideal into practice.

Fathers report feeling guilty at being away when children are born and then finding their children unrecognisable when they return. The father's return also poses problems for the family role and power structure. Wives having dealt with everything for several months, have to share roles, some of which they have come to enjoy. Jolly concludes,

> in most households, after an initial period of intensely difficult readjustment, family relationships return to normal. But, for some time, the returning husband remains an outsider. If he lacks the force of personality to demand his share of the decision-making, he becomes little more than a temporary lodger and his status in the family sinks, so does his sense of responsibility to them. In fact, many fathers spend time on leave away from their families, in the company of other servicemen.

This feature has been widely observed among returning war veterans; they find solace among colleagues who have shared their experiences and separate from their family again to solve the problems of return.

The process of family adjustment that follows a home-coming is long and complex. Jolly shows that for soldiers it begins with the arrival, usually joyful, sometimes emotional, always charged with underlying apprehension. And there is also shyness, some reserve. Jolly writes,

> despite all the *macho* talk about what they will do with, or to, their women, when they get home, for more than a few, the first days or even weeks bring sexual problems.

These include reluctance to accept intercourse on the part of the wife and impotence for the husband. Then,

> as both partners struggle to create a small space for themselves to begin the psychological readjustment of being together again, arguments, sulking and depression can occur. The family recoils instinctively from the intruder, but guiltily feeling that they should not be doing so. Father, for his part, cannot understand the children's truculence, or his wife's disappointment as her romantic illusions quietly evaporate. He loves his wife and children, he has missed them and, so they say, they've missed him, but they don't seem to show it.

Naturally, reactions vary among families from mild unease to blazing rows or stony silences, until the new way of life - inclusive of the new arrival - is re-established. At some point comes acceptance, as each member of the family stops feeling aggrieved. Rebuilding of the relationship takes place as husband and wife resume social activities as a couple and sex and rows assume more normal, even humdrum proportions.

The merry-go-round of family adjustment to loss and change is virtually continuous as the military posts its men from one location to another and sends them away on unaccompanied missions. As one would expect, the more upheavals a family has lived through, the less it comes to dread them, knowing it has coped and survived in the past, and is mature and open enough to be honest about the difficulties. As Tunstall (1962) shows in his study of trawlermen, some experiences can soften the traumas of separation and return; for instance, children may be pre-socialised for this life-style in education, by community values and by the frequent moves to live with relatives during fathers' absences. Nonetheless, people grow and change and a significant number of families do reach a point where they become tired of coping and compromising and making the best of things.

The return of fathers in well paid jobs to families they love may not appear to have many parallels for children looked after. However, some similarities will appear, for example, in the anxieties preceding the reunion, in the clashes and negotiations about family role and power, in the unease about the returner's secret activities while away, in the importance of the row for re-defining roles and power, in the gap on both sides between expectations and realities and in the slowness of the necessary readjustments. It also questions Rutter's (1975) suggestion that the separation anxieties of children looked after are largely due to the disturbed families they come from and return to. Even with auspicious beginnings, return is a long and difficult process for service families of all ranks and the problems of return are often resolved by further separations.

Conclusions

This evidence brings to an end the review of the research literature. It has looked not only at child-care studies but also the experience of other social groups. What conclusions can be drawn about return as it affects looked after children? Initially, it is clear that return is a common experience, affecting nine out of every ten youngsters. It is also complicated, every bit as fraught as separation, a process that has had far greater research scrutiny. It is equally clear from all of the studies that a child's return to home and community can only be fully understood in its wider context. This is because return will have been preceded by separation and may be followed by further departures. Hence, the reasons for prior separations and the skill with which they have been managed will be important determinants of return success. A longitudinal perspective on children's experiences while looked after would seem essential for a full appreciation of the re-unification process.

Secondly, although the studies discussed include young people who have returned from being looked after, their main focus is on children's situations once back. Hence, the findings highlight placement sequences and factors associated with successful reunion. Snapshots are provided of pre- and post-return situations with success evaluated on criteria such as whether the placement lasts. As the review has shown, this has been a fruitful approach. For example, new evidence on the high frequency of return from residential settings and the considerable changes that occur in children's families during the child's absence have surprised even child-care specialists.

However, there is also a clear need to view children's returns to home and community more in the context of their experiences and subsequent life-styles. Such a perspective sees family relationships as fluctuating and seeks to accommodate variations over time in children's emotional stability. Thus, some flexibility is introduced to the evaluations of outcomes. A prospective view of children's situations is needed to capture these dynamics and to explore the options open to participants at key moment in return negotiations.

These conclusions suggested the benefits of analysing existing longitudinal data further to see how looked after children can best be classified to clarify their return experiences. There is also a need to weight the influential factors to see which of those highlighted in the studies have an independent influence on children's successful return from being looked after and its aftermath. Since such an analysis is absent from the studies discussed, it was decided to undertake this exercise in addition to our scrutiny of return routes and patterns within representative child-care populations.

However, one consequence of the emphasis in the research literature on children once they have gone back is the lack of knowledge about the process of return, its psychological effects and what it actually feels like to be returned. The negotiations, accommodations and conflicts experienced by children and their families have been acknowledged but little explored. Neither has much consideration been given to the adaptations required from the wider family. Children's adjustment to outside situations, such as peer group, school and community, have also been given scant attention. While there is reasonably comprehensive information on the various return routes taken by children and some indications of the problems that young people subsequently face, these other processes remain uncharted and their effects unknown.

There is, therefore, a clear need to explore return in its own right and to examine the variety of adjustments that have to be made by children and families. Such an exercise needs to look wider than just the relationship between child and family, for a youngster's return can affect other relationships, such as those between parents and grandparents or between siblings. The child's behaviour in other contexts, such as school, may also be significant.

The literature review has sought to summarise the research information available about return home as experienced by looked after children. At the same time, it has revealed considerable gaps in knowledge and has suggested fruitful research approaches. This study hopes both to extend previous work and tackle issues that have, to date, been little explored.

Summary points

1. Many children other than those looked after experience return.

2. Research evidence shows that hospitalised children suffer separation and return problems but they are likely to be less severe than for children looked after because of greater family stability and clear reasons for the child's absence. Nevertheless, return is difficult for children and families and disturbed behaviour by children following reunion is not uncommon.

3. The periods of separation and return are also considerable for children in boarding schools but are tempered by the cultural context of the experience. The extensive pre-socialisation for departure, the clear and predictable cultural continuities and manifest status enhancement provide compensations. Nevertheless, many children in residential schools face similar problems to children looked after.

4. Studies of occupations where separation from and return to families is frequent, such as the armed services, show enduring difficulties of readjustment. Family roles and power have to be constantly re-negotiated.

5. To understand children's returns in their wider context and to fill gaps in existing research knowledge, longitudinal and prospective studies are needed both of large cohorts of children and of individual cases as they return home from care.

5 Designing the study

Here the variety of research approaches employed in the study of reunion are laid out. The study design combined both quantitative and qualitative research strategies and both retrospective and prospective stages. First, the return process was closely scrutinised in a study of 24 families containing 31 children where parents and children had been separated and where the professionals involved anticipated reunion at some stage. Second, existing data on the experience of 875 children looked after in the 1980s was re-analysed to identify factors associated with a successful return home. This involved multivariate analysis of factors predicting two separate outcomes - the speed and the success of return. Third, predictive factors identified and theory developed from the first two studies were tested prospectively on a second cohort of looked after children.

A major aim of the study was to chart the processes and return avenues experienced by children looked after for whatever reason and for whatever length of time. The study also identified children particularly vulnerable to return problems and looked at the different households to which children returned and the various styles of social work provided. Furthermore, the study sought predictive factors associated with successful returns from which to develop guidelines to inform social work practice. To these ends, three inter-related studies of return were undertaken. This chapter describes both the methodology and the rationale of each.

Study One: An in-depth scrutiny of the return process

An initial step was to mount a small pilot project involving people from outside child-care who might contribute to an understanding of the issues surrounding return. Members of the armed services, young men returning home from prison custody, a refugee who went back and a war veteran all participated. They helped to identify themes and experiences common to all return situations and highlighted the inherent stresses. From these interviews, it became clear that return is a long process involving complex negotiations. It was necessary, therefore, to study in detail the changing perceptions of participants at various stages in the return process.

In selecting the intensive cases, the aim was less to seek a representative or random sample than to identify a broad range of return situations. Thus, the intensive study needed to include those being reunited after short and long periods, those experiencing difficulties going home and those restored with relative ease. Social workers were asked to identify children for whom return was becoming an issue. Eighty-six families were put forward, but the time between separation and envisaged reunion varied considerably. Some of the children were arriving back on their doorsteps by the time the researchers were involved while in other cases the restoration was planned for several months hence. The children were therefore categorised into early, intermediate and long-term returners. The *early returners* were children away from home for six months or less, the *intermediate group* had been away for between seven and 24 months with the *long-term children* away two years or more.

It was clear that some of the 86 families suggested by social workers had a better chance of seeing their children returned than others and some reunions were more likely to encounter difficulties than others. Cases were therefore further categorised into the following four groups,

i. Children who would be likely to go home fairly easily.

ii. Children who would be likely to experience some difficulty in getting back.

iii. Children unlikely to go home despite the social worker's plan for them to do so.

iv.   Children who would probably go home but would move on fairly soon afterwards.

These four options when crossed with the early, intermediate and long-term returns described above produce 12 possible categories. Two families in each category were selected, and these 24 families had 31 children. These provided a broad picture of the stresses and difficulties surrounding many return situations.

The intensive study of the return process began with the identification of the child. Each case was followed up for 18 months, with the researchers regularly interviewing parents, children and other relatives as well as social workers and concerned professionals. As will be seen, some of the children rapidly returned home and stayed there, while for others the period between initial research involvement and the actual return was far more protracted. Indeed, an important finding from this exercise was that, despite the intentions and plans of social workers and the supposed imminence of reunion, many of the 24 families did not see the return of their offspring during the 18 month follow-up period. The intensive study is described in more detail in the next chapter.

Study Two: A retrospective study of 875 children returning to family from care

A second stage was to use existing data to identify factors associated with successful reunion and groups vulnerable to problems following return. Three data-sets were used for this purpose. Approximately half the cohort comprised the 450 children whose experience had been charted for the study *Lost in Care*. In order to include children returning home after long separations, the follow-up of these 450 children was extended to five years after separation. In order to include young people looked after for longer periods, it was necessary to turn to another set of data - the 104 teenagers who left the Youth Treatment Centres (YTCs) between 1982 and 1985. This study followed graduates for five years after leaving the centres and was thus able to shed light on those young adults who return to family after a period of independence as well as those whose route home is more direct.

The study was also fortunate to be able to include data from Farmer and Parker's study of children returning 'home on trial'. These 321 children comprised two groups: a 'care and protection' group of younger victims of abuse and neglect and a 'control' group of adolescents beyond parental control. The extended *Lost in Care* data, the follow-up information on Youth Treatment Centre and Farmer and Parker's *Trials and Tribulations* provided information on most categories of children in care, as the following table illustrates.

Table 5.1: Data on the return experience in the three data sets used in Study One

Care category	Return information	Lost in Care	Trials and Tribulations	YTC
Short-term care	Who returns	Yes	No	No
	Outcome	Yes	Yes	No
Long-term care	Who returns	Yes	No	Yes
	Outcome	No	Yes	Yes
After leaving care	Who returns	No	No	Yes
	Outcome	No	No	Yes

Yes = Data Available   No = Data Not Available

Where long follow-ups are required, a retrospective study is the only way to answer questions within a reasonable space of time. The advantage of this material was that it had been prospectively gathered by interviews and from case records, and thus yielded more extensive and reliable data than could be obtained by a new retrospective scrutiny of case records alone. Though the emphasis of the present analysis was different from the focus of the original work, this was offset by other gains. Indeed, re-working the data provided a salutary reminder of the opportunities such data afford. The exercise allowed the identification from a large study population of issues surrounding the management of return and the problems experienced by families and children, and enabled correlations between these and known outcomes to be made. It also suggested groups of children particularly vulnerable to return difficulties.

Study Three: Validating the results

The first two studies allowed the identification of factors affecting the speed of return, and the chances of its success. The third study sought to test prospectively the factors thus identified. Social research is very rarely subjected to this sort of prospective validation. Why was this third stage necessary? There were two principal reasons. Firstly, it is precisely because social research is so rarely tested prospectively that it is important to do it from time to time. It is much easier to identify factors associated with an outcome that is already known than it is to predict outcomes in advance, but it is the second type of knowledge that professionals, quite reasonably, demand. Since the large retrospective data set had been used to generate hypotheses concerning return, it was necessary to test these on another set of data.

Secondly, the completion of the first two stages of the research coincided with the implementation of the *Children Act 1989*. There was thus good reason to suppose that the British child-care system was changing by the time the findings came to be published. This was certainly the hope of those framing the legislation. This was more a problem for the quantitative aspects of the work than for the intensive study, for it is unlikely that an experience as fundamental as return will be much altered by legislation. Nonetheless, it was important not to give professionals any excuse to ignore the findings. A prospective validation also provided a unique opportunity to assess the extent to which the legislation had actually affected the experience of children and families in need. This comparative data is presented elsewhere.

The third study involved monitoring 463 children separated from relatives, nearly always parents, to commence a fresh period of being 'looked after' in 1993. Seven contrasting local authorities participated in this stage of the project, ranging from London boroughs to mining areas recovering from the effects of the pit closures of the 1980s to large Shire counties whose concerns were rather more agricultural. All children separated from relatives in the study period were included. The demography of the sample reflected accurately the characteristics of children looked after according to contemporary national statistics published by the Department of Health.

The children were followed up for two years after separation if they remained looked after for that long, or until they returned to live with relatives or were adopted. Those who returned to relatives were followed up a year after the reunion.

The three principal elements of the research design have now been described. Concepts such as 'career' discussed in the opening chapter and the aims of the research as described have both guided the fashioning of this research approach. A child's care career involves individuals making choices between available options and adapting to particular situations. The decision to use this perspective as a way of understanding aspects of the lives of children looked after suggested a need for both quantitative and qualitative approaches. This methodology is innovative in that qualitative and quantitative approaches have been linked in a fruitful way at each stage of the research (Bullock, Little and Millham, 1992). It is also hoped that a good foundation has been laid for further confirmatory research studies.

The remainder of this book presents the results of these three studies. The intensive study is reported first. Chapter Six discusses in more detail some of the problems associated with qualitative analysis and explains how consistency and reliability were ensured in the current study. Chapter Seven presents some general themes from the analysis. Chapters Eight to Twelve describe in some detail the episodes identified in the return process while Chapters Thirteen to Seventeen discuss findings from the quantitative parts of the study.

Summary points

1. This study of return seeks to combine qualitative and quantitative, retrospective and prospective approaches, in order to make best use of the strengths and compensate for the weaknesses of each.

2. An initial prospective scrutiny of 31 children from 24 families sought to examine in detail the ways in which children, parents and professionals managed the return process, for better or worse.

3. A simultaneous study looked again at 875 children from three previous studies. Factors predicting the timing and the success of return were identified by multivariate analysis.

4. A third study tested prospectively hypotheses generated by the previous two studies.

5. The large numbers of children involved and the combination of approaches applied ensure that the results presented in this report are derived from a uniquely robust set of data.

6 The intensive study

This chapter describes an intensive scrutiny of 31 children returning to 24 families. In later chapters the process of reunion will be explored through a sequence of episodes that highlights key moments and issues as return gathers momentum. Four contrasting groups of children are represented: a) children likely to go home without serious problems b) children likely to experience some difficulty in getting back c) children unlikely to go home despite social work plans aimed at reunion and d) children likely to return, but not easily to settle.

It will be recalled that for this intensive study, twenty-four families awaiting the return of children looked after were selected from the 86 proposed by social workers. In eight cases, children were likely to be away less than six months; in another eight the reunion was expected to occur between seven and 24 months after separation. The final eight families had been separated for two or more years on reunion. As some families contained more than one relevant child, 31 children were included in this part of the research.

Four contrasting groups were identified. These comprised: (i) children likely to go home without serious problems; (ii) children likely to experience some difficulty in getting back; (iii) children unlikely to go home despite the social work plans aimed at reunion; or (iv) children likely to return but not easily settle. The sample aimed to be comprehensive, in incorporating as a wide a range as possible of possible participants and return scenarios. The combinations of timing and predicted outcome are summarised in table 6.1 overleaf.

What were the characteristics of the 31 children? The intensive study included more boys (22) than girls (9) but the age distribution was evenly spread among the 31 children, including four babies aged two years or less and six adolescents aged 16 years or more. Just over half (16) of the 31 children had been looked after voluntarily with the remainder being subject to care orders. Using Packman et al's (1986) classification of the circumstances which lead to being looked after, six of the 31 could be considered victims of abuse and/or neglect, 11 were beyond parental control or were offenders, leaving 14 where parents requested their children be accommodated The intensive study included four children from minority ethnic families, one of whom was Asian, and one girl whose mother was Irish and father West Indian.

Table 6.1: The distribution of cases selected for the intensive study

Research team predicts:	Early returner	Intermediate returner	Long-term returner	TOTAL
Easy return	2	2	2	6
Difficult return	5	5	3	13
Unlikely to return	3	2	2	7
Return & breakdown	2	2	1	5
TOTAL	12	11	8	31

The 24 families were followed up for 18 months, all the participants in the return being interviewed regularly during that time. Before presenting the results, however, it is necessary to describe in greater detail of what exactly these interviews consisted. Woods (1986) suggests that research interviews ought to be 'democratic, two-way, informal, free-flowing processes', but this approach carries a danger that the articulate will get a better hearing than the taciturn. To achieve consistency, a set of principles guided the interviews. For example, it was decided that in order to avoid distortion by third parties, only members of the research team would talk to respondents. To overcome the danger that certain returning children would capture a disproportionate amount of interest, two researchers were assigned to each case and shared interview material with each other. These practices ensured consistency in the conduct of the interviews and scrutiny of the evidence.

Ensuring reliability of the interview material

Such an approach to consistency also assisted in validating the interview material; there was the familiar research problem of not knowing whether the information collected was true or typical. This problem is particularly thorny in the social sciences because deception and concealment by respondents are not uncommon and although, as Hammersley and Atkinson (1983) found, a loss of accuracy may be balanced by the insights gained, reliability is still a problem. It is our experience that distortion is less easy when the interviewer is well-versed in the subject matter. As Whyte (1982) found, the plausibility of accounts can be checked during the interview and, as Little (1990) discovered, deception seldom endures over several meetings or the scrutiny of a group of respondents. Nonetheless, attempts were made to minimise, where necessary, the confusion that can spring from recollection. Whenever possible, interviews took place near to key moments in the return process. When people were asked to look back over even short periods of time, the systematic bias that occurs in long-term recall was reduced by using the methods employed by Quinton and Rutter (1988). They recommend,

> until the question of experiences, memories and reaction to childhood experiences are better understood, it is preferable to place most weight on discrete events located within broad time periods; to place more weight on clear descriptions of events and relationships rather than generalised recollections and to use the reconstructive nature of memory to locate events within a coherent life-history framework.

Observation of family life

The study of individual cases also benefited from observations of the interaction between family members and, in some instances, the actual return of the child. A considerable amount of discussion about research methods has concentrated on the ways in which researchers can best obtain such data (Giddens, 1976; Denzin, 1970; Filstead, 1970; Hammersley and Atkinson, 1983). Many are at pains to show that the researcher can become a member of the group under observation without affecting its structure (Becker, 1958; Becker and Geer, 1960).

However, in child-care research, it is extremely difficult to be a participant observer and slip unobtrusively into private family moments; nevertheless, the principles and aims of the method had obvious attractions and there was a viable alternative in non-participant observation (Woods, 1986).

Non-participant observation can be defined as 'participant observation where the people under scrutiny are aware of the researcher's role'. The researcher may change the dynamics of the group being studied but the effect can be minimised as participants become acquainted with and feel at ease with the stranger'. During this research, considerable time was spent with the families of returning children and observations made on the state of the child's home, whether the child had any belongings there and, particularly important, if a bed was available. The researchers also looked at the physical preparation for the child's return, the buying of gifts and redecoration that took place. In addition, they observed the actual return, looking at who greeted the child, whether neighbours and friends were involved and so forth. As will be seen, in some cases the return was a marked event with identifiable rites of passage, while in others the actual moment of reunion was hard to place as the child gradually re-integrated with the family or drifted back home in an unplanned way.

The analysis of material from the intensive study

The information produced by both the observation of children's returns and the structured and in-depth interviews was used in two ways. Firstly, it contributed to a profile of each individual family and the changes that occurred as the return took place. The experiential evidence provided unique material about respondents' fears, expectations and adaptations, their need to negotiate role and territory, their perceptions of home and their feelings of being returned.

Secondly, both the qualitative and quantitative evidence were used to develop the theoretical perspectives discussed in later chapters. In doing this, the thorny problem of generalising from case studies and the danger of considering only those cases that fit pre-established theories had to be faced. Theoretical generalisation was sought for the qualitative material in the following way. Initially, the material was examined for key concepts and themes that were frequently mentioned or observed and typologies were constructed. However, as would be expected, there were some ambiguities and these were examined in the light of the context of each case and the significance of the personalities of respondents. For example, misplaced optimism about a child's return can follow from the renewed interest of a parent long absent. Next, contrasting theoretical perspectives, such as functionalism, conflict theory and also common sense were applied to ensure that all possible explanations of the data were considered. Further checks involved bringing in external judges, including some respondents as well as academic colleagues. For example, a consultant psychiatrist commented on our interpretation of events in individual cases. The procedure seems the most effective way of ensuring rigorous scrutiny of qualitative data.

Episode analysis

One result of this approach was a realisation that there were several stages in the return process. However, long experience of longitudinal research has led us to be wary of identifying clear stages in the lives of looked after children or their families as individuals' lives do not fit into neat packages and apparently distinct phases rarely accommodate the experiences of every family member. Indeed, although it became clear that the return process could be broken down into segments each of which was meaningful to the participants, it was more difficult to understand how one part of the reunion led to another. Some children or relatives skipped what seemed important stages for others, for example the preparations for the homecoming. Furthermore, a step towards restoration lasting a matter of days for one family could take several months for another.

The need, therefore, was to find a more fluid schema for analysing and presenting the intensive data. Using a procedure developed for Little's (1990) study of young men in prison, the key episodes in children's returns were identified. An episode is defined as a variable period of time surrounding a particular phase of the reunion. As Lofland and Lofland (1984) point out, episodes are by definition remarkable and dramatic to the participants and, therefore, to the researchers as well. Episode analysis has been used in several disciplines but mainly to make sense of past events. For example, Keegan (1976) describes twelve episodes in the battle of Agincourt. In this study, by contrast, long-term outcomes were unknown.

Even when used prospectively, the great strengths of the episode analysis adopted for this study are its contribution to an understanding of the meanings and perceptions of the children and their family members over time and the opportunity it gives to wield control over the enormous mass of qualitative data assembled. There are, of course, some deficiencies in this approach; for instance, the reader is often left to fill in the gaps or make the links between the episodes and it does not lead to relatively straightforward, deterministic explanations. Indeed, it demands that the reader keeps a number of competing notions about return simultaneously on the boil.

Seven episodes were identified as particularly important:

- the initial separation
- subsequent changes in family circumstances
- the point at which return becomes an issue
- the point at which return occurs and the first few days at home
- the honeymoon period
- acrimonious negotiations between family members, and
- the point at which a new *modus vivendi* is established

Whilst certain events might overlap several episodes and some episodes might be missed altogether, this approach to the qualitative material has considerably helped with the analysis and presentation of findings. The following chapters look in detail at both the general themes that apply at all stages of return and in each of the above episodes. In each case, evidence from the various participants to the return is offered, along with the main themes drawn from the analysis.

Summary points

1. The 31 children in the intensive study cover the range of return situations. The sample ranges in age from babes-in-arms to young adults past school leaving age. The problems leading to separation range from abuse and neglect to offending and family breakdown

2. A protocol was drawn up to ensure the consistency and reliability of the research material.

3. Interview material was supplemented by non-participant observation of key events in the return process.

4. The data generated were analysed by colleagues from a number of disciplines, and by respondents themselves in some cases, and using contrasting theoretical perspectives.

5. The most useful approach to the data was that of episode analysis.

7 General themes from the intensive study

Themes of continuity, role and territory occur in each of the episodes in the return process.

Continuity

Maluccio, Fein and Olmstead (1986) open their study *Permanency Planning for Children* with the words

> in order to grow up satisfactorily, children need to know that life has predictability and continuity. They need the reliability of knowing where they will be growing up.

Continuity is also stressed by Kellmer Pringle (1975) who writes,

> a child is most likely to develop to a maximum level if he has an enduring relationship with at least one person who is sensitive to his individual needs and stages of development.

Several writers have explained that families and wider social networks provide children with that sense of continuity and security from which to plan and help fashion their identity and sense of worth. Kahan (1979) in her perceptive study of young adults recollecting their careers as children in care comments that

> families and what they mean to individuals not only as children but in adult life were of great significance to all, whether their families were related by blood-ties, by remarriage or by adoption.

She also highlights young people's need to belong:

for a pattern and for that pattern to be an orthodox one, it is vitally important for the child that everything is done to avoid any thought of being different from any other child.

Whitaker, Cook, Dunne and Lunn-Rockliffe (1984) in their study of children in residential care comment

the most important areas of concern from the point of view of the children were families and friends. This pre-occupation was present in a wide range of circumstances.

Indeed, the authors go on to emphasise the importance of the wider family and social networks of children in providing a sense of belonging for the child and offering explanations for present situations. They comment

persons in the child's network and, of course, the child him or herself, form opinions and hold views about key issues, such as the reasons for entering care, or on a child's history and its likely influence on present and future. Network members are inclined to identify certain turning points in the child's life and emphasise subsequent events in terms of them.

The research team found that interviews helped reconstruct the child's history in network terms,

as in time-lapse photography, one could see those points in a child's life at which significant network changes took place.

Indeed, the value for the child of strong family links and the sense of continuity and belonging that these provide are all explored at length in the Dartington Research Unit's studies *Lost in Care* and *Access Disputes in Child-Care*. A sense of continuity is often taken for granted but for those without it, the past and its meaning become constant pre-occupations. Continuity and security are viewed as particularly important in satisfactory child development and any child who fails to enjoy such a birth-right faces considerable difficulty.

I had three foster home placements in the two years after I was taken into care and then I ended up in a children's home. I hadn't much clue as to where I came from and none about where I was going. Nobody seemed to care about me, they never asked me what I wanted or what I felt, never showed any interest in what I did, either in school, in sport or in anything. Unless, of

course, you nicked something or kicked up rough, then there was
hell to pay and everyone put their nose in.

Another boy comments,

> I was at an O and A centre for months waiting for a foster home
> but nothing came up, everyone needs to belong somewhere and
> to somebody. How can an observation centre replace your
> parents?

Indeed, if continuity and a sense of belonging do not materialise,
then children will create them and fantasise a past which usually bears
little relationship to fact. Many observers have also commented on the
value of possessions, photographs and other mementoes to help
maintain links with those absent and continuity with the past.
Whitaker and colleagues comment that

> while all concerned constructed explanations for events, for
> example why a child was in care, the children themselves had
> little life experience to bring to bear and sometimes accepted or
> ascribed blame inappropriately or held incompatible views.

Thus, children comfort themselves with fantasy and myth.

> When I leave care I'm going to go back and find out exactly who
> my father is. Maybe he's a Duke or Lord or something and then
> everybody will be sorry and want to know me.

Kahan offers us a most poignant example of a child seeking
continuity and a sense of belonging.

> About three years after I went into adoption, I used to go down
> to the children's home, River-Side, to see if there was anyone
> there I remembered and took a big chunk out of the wall and I've
> still got it. In fact, I've heard the place is going to be pulled
> down, I think I'll get in first and ask for the name-plate. The
> chunk of wall is out in the shed somewhere, I wouldn't part with
> it.

But a need for continuity, a sense of belonging and the security that
comes from a sense of place are not only needed by children; adults also
seek to maintain continuities and to put separations and returns into
context. According to Yitzhak Kashti, a survivor of the holocaust, many
middle-aged Jews long settled in Israel remain haunted by the villages
and towns of central Europe from which they fled, often under terrible

circumstances, fifty years ago. They frequently revisit their origins. He comments on his own return to Hungary,

> You go back alone, it is the loneliest of experiences and everything floods back, very little things trigger off memories you've entirely forgotten. But in the end, you realise you cannot really return, all you can do is integrate the separations and returns into the battered identity you present in everyday life.

A middle-aged woman who with her sister fled from the Warsaw Ghetto in 1940, recollects the experience long after and the way return helped make sense of the present.

> I went back to Warsaw with my younger sister, it was heartbreaking, absolutely nothing remained, nothing that is except the bitter anti-Semitism of the Poles, everything had gone, now my sister's gone as well. Yet, in some ways there is comfort, we did go back together and the hatred itself provides some sense of continuity. Jerusalem makes much more sense to me now even though we have lived here fifty years.

Hence, when writers raise the issue of the needs of belonging and family links for children, there is often implicit in their writing this greater sense of order, sequence and continuity.

However, even these brief illustrations would suggest that authors differ considerably in their ideas on continuity. Generally speaking there is a contrast between definitions of continuity produced by academics seeking to refine theory and the ideas developed by those working with children to describe family and child situations. There are also contrasts between ideas about continuity produced by sociologists and those of social psychologists and psychiatrists, although all would agree that disruption and abrupt change in life patterns can be damaging.

Continuity might also be defined as that sense of meaning and order which people impose on a sequence of life events. These events may be unexpected or random, they may even be traumatic experiences such as a child being accommodated or the loss of a parent. Therefore, a sense of continuity is a way of maintaining psychological health. One can also perceive different types of continuity, for example, there are 'expressive continuities', those that endure over time and change very little. Some of these have macro aspects, such as national and regional identities and perhaps religious, moral or political beliefs, but they also come in the form of feelings for those long departed or the rights of 'family' over friendship. Secondly there are temporal continuities which do change over time. Indeed, such continuities may wither and be replaced by others such as changes in career or marriage. One might even suggest that there are conflicts between expressive and temporal continuities. As will be seen in the coming pages, return can cruelly expose these contradictions.

In asking children what going back is like, two themes constantly emerge. Firstly the complexities and difficulties in the resumption of roles and, secondly, the problems they encounter during the re-colonisation of lost territory. These concepts of role and territory are part of the continuity sought by those who are separated, whether child or adult. The ideas that both separation and return are not discrete events but part of a process and that separation from home for the majority of children is negotiated with return in mind are very important. Both for eventual return to home from care or accommodation and for the success of any reunion, the existence of strong links with family, particularly with the mother, is of great importance. It is possible that stressing these continuities to the absent child, highlighting continuities of relationships with family and neighbourhood and emphasising the likelihood of eventual return will facilitate reunion and lead to a successful adjustment.

On return, children's sense of continuity and security is likely to be much affected both by changes in the roles they are expected to make and by the space they seek to re-occupy.

Roles

Many years ago, the Dartington Unit studied the Byzantine world of the English boarding school, a set of institutions which would have warmed the heart and stimulated the pen of Goffman, institutions beside which other asylums pale. While the relevance of schools to the return of luckless children from being looked after might at first sight seem rather distant, the complexity of the roles children played within the boarding schools, the demands made upon them and the skills necessary for adequate role performance were of great interest.

Roles in the boarding schools could be classified in three distinct categories. These may have some transfer value to the roles played by children within families. First of all, there were *instrumental roles*, those concerned with acquiring skills and proficiency. Secondly, there were *organisational roles*, those concerned with oiling the wheels of the organisation, keeping the show on the road and, thirdly, there were *expressive roles*, those which were concerned with beliefs, states fulfilling in themselves and roles which had a spiritual dimension. Now within the school, children performed and moved between these roles swiftly, but not quite effortlessly. Their role performance often conflicted with others and there were tensions within a particular role.

This classification of roles is not quite as complicated as it sounds. For example, a parent taking a cookery class might be part of an *instrumental role*; cleaning the kitchen floor an *organisational* chore, a role which hopefully prevents children from breaking their necks; and, thirdly, counselling, supporting children and offering pastoral care are *expressive roles*. Neither should such a classification of roles be viewed as exclusive. For example, one may invest either the balancing of accounts, the stacking of supermarket shelves or even a gleaming kitchen floor with expressive dimensions.

Roles often overlap and, in many role performances, *instrumental*, *organisational* and *expressive* dimensions are closely interwoven. Indeed, one of the problems families and children face on return is that many apparently *organisational roles* within families, such as washing up, making the bed, cooking the chips and taking the dog for a walk, have expressive dimensions which pass largely unnoticed and family members have expectations and investments in these roles which can easily be violated. For example, a mother comments on a returning daughter,

> I thought she would be delighted that I had got a second-hand dish-washer, because we used to row about whose turn it was to do the washing up. But she wasn't pleased at all, she moaned about being done out of her job and actually hardly ever used the thing.

Very often within families certain roles have considerable status and power, as anyone clasping the television's remote control well knows. Thus, on return, the child finds many seemingly trivial actions deeply invested with other significances, each invested with rights and obligations, all forgotten or ignored at considerable risk. Indeed, when *organisational roles* in a family are invested with expressive dimensions, conflict and tension are likely. An armed services' wife said,

> A moment comes when I know that he is gone and that everything, kids, home, finance, everything is up to me. That realisation comes last thing at night when I go round closing the windows and bolting the door, I hate it, I feel guilty and angry at the same time. It's his job and he should be here to do it, I say to myself, he should protect me and the children. In fact, locking up at night can easily bring on tears and then I feel bad and stupid and say to myself, 'you wimp, without him you wouldn't have children to love or even a door to lock up.'

Hence, part of the management of return should be a keen awareness of the different dimensions operating within each role and that even the simplest of roles have expressive dimensions. It is also true that various family members, including the returning child, will have different perspectives on the meaning implicit in role performances.

Naturally, the holder of the television's remote control reminds others of the power dimension behind any role performance but he or she is highly likely to conflict with others when football coincides with *Coronation Street* or *Top of the Pops* and the arbiter of the evening's viewing will be reproached with comments from others such as 'well I bought the damn' thing,' 'who paid for the licence anyway?' 'I thought it was my Christmas present', or deftest strike of all, 'but Mum I'm supposed to watch *Panorama* for my homework.' Naturally the more key the role, the more derelictions in performance are noted. 'It's never worked properly since you let the dog gnaw the damn' thing.'

Not only do roles conflict when different individuals simultaneously seek to play the same role but also within roles there can be conflict, for example, between the parents' need to control, to be fair, yet to encourage and empathise with their children. In addition, conflict can be omnipresent, built into roles. For example, the role of an adolescent or of a step-parent or step-child has built into it conflicting loyalties and difficulties in meeting the expectations of others. This glimpse of the complexity of family roles no doubt would encourage the socially sensitive to take refuge in the role of the recluse or anchorite. But, actually, the gradual way in which roles are learned and changed and the loving environment in which performance takes place mean that most families are not arenas of endless dispute and tension. Nevertheless, the complexity of family roles illustrates how a child long separated from home will find reunion difficult and amply reinforces Winnicott's (1984) comment that

> insecure children can have all the feelings they can stand within their families or within a few yards of the doorstep.

Obviously, separation and return cause difficulties in any role performance. If absence is lengthy, children forget those signals which direct and reward appropriate behaviour. On return these signs have to be re-learned. While away, the child may adopt role behaviour very different from that expected at home and on reunion find an unappreciative audience. As one mother described,

> he came back from the assessment centre swearing like a trooper and throwing his weight around, that was at least until his father heard him and then gave him a belt.

It is also true that things have moved on both for children and their families, although separation tends to freeze the picture for those apart. The families of children who are looked after display a wearisome procession of arrivals and departures, a turbulence and movement which make reunion difficult. The households from which children were removed may not be those to which they return; going back may involve them in reunion with siblings also separated by a looked after experience. In addition, during the interim, families may have welcomed new members or may have had lodgers thrust upon them. The passage of time means that there is a gap between the roles the children wish to take up on return and those that the family are willing to accord them. Their departure may have encouraged others to usurp their role and occupy their territory at home, thus resenting their return, particularly if the welcome proffered at reunion seems disproportionate to the trauma and reasons for the original separation. Indeed, the Bible's finest parable says it all with admirable brevity:

> And he was angry and would not go in: therefore came his father out and entreated him.

And he answering said to his father, "Lo, these many years do I serve thee, neither transgressed I at any time thy commandment; and yet thou never gavest me a kid, that I might make merry, with my friends. But as soon as this thy son was come, which hath devoured thy living with harlots, thou hast killed for him the fatted calf".

And he said unto him, "Son thou art ever with me, and all that I have is thine. It was meet that we should make merry and be glad: for this thy brother was dead and is alive again and was lost and is found".

Children and adolescents, unprepared for the tensions and difficulties of return, will react aggressively and appear to the family to be recalcitrant and even less attractive than they were at the initial separation. As a thwarted adolescent girl illustrates,

> My new step-sister took the kids off to play group like some mother hen and Mum said 'there, that Angela is really good with them. You never liked the job and she does it without any fuss'. Well there was a fuss 'cos I burned that little shit's bus pass and she had to buy a new one.

But there are ways in which the role conflict inherent in return can be managed and minimised. When counselled and assisted, separated children and young people can become more objective about the roles they and others play in family life and more accommodating to the needs of others. Distance encourages a cooler look. In the same way the arrival of step-parents and step-siblings, although initially threatening, can stimulate new interests in family members. Families can do much by their efforts to keep alive the image of the absentee within the household, remain mindful of his or her preferences and, where possible, seem anxious for the return and be instrumental in its achievement.

A girl removed with her younger sister from a depressed mother comments,

> It was difficult when I was at home, I couldn't understand why Mum was lonely or depressed or what to do about it. She just used to sit in the pub or lie in bed. We used to row all the time. Being here makes me realise how little she has to look forward to while I and my sister have a lot, so now when I go home at weekends I try to be different to Mum. We go shopping

> together, watch T.V., sometimes it's quite a laugh. Now I'm looking forward to going home. Nicest thing is that Mum has been on to the social worker asking if we can go back.

In a similar way, a returning adolescent becomes reconciled to his new step-brother.

> I didn't like the idea of a step-brother at all and things were a bit dicey at first. We both liked football and I was much better than he was. We go to matches and we have just bought a motorbike between us to go racing. Most of the time it's in bits but now we get on fine and Mum is over the moon about it all.

A lad returning from youth custody comments,

> Going back was easier than I thought. I felt bad about the trouble I caused everyone and they, I know, were none too happy at kicking me out in the first place. But when I went through the door everyone was smiles, my photo in the army cadets was in its old place and Mum had my favourite meal ready. My step-dad offered me a can of beer, so even he was trying hard. It's been like that now for a couple of months, I've got a job bringing in some money and they look at me different now.

Of course, what children find most distressing is inconsistency in parenting behaviour, a lack of forewarning and unreliability in adult role performance. This uncertainty is manifest in families where key members suffer from the mood swings associated with depression and/or the aggression and unpredictability inherent in alcoholism.

While re-negotiating a new set of roles on return may present problems, children also have to re-adapt to familiar places. In some cases they enter new households and other unfamiliar territories. The next section looks at the ways in which 'territory' affects their return.

Territory

In terms of outcome the mystery of criminology has not been among the most productive of social sciences. Nevertheless, one of its more interesting by-ways has been geographies of crime and the territories of offending. Intriguing, possibly even useful, is the knowledge that one is most likely to be murdered, not by some mindless thug, but by one's nearest and dearest. In addition, the kitchen and bedroom, where presumably our keenest appetites are aroused, are territories of maximum risk. Would it be wise in moments of high family tension to abandon eating and sleeping or, like children, retire strategically to the toilet?

Although these issues might seem adult pre-occupations, territory and the personalisation of space are of equal concern to children. If the usurpation of role is also accompanied by the seizure of territory then tensions will quickly mount. As a mother swiftly learned,

> I thought he would be grateful the boy next door had looked after the rabbits. Well, he wasn't. He said he'd built the hutch, the rabbits were his and nobody else would look after them properly.

It is accepted good practice that separated children take something of home away with them, mementoes and keepsakes, the loss of which can be very distressing. In the same way, during separation children's private places, their bed, cupboard, drawer, cluster of photographs and prized possessions should remain undisturbed and inviolate. Change can immediately be recognised and resented even after an absence sufficiently long to have contributed to forgetfulness. Neither does age act as a filter to a sense of violation, as adolescents are quite as sensitive to changed territories as younger children. Anyone managing return should explore the young person's expectations of what his or her territory is going to be like, what changes might have occurred, in order to forestall disappointment. Naturally, bountiful additions like a new chair or bedspread may be welcome if the chance to retain what has gone before remains open, but the disposal of anything, varying from a pair of odd trainers to a pile of battered colour supplements, is fraught with risk. A naval wife copes with an upset child,

> I was amazed. Anne is only six and we had been in Gibraltar for three years. When we came home she was in tears because her bedroom was different. All that our friends had done while they stayed was to move the wardrobe and chest of drawers a bit. Anyway, she was inconsolable until we moved them back again. I didn't even realise they had been shifted, but Anne did and didn't like it one bit.

The gradual re-colonisation of lost space is also a strategy to ease return, as a mother recollects the designs of her adolescent daughter in seeking reunion.

> I knew she was worming her way back in, each weekend she would leave more and more stuff behind, shampoo in the bathroom, clothes, magazines, anything. Gradually she took over the bathroom shelf and all my stuff went on to the window-sill.

The scattering of one's property not only helps regain lost territory but possessions themselves are symbolic of one's rights and place in the home. Indeed, possessions can be sacrosanct and the unauthorised borrowing of gear, however trivial, can allow tensions to focus upon the culprit. As a returning adolescent girl comments,

> That scrubber my dad brought home had the cheek to borrow my skirt, then she complained it was too short, too tight and needed cleaning. 'Wash it yourself' I said 'then it will be even tighter for all your friends, like dad, with wandering hand trouble.'

Winnicott (1984), slightly less acerbic, neatly summarised these issues fifty years ago as the dust of war settled on parents awaiting the return of their children. He reminded them that the child who came back would be different from the waif, brown label round the neck, that tearful mothers had seen off several years before.

> In two or three years of separation, both mothers and children will have altered, more especially the child out of whose life three years is a big chunk. After three years, he is the same person, but he has lost whatever characterises the six year old because he is now nine. And then, of course, even if the house has escaped bomb damage, even if it is exactly as it was when the child left, it seems much smaller to him because he is now so much bigger. It must also be difficult to come back from a farm to a room or two in a block of flats in a big city.

Thus, the re-occupation of lost territory is as important as the resumption of family roles on any return from separation. Role and territory are often closely associated, and sometimes invested with considerable expressive significance. So, it is not surprising that, after a brief honeymoon period, rows and tensions between family members and the returning child manifest themselves. Far from offering forebodings that *rapprochement* is not working, quarrels are likely to signify that reunion is on course.

Conclusion

Clearly, reunion with parents and the wider family will not be easily accomplished by the child or adolescent and going home is likely to be as stressful for those who afford a welcome as it is for those who return. Hence, careful management of return should be part of any social work intervention and the same effort that goes into smoothing the pains of separation should also characterise return.

It is also clear that separation and return are part of a long process. Indeed, they may never be accomplished, but, like so many relationships, hover in a limbo of uncertainty. Seeing the child back through the door is not sufficient because breakdowns in reunion are not necessarily rapid, clustering in the first few weeks. Rejection and withdrawal take time to negotiate and hope dies long after going back.

Far from being a moment in time, it is difficult to say when a return has actually taken place, just as not being with someone does not necessarily imply separation. Is return the thudding of heavy boots on the doormat? Is it the passionate, unfeigned embrace? Is it the inevitable row when tensions over role and territory become explicit and, hopefully, lead to rapid re-definition? Is it when everything is back to normal and the separation can be recollected with nostalgia and a guilty smile?

In a process perspective, separation and return cease to be discrete events but colour each other. What happens at the outset will influence the ways participants view subsequent events, as the parable of the prodigal son beautifully illustrates. What happens on return will alter perceptions of and give meaning to the initial separation. Each episode informs the other and an exploration of 'return' can benefit from the adoption of this longitudinal perspective. For example, looking at the episode of the initial separation participants might ask why the child needed to be looked after in the first place. Who, if anyone, was deficient? How much was everyone a victim of circumstance? The answer to these questions will obviously colour the ways in which links are maintained over time between family and separated child and will also affect reunion.

Thus, it is best to cease to view moments of separation and return as discrete events but perceive them as part of a continuing process of adaptation in the child, as he or she strives for continuity, meaning and identity. After all, there may be many separations and several attempts at reunion, the return itself will be blurred by preparatory visits, by subsequent departures and by the uneasy mobility of the young person even after re-unification with the family. There is a difference between 'returning', which is a process brimming with fraught possibilities and 'being returned'; indeed, many respondents suggested that long separation fundamentally alters the ways in which they perceive others and themselves so that reunion is never quite the same as the union which preceded it. In that sense, return is never possible.

While, on return, a voyager may expect people to be the same as at the moment of departure and they similarly expect a facsimile of the person who set out, time and experience irrevocably change any actor's performance. In some, those returning from ordeals and trauma, such as hostages and servicemen, the gap in comprehension between those coming back and those who stayed can lead to breakdown.

To return home, children and adolescents have, once more, to separate from those carers and friends with whom close relationships may have been forged during separation. Adolescents are highly likely to have reciprocated relationships with other young people far from the home front. Even the prodigal son might be forgiven for occasionally twitching in nostalgia for past harlots and riotous living. Thus, however welcoming the natural family proves to be on return, some oscillation in the young person's involvement and contentment is to be expected. There is also evidence that separation and withdrawal are effective strategies for coping with stress and that, once learned, such devices are not unattractive. Thus, a young person's movement round the wider family may not be particularly detrimental; indeed, in late adolescence such movement is a well-tried avenue of breaking away from the nest.

While return may be problematic, most children and adolescents achieve some sort of reunion with their families; in fact, the majority of these are successful. Neither does breakdown among those who go back necessarily imply a failure of reunion, in the same way as divorce does not necessarily signify a marriage devoid of satisfactions.

This chapter has charted the difficulties a returning child may experience in resuming lost roles and territories within the family. Nevertheless, for most young people, return also involves re-entry to the neighbourhood and re-integration with friends, whose mobility and transience will complicate re-acceptance. The majority of children and adolescents will go back to school, to employment or to some form of training. It is unlikely that these looms of youth will provide an entirely smooth passage for those who shuttle to and fro. The greatest challenge to those seeking resettlement may not lie within their families but in seeking jobs, in resuming school and community membership. Indeed, when the difficulties inherent in family reunion are compounded by re-adjustment problems outside the home, then return may swiftly end in defeat and flight.

Looking at those episodes significant in the process of reunion, beginning with the stresses and perceptions engendered by the initial separation, illuminates the clusters of adaptations, both within and outside the family, that all returners have to face.

That continuity, role and territory are important at several points in the return process and the messages learned can be used to plan for children's restoration before, during and after the separation. The chances of success are much greater where

1. There are continuities in the child's life (including family relationships, education, cultural identity and social networks).

2. The child retains a role within the family at each stage in the return process.

3. The child retains territory in the return home either by having a room, a bed or by the leaving of toys and other personal possessions or by the retention of keepsakes.

However, during different episodes in the return process, other factors become apparent. The task of identifying these begins with the first episode in the process, the events and negotiations surrounding separation.

8 Separation from home

Many subsequent negotiations, including reunion, between parent, child and social workers are coloured by early events in the looked after experience. This chapter focuses on early episodes in the looked after career, both the point of separation and the first few weeks thereafter. The significance of these experiences for families and children as they negotiate reunion is illustrated.

Earlier chapters have documented the increasing focus in both child-care policy and legislation on speeding the return of children looked after by local authorities back to their parents. Today, ideas of child rescue are unfashionable and families are now seen as the mainstay of children's lives, even of those children who are abused, neglected or beyond control. Thus, preventative work which obviates the need to remove the child from home has once more become a high priority and where this fails, the sharing in the care of the absent child between families and social workers is obligatory. After all, it is to the family that the child will eventually return and any improvements made in the parents' capacity to care will be of considerable value.

Getting the child home quickly has high priority with social workers and a strategy for return ought to assume considerable salience in a 'care plan' for the child, just as, in the halcyon days of the reformatory schools, 'after care' was supposed to start as the boys came through the gates. Hopefully, for children in care, this ideal should come closer to realisation than it did for young delinquents.

The alacrity and success of any return is bound up with the processes by which the child became looked after and the reasons he or she needs to remain away. Children will have been referred for help by a wide variety of agencies, including schools, police or health authorities, all of whom maintain some interest in the solution of the problem. Some candidates for care or accommodation present themselves; others are identified by families and neighbours. While most of those who come to notice merit little action and remain 'known to social services', a minority of referrals are swiftly removed from home, often in crisis circumstances. These precipitate departures colour the way parents perceive subsequent interventions.

The outcomes of welfare or educational interventions with children and adolescents can only be evaluated and understood if antecedents are explored. It is important to take a long-term view when scrutinising the situations of children and adolescents because what is a disaster at one moment can easily herald subsequent success. The swiftness and success of any reunion is likely to be much influenced by what has gone before, by the preparations made for return, by the legitimacy of the original separation and by the resolution of problems while the families are apart. Like the young men of Alsace, who long kept two military uniforms in the cupboard, one German, one French, successfully coping with any return implies a keen awareness of and accommodation to preceding events.

Subsequent chapters identify key moments in the process of reunion. Initially, however, it is helpful to describe the situation of the 31 children and 24 families who participated in the intensive study at the time of separation.

Episode One: Separation

Children are looked after for many reasons and by many legal routes. Of the 31 children in this intensive study 16 were accommodated under voluntary arrangements, leaving 15 who were on care or emergency protection orders. The expected lengths of children's separation varied depending on these and other factors.

Short-stay admissions are usually voluntary arrangements between social workers and families and most follow temporary family breakdowns, usually a mother's illness or confinement. In the majority of these cases families view social services in a very positive way. Such separations involve many younger children, often sets of siblings, most of whom are placed in foster care. This scenario characterised eight of the families scrutinised in this part of the study. Their needs for an alternative family were short-term and social workers hoped that reunion would be possible within six months of separation. Indeed, in two cases, the child was already at home by the time of the first interview. As might be expected, these short-term separations posed fewer problems on reunion than others.

The intermediate and long-stay returners, in contrast, included more children who had experienced severe abuse or neglect as well as adolescents seriously beyond control. Residential care and placements with relations and friends were more common for these young people and, in these cases, social workers viewed return as a more delicate task.

Whilst for some the initial separation was precipitate, 16 of the 31 children studied were well known to social services and ten had been looked after before. These proportions mirror general patterns. Prior to separation, therefore, considerable negotiations had taken place in many cases between families, children and social workers. These initial contacts were also likely to colour the ways in which family and children perceived separation, particularly when, as Packman et al. (1986) have demonstrated, the degree of choice for families was restricted.

The decision to look after a child poses a variety of immediate problems. Social workers have to choose the appropriate legal arrangements, decide where the child should live and, wherever possible, negotiate access between families and absent children. In making these plans, much will depend on the length of time the separation is expected to last and on factors such as the reasons for separation, knowledge of the family and the availability of resources. In addition, the involvement of outside agencies, such as police or courts, not only complicates social work decisions but also affects the ways in which families and children perceive the legitimacy and wisdom of the separation. Police intervention may outrage families and sour subsequent events, while health visitors, for example, are more amicably accepted. Subsequent decisions crystallise these initial perceptions, emphasising certain options and closing others.

As the child enters care or accommodation, parents have to cope with the loss of their offspring in circumstances that are generally stigmatising. They have to handle a mixture of feelings, such as failure, anxiety, mourning and anger, and develop coping strategies, such as what to tell relatives and neighbours. In most contexts, their views will be forceful.

> If I could stand up in court and tell the judge everything, he'd understand and let me have my babies back

said one resolute mother whose access had been restricted.

> My daughter is ill and needs help, it was quite wrong to take the children from her

appealed a grand-mother in a letter to us, while another aggrieved parent added,

> I went to social services for help and what did I get? They took away my children and made me feel like a criminal. When they come back I'm clearing out somewhere else where social workers will never find me.

For children, too, care or accommodation involve major transitions, even traumatic upheavals, with all the disorientation, stress and adjustments associated with such moves. Even for them, tears are not necessarily a barometer of feelings.

> They took me to a foster home. I didn't know where. I still don't know why. Everything I knew went and I've never got it back.

In contrast, some children see the changes as necessary and find them easy and enjoyable.

> When Mummy's ill, we go to Mrs. Fraser's; we love it. They've got a hamster and a goldfish there and Mr. Fraser acts silly and makes us laugh.

Before and after separation, various negotiations have to take place, some reassuring, some less so.

> I didn't know what to tell my mother; we meet in Kwik-Save every Tuesday, so I said I'd got the 'flu and didn't go but she'd heard about the kids being taken away from our Pamela (my sister).

> They said Amanda would go to a special centre where experts would get her back to school. They said it was a treatment place and she'd stay for six weeks. I was so worried that I just nodded. But after they'd gone, I thought how the hell will they get her to

school when I haven't been able to for a year? They came back after a fortnight and said she needed intensive care and now I don't see her at all.

In all these negotiations, return will be on the agenda from the start, either as a clearly expected outcome or as a generally desirable aim; on the other hand the issue may remain significant simply because everyone ignores it, as the following examples show.

One mother recalled,

> I went to this meeting and they explained where the twins were going and it sounded very nice. It was all about how I could visit and what the foster parents were like. I got home and Stuart (partner) said 'when are they letting them come back?', I just looked blank and said, 'No-one mentioned anything about that'. He said I was an idiot and we had a row.

The social worker in talking to the above parents at a subsequent meeting said reassuringly,

> Of course we want the children back, Mrs. Campion. We're not being critical but we have to be sure it's right for them and that might be some time. You need to sort yourselves out first.

In an interview, the social worker elaborated,

> I can talk to Karen (the mother). She knows I'm on her side. She knows that I opposed the adoption when the psychiatrist suggested it and recommended work towards rehabilitation as soon as possible. Basically, she loves the children and vice-versa. She's a bit unstable mentally but the most she's ever threatened was that she'd once felt like she might harm them and when I said 'how?' she replied, 'by hitting them.' It really annoys me when the senior talks of child protection because I've never seen any evidence they need it.

The response of families

The 31 children in this intensive study illustrate the wide variety of situations that can lead to a child being looked after. Some left home willingly, while two left swiftly under emergency arrangements. Six of the families involved groups of siblings but the others departed alone. Some parents felt their child's departure as a bereavement, whilst others viewed separation as a familiar recurrence and three mothers could not face the event at all. Similar variations were seen in other aspects of the arrangements, in the role taken up by social workers, the receptions offered by carers and the style of interactions that accompanied the children's initial separation.

The way separation is handled has important consequences, and initial perceptions colour future relationships between families and social services. Aggrieved parents can respond in many ways but bad early experiences rarely lead to co-operation and, even less, to participation in social work plans. Similarly, difficulties encountered in early visits cause parents to withdraw from their child's life, engendering problems for later returns. At the moment of separation, parents are highly likely to be preoccupied with their own problems and changes at home, particularly new relationships and reconstituted households. They may find the traumas of separating from their child overwhelming or may use the stress of separation as an excuse to avoid facing the problems that necessitated the child's removal.

The child's separation is, therefore, an outcome of a long and complex family history and much of what follows, including the eventual return, is affected by both the reasons for the child's absence and its style of implementation. Thus, the management of return is specific to each case and needs a thorough understanding of all the antecedents leading to a child's separation.

Bitterness can endure, as this poignant quotation from a child's letter to a dying father shows:

> I am sorry you are gone. I wish we could have had some more good times together. In some ways I am glad it is over. I wish you could have been a good adviser like the staff here. I have a lot of complicated feelings and I do not know how to put them. From your loving son, Dan.'

The response of children's relatives is particularly affected by the way that the separation was seen to have been handled. If the child's departure was well managed, there was less anxiety and bitterness. One social worker explained why he had overridden parents' request for fostering with relatives and outraged the wider family.

> It's all very well them talking about the extended family. Mother's relationship with her mother was explosive. So

suggesting that Darren might have gone to his grandparents opened up all the old wounds. Putting Darren with grandma and grandad would be like sticking him in lodgings and he's only six.

It was clear that some families and children were far more prepared psychologically and culturally for separation than others. This anticipation had several aspects: in three cases, parents had been in care themselves and the pre-socialisation took the form of inter-generational awareness.

I and my sisters were in care six times. I think my gran was in an orphanage in Ireland as a girl as well. I was fifteen before I realised that every child did not have a social worker.

In three other cases, there was a cultural tradition either of private fostering or of high geographical mobility of wage earners and a sharing of care amongst female relatives.

You must realise that in the Caribbean the family structures are different on different islands. In Jamaica, the men worked away and the women looked after the children.

As a consequence, preparations for separation varied considerably. One mother shopped in Boots as if her child was off on a school trip, while seven others claimed to have been neither consulted nor informed until the day of departure.

Certainly it would seem that the ease and success of return are influenced by the quality of social work offered at the time of separation. Many parents are numbed by numerous anxieties not all associated with the loss of their children. When the problems leading to separation are perceived as likely to be ameliorated or resolved by a separation and the intervention is seen by the family as legitimate and in the best interests of the child then return will be less difficult.

Nevertheless, at this stage, there is still a great deal that social workers can do to obviate problems later on. By bridging the two worlds of the child and keeping parents involved in decisions, social workers can ease parents' sense of personal failure and reduce the likelihood of children fantasising which, as will be seen, can complicate reunion. Particularly important is to avoid the sense of mutual loss. This means helping relatives and children anticipate and interpret what the return will be like, for example by getting parents to chart the changes in their household and the consequences of these for the home-coming.

Does a successful separation affect return? For all parties, each separation proved extremely stressful, more because of expressive failure than poor organisation. The actual dynamics of the transition were viewed as well-handled in the majority (70%) of cases and, although most children were understandably anxious, most found the experience less stressful than expected. In fact, while a few families spoke of a sense of release, many families and children found the event something of an anti-climax.

It was the affective component of separation that raised most anxiety. Parents felt guilty, especially that they had failed their child and let down their wider family. In the eyes of others they had fallen short. Children felt rejected, partly because of the rift and partly because their families seemed powerless to help them. Their worries focused on matters such as territory, that may seem trivial to an outsider, 'Will my brother get my toys?' 'I bet she'll pinch my gear'. But such apparently superficial concerns reflect much deeper insecurities about their situation. Often, the long-term viability of their family is questioned. Is it a family in anything but name? As one child recalled,

> One night I dreamt the phone rang, I picked it up and it was Auntie Kate. She just said 'Your mother's dead'. I woke up sweating and couldn't get back to sleep. Did I have a family or was I like some orphan in story books?

Return also has an affective dimension, testing perceptions of whether children really are wanted back and whether parents are keeping memories alive while children are away. Unfortunately, during this episode, return was rarely discussed as part of the care plan, other than in very general terms of how long the child would be away and what home visits should take place. But for most children it was the only question that mattered. All kinds of symbols indicated to them the priority afforded by parents and social workers to return. One eight year old, Jason, correctly interpreted his mother's casual comment to a neighbour about taking in a lodger as a sign that his speedy return from being looked after was unlikely, despite the social worker's repeated assurances. Another six year old was reassured by his mother's romantic suggestion that at bed-time they should both look at the moon and they would know that each was thinking of the other. Return is built into the strategy of separation and its possibility and imminence should be honestly faced by everyone. Expressive continuities are, for youngsters, constantly threatened by temporal continuities and children's sensitivity to the symbols, actions and expressions of adults, siblings and peers should not be underestimated. Children only too easily get the wrong messages. Anxiety makes them distrustful.

The stresses caused by separation also vary; they arise for different reasons at different points in children's looked after careers. On the first occasion, there is considerable fear of the future, but as time passes the focus of anxiety changes. But the distress experienced by children does not seem to diminish on repeated separations, an anxiety noticed by researchers studying children who oscillate in and out of hospital.

Why do repeated separations feel more difficult? It may be that the failures and disappointments of previous reunions suggest to children and parents that their problems are insuperable. Separation, far from being an unwelcome incident in life's rich pattern, is likely to become the pattern itself. On the other hand it may be that the focus of anxiety changes; the threats posed to children by the mechanics of separation fade with familiarity, allowing feelings of insecurity, discontinuity and rootlessness to assume greater salience.

The initial separation can be viewed, therefore, as a key moment in the process of return. Sensitively managed, the rift need not hinder eventual reunion but all too often the anxieties and violations of the episode linger and magnify. On departure, roles change as the absent adolescent becomes the prodigal and as parents face up to feelings of bereavement.

Of course, the absentee rapidly learns that emotional and physical territories are vacated and may be occupied by others. There are many rites of passage in this process. Some of these are overt, such as case conferences, the signing of papers and the packing of clothes; others are covert, such as the moment when being looked after emerges as a possibility, gaining importance as the family's problems refuse to budge. These moments of truth are very clear to children and families and markedly contrast with the few signposts which characterise and ease return.

In order to ease the pains of separation, continuity is stressed both formally and informally as children leave home. Social workers mollify all parties, stressing that the absence will be as short as possible and that contacts between children and families will be frequent. In all too many cases these reassurances markedly contrast with what actually happens which leads families and children to feel betrayed. Other continuities of experience may also be promoted, such as keeping the child at the same school or maintaining the child's racial identity. Even at this early stage, the extent to which expressive continuities are maintained lays the foundations for the ease of later returns.

The separation experiences of looked after children, therefore, should not be viewed in isolation but as part of a sequence of events in which family and children have had to accommodate many disintegrating experiences. Separation may solve the immediate problems facing a family and child and, hopefully, should promote or protect the young person's welfare, but for some, particularly for those whose stay is extended, the experience of being looked after can open the door to new problems - the secondary difficulties of coping with separations, managing new relationships and mastering changed living situations. Indeed, interactionist psychologists have suggested that these can prove overwhelming, even displacing the primary problems for which intervention was originally deemed necessary.

> Jason came here for assessment but we're now thinking of at least
> 18 months in our treatment unit

said one group worker, reacting to the discovery referred to earlier that Jason's mother had let his bedroom. The fact that his sister had been accommodated with him and was also likely to stay as a result of this decision aroused little concern from relatives or social workers, despite the fact that her needs were somewhat different.

The changes which follow separation and entry into the looked after system have been well documented. Indeed, it was anxiety over the instability of many children's placements and relationships while separated that encouraged the development of concepts such as 'drift' and 'permanency planning' in the 1970s. But it is only in recent years that their extent and complexity have been fully appreciated. Nonetheless, return is likely to be more successful when family and children perceive the problems necessitating the original separation to have been resolved or to have been much assisted by the child's being looked after.

Episode Two: Changes in circumstance

What happens in the days and months following separation? One consistent finding was that the composition of the natural family was highly likely to change during the child's absence. New babies and step-parents greeted returning children while previous household members well-known to the child departed. Children also often returned to new and radically different households and experienced considerable movement both while in care or accommodation and in their home circumstances. Links between families and absent children declined even in situations where everyone wished them to flourish, looked after siblings were separated, parents felt de-skilled and played a diminishing role in their child's life. Social work contacts with the natural family became infrequent or were lost altogether.

This cluster of events characterised the histories of children who had become 'lost in care' and affected as many as one in seven of the long-stay group. These residual cases were highly dependent on the welfare system. For example, they had no friends outside care or accommodation and they were culturally and socially anomic. Unfortunately, many of the adverse effects of separation do not become apparent until the child's return home becomes an issue.

Several factors highlighted by the intensive case studies are important here. First, there is a tendency for new information to emerge about children and families as a result of the increased scrutiny which accompanies the child's stay away. Some of this new knowledge radically alters care plans, preventing the return of many children. But, equally important is information that would never have been discovered had the child not left home. This often has the effect of reducing social worker's confidence in parents' ability to care and engendering misgivings regarding return plans.

> I was quite happy about mother's competence and her ability to care for Tracey until I found out that as a teenager she had given birth to a child which she tried to keep but which had to be removed for protection and was ultimately adopted. This really threw me. It delayed Tracey's return for six months until I was sure the home was O.K. I know it's silly but I just lost my nerve. I couldn't take the risk and I'd done ten years in the mental health team.

Tracey's mother, too, noticed the change:

> I always got on well with Mrs. Thomas (social worker) until one day I told her my own life history and how I didn't want Tracey to suffer the same things as me. She seemed to turn off and on the next visit when I asked 'will Tracey be home for Easter?' I got all sorts of excuses.

A second problem results from the diminishing contacts between social workers and the natural family during the child's absence. Not only do links between family and absent child wither but when social workers have no contact and no means of re-establishing it, currency between social worker and family is devalued. Entry to reconstituted families poses particular problems when new arrivals take leadership roles.

Contact between parents and absent children is maintained in several ways. There are visits, letters and phone calls; there are feelings of belonging to home and community; there is the currency of news and information, perhaps acquired through third parties; and there is children's awareness of their parents' power (if any) to act in their interests. If this currency is devalued and squandered, families have little to talk about.

Respondents emphasised the importance of fantasy in maintaining contacts between separated people. It was often hard to distinguish fantasy from reality in the comments that parents and children made. For example, one 17 year old who had been completely rejected by his family but still hoped to return to live nearby told us that at week-ends when they did not telephone:

> I bet they're out finding me a nice flat.

A mother told us how she longed for her children's return and while waiting passed her time in the following way:

> I'm pretty hard up and often feel lonely, so about three times a week, I spend the evenings in town looking in the shops and gas and electric showrooms, imagining the things I will buy to make a nice home for the boys.

Clearly, such perceptions serve to sustain relationships during the separation but can become so essential a coping strategy that they remain unmodified, even in the face of clear contrary evidence. Return becomes a moment of truth, a situation in which reality and fantasy meet. It is these gaps in perception and the fear of their exposure that makes return so difficult for all concerned.

The Child's View

Nowhere are these contrasting perceptions of return more poignantly demonstrated than in talking to children. It was difficult to gauge how far the children interviewed could perceive alternatives to where they were and so have some understanding of what return would actually mean. Nonetheless, the children all had a clear perception of 'home'. They knew who was in it and all but six of them wanted to be there. But it was a static view of a situation as they had once known it, a perception reinforced by the endless 'waiting' that seems such a feature of children's looked after experiences and which is so often exacerbated by chronic anxiety. Any subsequent change in the home situation, therefore, proved very difficult for children to comprehend. In addition, the young people displayed considerable anxiety that their home would disappear. Several explained vividly how they thought that their mother and siblings might simply go away and nothing would be left for them. Children seem to be aware of the fragility of the family home even if changes in its structure and membership are less easy to assimilate. Amanda, a 15 year old long looked after has already been described. She confessed

> I worry it will all disappear. I'll go back and there'll be nothing, just a big space.

Such views may, of course, reflect the children's desperate attempts to make sense of what has happened to them. Indeed, many children felt extremely guilty that they had been or could be the cause of the family fragmentation they feared. This is exacerbated by the child's perception that something damaged can never be repaired. It was also clear that, in their anxiety to return, children pick up and distort information not intended for their ears.

Particularly affected by the static view of the natural family were children's views of other youngsters in the household. A likely effect of family dislocation and reconstitution is an increase in the number of siblings, whether natural, half or step, and of 'cousins' who can be numerous in large families. As Wedge and Mantle (1991) have shown, permutations of relationships within a family are greatly increased with the addition of a new child.

This difficulty in incorporating the changes taking place at home can lead to surprises when children re-encounter their siblings as a two year period produces considerable changes in children and adolescents. Teenagers, for example, quickly graduate from motor-bikes to the opposite sex or from romance magazines to the real thing. Thus, the time span of looked after careers is even more significant for sibling changes than it is for parents' situations.

It is difficult to conclude what precisely children in care and accommodation can and cannot comprehend about future return to home and community. They can certainly remember people from their past and speak affectionately about them. They also have a clear perception of home, static as that view might be. Yet, under the stresses posed by an impending return, they clearly find it difficult to think logically or organise their feelings.

Important changes occur in the situations of looked after children and their natural families. The problems posed by separation have to be tackled, family compositions alter, children move around and contact between social workers, children and families declines. These changes are not always apparent until return is considered. In addition, the new situation is compounded by the effects of new information that emerges from increased professional scrutiny and the difficulties social workers face in negotiating with reconstituted families. The diverging views of participants and the gaps between fantasy and reality also come into play, making it difficult for children to understand their situation.

Conclusions

Considerable research attention has focused on the deleterious effects of a child's separation from home but few investigations have explored the influence of the removal from home upon subsequent reunion. This chapter has used the experience of the 31 children in the intensive study to address this issue.

The majority of looked after children are reunited with parents or other relatives and social work planning can accommodate the prospect of return home by an inclusive approach to the family. But separation can muddy even the clearest waters; parents can become mistrustful of social work efforts; children lose whatever security is afforded by their family life and expressive continuities which have given coherence to their existence are questioned; social workers find that their initial perspectives are complicated as new information on the family comes to light.

Very often, the tensions and anxieties associated with removal from home do not surface during the child's separation, but it is unlikely that they have evaporated. Indeed, as children and parents cope with the immediate problems of being apart, the causes and consequences of separation can be suppressed but they eventually surface in the days that follow reunion.

9 Return becomes an issue

For the majority of children, return becomes an issue early on in their looked after careers, for others many months may elapse before reunion is considered. Here, the moment when social workers, children and families begin to face up to the challenges posed and realignments necessitated by reunion is examined. Family roles will have to be re-learned and re-defined, cherished territories abandoned or shared. The first few days at home are also explored as an episode, highlighting the anxieties and false expectations engendered in many children and families in the early stages of reunion.

There is usually a point in the child's career when return home becomes an issue. This is not to say that rehabilitation has not previously been considered, indeed, for short-term cases, return plans are probably formulated at the point of reception. But there comes a time when social workers bend their minds to returning the child.

For ten of the 31 children reunion had been part of social work plans on the day of separation, although for one young girl, several previous attempts had failed to achieve restoration. For others, return plans began much later and, in five cases involving adolescents, they had begun two or more years after separation. The reasons which stimulated plans for reunion varied with each child. In some cases home circumstances improved, in others, children's behaviour calmed down, while occasionally time and options simply ran out. Indeed, for ten children, return home was precipitated by events that were largely external and unexpected.

Episode Three: Return becomes an issue

As reunion began to loom large it was clear that even the mention of return generated widespread anxiety among children and families, foster carers and social workers. Return is invariably stressful but even the thought of it seems to be frightening and occasionally disturbing, no matter how much people long for or expect it. As one young person said:

> When Mrs. Dass said, 'I think it's time we got you home', my stomach turned over, my heart beat fast, my hands sweated, I wanted to go to the toilet and I tried to change the subject. Yet, it's what I'd wanted her to say for ages.

For parents, too, reunion meant disruption, extra responsibility and additional expense. As a mother said:

> I know it's awful but we've got used to him being away and enjoy his coming home for short stays. The thought of having him back for good worried us, all the noise, washing, cost, getting him up for school. We couldn't sleep all night worrying about what to do and could we cope.

Social workers also feared that return might signal a repetition of previous difficulties, especially in abuse situations.

> I wanted him home. I could see him getting institutionalised and the proper place for a child is with their family. But he had probably been physically abused and certainly he was neglected. Frankly, it's a risk to say that it won't happen again. I sometimes envisage a scenario of a High Court judge as the arresting officer and me as the hapless social worker.

The reasons for these fears are many. First, there is the fact that the fantasies which sustain the separation, described in the last episode, come under scrutiny. The idea of return questions their validity and raises suspicion about their shaky foundations. Indeed, several children who were interviewed implied they had forgotten what living at home was really like, just as some parents said they could not remember how life was when the children were there. While fantasies may be functional for surviving a separation, there is certain to be a degree of 'let down' when return actually occurs. Naturally, the severity of the disappointment will vary according to the situation, the investment each has in the reunion and the extent to which reality accords with happy anticipation. Unfortunately, some aspects of reunion are not open to negotiation and fantasy reconciliation, such as a new baby or fresh neighbourhood; one simply has to get on with it.

Inklings about these future disappointments begin to nag as return becomes an issue. As Lord Macaulay wrote,

> Dark and terrible was the day of their flight; far darker and far more terrible will be the day of their return.

As a mother described,

> When our social worker left (having discussed plans for reunion) I remember exactly how I felt. I've only ever felt like it once before. My father died one March when we were young and everyone was very kind. They said everything would be all right and we'd got the light nights to look forward to. But I remember after the funeral, everyone just went. Me and my sisters and my mother were left sitting there to face everything with no money or anything. That's what it was like when I heard they wanted Christopher to come home; I was suddenly frightened and felt I'm on my own.

Secondly, fears of return are aroused because roles often change when people live apart. Yet children and families learn new roles and assume them whole-heartedly; they create new routines in a way that seems to deny and shut out the past. Indeed, so great can be the attachment to new situations that there is a vested interest in maintaining the separation. Thus, return is seen as a threat to the *status quo* and so creates anxiety.

A different coping strategy is oblivion, where children and families appear to forget the fact that they are separated and carry on as if nothing had happened. The pain of separation is denied and preoccupation with the trivial and immediate blocks out any regret. This response is sometimes interpreted by social workers as indifference. Children and families fail to involve themselves and are happy to drift along, they seem unaware of the damage done to their situation by separation. Both these adaptations strive to maintain continuity in shattered lives; but each has different implications for the fulfilment of return plans.

While the thought of return is universally stressful, the preparation for the event is equally difficult. Nevertheless, there will usually be clear social work strategies, such as encouraging frequent access between relatives and absent children and regular weekend visits with over-night stays. But while *Lost in Care* showed that these are essential conditions for re-unification, they are not enough on their own, particularly when relationships between children and families are poor.

Week-end contact is, of course, easy to arrange. It has the added advantage that it can be convenient to carers and is generally perceived by all as a good idea. Students, lovers and families the world over reserve week-ends as a time for the deeper things in life. In practice, however, both looked after children and their families find such arrangements quite difficult to handle. Paradoxically, the amount of access between parents and absent children gives little indication of the problems likely to arise on return.

In managing return, social workers usually focus on organisational issues such as facilitating access, arranging suitable accommodation and, wherever possible, meeting the wishes of families and children. Issues important to families facing the return of their child, however, are much more likely to be concerned with affective, emotional and even spiritual matters. Relatives will be thinking about how the returning child is perceived and asking whether he or she is really loved.

The evidence would suggest, therefore, that weekend visits are an appropriate preparation for return provided they do not become routinised or used as a reward. As previous studies on children's family links have shown, contact between children and families has many functions. When return becomes an issue, there is a need to distinguish between access as a means of securing reunion and access for its intrinsic worth, for example, to maintain continuity in the child's life.

Working for return has to be seen as a negotiation of a set of roles, both instrumental and expressive, rather than simply regaining everything that was lost. This is why seemingly trivial things can become the focus of return hopes and negotiations. As one adolescent recalled:

> I remember when I was away in care last time, I kept thinking of
> my things at home. I lay in bed and I was thinking about my old
> records and one in particular. I felt if I could get back and play it

everything would be alright. Funnily enough, when I got home, I don't think I ever put it on.

In this context, weekend contacts and other access arrangements merely serve to facilitate the child's return. The danger is that they may not provide sufficient time to clarify or practise the new roles required. Short visits can be honeymoons and regular access is not a normal style of contact between children and parents. Both may give insufficient time to prepare everyone for establishing the *modus vivendi* that must follow the return.

While all but a few children experience return, the contexts in which it takes place are varied indeed. There are different levels and patterns of return and different grades of 'fixedness'. Nine major dimensions in which return contexts differed can be identified. Each suggests questions that need to be answered when considering the way a child's return takes place. They are: have there been previous separations and reunions? Who initiated the return process? Does the child's situation carry stigma? Are the child's or parents' expectations of return unduly high? What rights, formal and informal, does the child have to return? Have either the parents or child used delaying tactics? Has the memory of the absent child been kept alive in the home? Do parents and child feel that past problems have been resolved and is there a refuge for the child if things go wrong?

When return becomes an issue, family, child and social workers begin to reap what was sown at the time of separation. Anxieties are aroused and conflicting attitudes and perceptions will be stringently tested as return plans proceed.

Indeed, at the point at which (according to social workers) return was under active consideration, it was clear that many families and children were still depressed socially, psychologically and economically even though reunion was imminent. Separation often eased situations by reducing the demands on parents and children but it was equally clear that to facilitate return, people's resilience and resolve have to be built up. This requires several strategies from social workers. There are relatively straightforward matters of housing and finance: incidentally, a constant concern of parents was the need to get child allowance paid quickly after the young person's return. But equally important are the conditions just described and the need to boost participants' self-esteem, clarify outstanding issues and give people confidence that things will work out.

Planning for return once more stirs the waters first clouded by the separation. Parents', children's and social workers' anxieties heighten. Even if an inclusive social work approach has been adopted, participants' perceptions have been realistic and looking after the child has resolved some of the problems which led the family to social services' door, when return becomes an issue new complications will arise.

From the intensive data on 31 children, three indicators in this episode were identified as useful pointers to whether or not a separated child will go back to live with parents or other relatives. These are: whether participants absorb and identify with the roles generated by the child's return; whether the child and family see the care situation as negotiable; and whether the problems necessitating the original separation are perceived as having been partially resolved at the point at which return becomes an issue.

Episode Four: The first days at home

Despite social workers' belief that the return of the child was under urgent consideration, and in some cases was imminent, not all 31 children went back home. Indeed, it was the anxiety aroused in everybody by raising the possibility of reunion that foiled return in many cases.

Thus, only 20 of the 31 children under scrutiny actually went home to live in the 18 months of the study. Some went back soon after separation, others were reunited with new relatives after prolonged periods apart from their family but in many reunions it was difficult to isolate the actual moment of return. Even for the 12 children whose restoration was planned by social workers, it was difficult to say when reunion was complete. In four cases, the child drifted back home and another four children, voting with their feet, ran back to their parents not knowing if they would be able to stay.

Although social workers and relatives, sometimes independently, made quite elaborate plans for children's restoration, aims and objectives seldom came fully to fruition. Even when social work plans seemed to be working especially well, a family's anxiety to hurry things along to a successful conclusion often encouraged parents to circumvent arrangements and, once begun, some returns assumed a momentum of their own. For example, one mother explained:

> Well, everybody at social services was very happy but not much seemed to be happening. So we kept making arrangements with the foster parents to keep Chris for a bit longer and then a bit longer and so, although she's not due back now until (three weeks time), as you can see she's here with me. I don't think everybody's happy but on the other hand they are leaving well alone.

Clearly, it is difficult for social workers to delay reunion in order to allow family members to overcome possible obstacles. So, even in planned returns, it was difficult to isolate the moment of return. This speeding up of events does not appear to be detrimental to the eventual success of the reunion, although it was clear that parents missed the opportunity to mark the event in a formal manner. This is illustrated by a mother who said to us:

> He was back before he should have been, as you know. And that was what we wanted, but we missed the chance to make a bit of a fuss. My first husband had been in the Navy and the days he came back were sheer joy. Most of the time we hated each other, but I loved those days and I wanted the same for Dan. They made a big fuss when he had to go away and it would have been nice to say "great to have you back".

For those children who drifted back to parents, the day of return was even more unclear. Visits turn into overnight stays which become a week at home, only to be punctuated by a trip with the foster family. However, parents and children often retrospectively impose a point of reunion on complicated situations. So John, a 12 year old boy separated from his mother at the same time she left his father, was able to comment:

> I was sitting at home on Sunday having tea. I'd been out all day with people 'round here, Granny was here, Phil (the new step-father) was back from the pub and we were watching telly. I didn't say much I suppose, but it was a really nice day. And then Mum asked me about going back and I said 'I'm not going'. And

she didn't say anything so I suppose it was alright and I've been here since really.

Parents similarly marked the point of reunion with the benefit of hindsight and this moment often occurred before the child came home to stay. A revitalised sense of belonging, triggered by a shared moment remembered, was often cited as the point at which parents felt their child was back.

For the remaining children who ran back to their parents, the point of reunion was, in one sense, clearly identifiable and memorable. However, the anxiety which followed seldom made for clarity of purpose or perception. Children were seldom sure their parents wanted them home, relatives felt concerned that social workers would object to a precipitate reunion and, indeed, social workers were always uneasy in such situations. So once again, the point of return was not always clear; was it the day the child ran home; the day the parents decided the child's return was a good idea; or when the social workers acquiesced in the train of events?

The evidence from the intensive study leads to the conclusion that the moment of return occurs when sufficient family members feel that the child has come home to live. It is rare for all participants in a reunion to see the event in a positive light and, indeed, most will harbour lingering doubts. Relatives' and children's views on reunion will be coloured by their experience of separation and they are seldom entirely confident of the future. Nevertheless, their judgements of progress were usually reliable, even in apparently cursory remarks, such as 'I'm home to stay now' or 'It's not quite right, yet'.

Expectations and emotional upheaval

In comparison with the first episode in the return process, there are few rites of passage to mark a child's restoration. The clandestine way in which parents short-circuit social work plans or the slow drift home which characterises other reunions make it difficult for the family to celebrate. This may be an area in which social workers can help, making return something of a celebration. One should remember that the 'leaving prize' or retirement gold watch not only signifies the end of a long experience and the start of something new but, for the recipient, such moments mean that previous roles and territories cannot be resumed. Whilst there cannot be a general prescription appropriate to all cases, providing families with a date and means to commemorate formally a homecoming would be welcomed in many of the cases studied.

It is difficult for social workers to plan a child's return and, if the family takes increasing responsibility, the outsider's role in the home can be less than straightforward. However, the evidence would suggest that simply taking the decision that a child's best interests would be served by being at home and making plans for the reunion do not, in themselves, guarantee success. More important are the participants' perspectives and their feelings that events are going at the right pace.

Several factors appear to influence participants' experience of the reunion. Initially, family members, especially the adults, are guided by cultural expectations, that is what they feel they are supposed to do. Memories of past separations and reunions also play their part and contribute to the reunion's being emotionally charged. However, with no rites of passage into which these emotions can be channelled, anxieties linger, though often neutralised in a short honeymoon period during which everybody is on their best behaviour. However, some family members are not fully involved in the reunion. Step-parents, for example, who have moved into the home during the child's separation from mother or father watch the return with suspicion and they too help to shape the way in which other family members view the event.

Family members often sensed that they were under scrutiny, that they were being assessed, especially during the days that surrounded the return. To an extent their apprehension was correct, for many social workers did notice a change in behaviour and expressive roles as the final restoration of child to family neared. One social worker commented:

> They're suddenly hugging for the first time ever. He walks in the door and Joan (the mother) gives him a big hug. I've been taking him on home leaves for two years and normally he walks in the door and nobody bats an eyelid.

There is a contrast between those aspects of the return which are conducted in public and those which are private, involving only the family. For instance, neighbours may provide an audience for reunion and parents also put on an overt display of affection. However, when the family is alone, displays of affection can lose their function and the reunion becomes a disappointing, low-key affair, especially when parents contrast the event with cultural expectations. One mother illustrated this when she said:

> I had this idea it would be like something out of the movies with violins and everybody happy and we wanted to make a fuss but it wasn't really like that. It was all a bit empty really, I can't explain it to you.

In the few cases where the final return was more clearly marked, the participants' satisfactions with the event were much greater. Mrs. Abbot who went with the social worker to collect her child John and his possessions from the foster parent's house obviously felt everything had gone well:

> We got everything ready and said our farewells to Brian and Sylvia (the foster parents) and I thought, I know this doesn't sound nice, but I thought you're not needed any more. I thought from that moment that I was back in control. Then we (mother and child) chatted in the back of the car on the way back, got rid of the neighbours and Steph (the social worker) and had a little party just ourselves. It was quiet, but it was just what we needed.

Often participants' memories of previous separations and reunions were suddenly evoked, particularly for those parents who were in care themselves. Several parents broke down as they tried to recount their experiences at the moment of return:

> It all came flooding back to me. I didn't know what set me off. I was nervous and I opened the door and he was standing there in his school uniform looking all smart and I thought "I should never have let him go, what was I thinking of, letting him go" and I thought "never again, you're never going to leave me again". And I was crying my heart out and holding him tight, I don't think he knew what was happening but he was a bit tearful too. It was supposed to be a happy moment and it was really, but I was in a terrible state.

Clearly, people have high hopes of return, expectations which cannot always be met in reality. In addition, participants are fearful about the reunion itself and the days following. When combined with the sense of guilt and all the other problems of separation, the reunion becomes emotional. Unfortunately, in none of the returns scrutinised did parents express their fears and feelings to social workers or, for that matter, to anybody else providing support. As such, the restoration often had the effect of breaking down defences carefully erected during the child's absence; indeed, the strength of emotions released took many by surprise.

As on any occasion when emotions are running high, mistakes occur during the reunion and participants display behaviour which might be misconstrued as petulant or selfish. A mother contrasted her obvious delight at her eldest's return with her somewhat unwelcoming behaviour:

> I felt all this love brimming up, but I couldn't say anything. I had a list of things I wanted to say about how it was partly me that had done wrong in the past and how I was going to make a fresh start, but when he came in I was sort of speechless. And he didn't seem to notice me at all and after ten minutes I lost my temper and told him off because he hadn't wiped his feet and he'd walked muck all over.

The moment of return may be emotional but not all participants are ecstatic. For example, one aunt said,

> I've never seen such a performance, all that hugging and kissing. Before, they hated each other, they still do in fact.

In this episode, however, the most difficult role is reserved for the step-parents, or others, such as step or half siblings, who have joined the family during the child's absence. They are required to display a welcoming attitude when they often feel deeply ambivalent. The limelight during the actual return falls upon the one coming home. The event is not viewed as the creation of a new family in which other recent arrivals are also going to play a part. As such, although pleased to see mother and child back together, many step-parents were far from enthusiastic:

> It was all very nice and I tried to be as nice as I could. But if I'm really honest with you I'd have to say really I felt a bit pushed out. You see, before it was our house, me and the wife, but suddenly on that day I felt I was in somebody else's home again.

The evidence from the intensive study clearly shows that the participants' experience of return is shaped by a range of factors. Cultural expectations are important as are previous experiences of separation and restoration and simple self-interest. However, the features which contribute to a return pull the participants in different directions, with parents in particular finding it difficult to reconcile the need to put on a show for the social worker and neighbours with the attempt to accommodate guilt and anxiety resulting from the separation and make sure the child is happy. Not surprisingly, therefore, emotions run high and more tears are shed at reunion than at separation. As these emotions are difficult to control or engineer, planning for a successful return is not easy.

Parents have high expectations of return and most have to cope alone with the elation, anxiety and disappointments associated with reunion. The actual return produces emotions which are difficult to understand, especially for those unused to examining their own feelings or to empathising with the anxieties and needs of others. It is easy to forget that these skills are learned over time in optimum family, school and other social settings. Many parents, through no fault of their own, simply do not possess these skills. Indeed, families may need their greatest support at the point at which the social worker feels withdrawal is the most appropriate strategy. Thus, it is not difficult to understand why eleven of the twenty children who returned swiftly experienced another separation.

Nonetheless, the moment of return is a happy one for most families, whatever the future may have in store. 'I felt we were a family again' was a common sentiment. As such, the honeymoon period which immediately follows return is functional in that it neutralises the emotions previously discussed and allows some recovery.

Change crystallised by return

The study has emphasised the continuities which bind together the participants to the restoration. However, at the moment of return certain aspects of their lives change and these can threaten the success of the reunion. Initially, return means that participants separate from a lifestyle to which they may have become emotionally attached or at least have got used to. Secondly, the return leads family members to review each other and the home, to think again about what has happened. Indeed, as will be seen, a returning child can change the relationship between all family members.

Mrs. Abbot's sense of triumph when she collected her son John from foster parents has already been discussed. In interviews with John immediately following the return, he found it difficult to disguise his sense of loss of the foster parents. He was very sad to leave them behind, but his greatest anxiety was that his mother would discover his thoughts wandering back to the substitute family. He said to us,

> I don't like to talk about Brian and Sylvia (the foster parents) in case it do upset her (mother).

Consequently, John found himself back at home with little to talk about, a silence which added to the growing anxiety in the house.

Many returning children expressed this sense of loss of their previous placement and the people associated with it. For older children, this included boyfriends and girlfriends, some of whom were unknown to the natural family. Foster parents, too, felt the wrench and wanted to keep in touch. This aspect of return highlights conflicts between the instrumental and expressive functions of child-care placements; putting down roots complicates return. For the host family the return meant separation from a previous lifestyle, an existence often made easier by the absence of the child. Parents got used to being by themselves and enjoyed the reduced responsibilities. Even parents receiving children after a short separation were surprised at the change and some mothers compared the reunion to the birth of a new child. For example:

> It's like the birth, it's marvellous when it's over and in the hospital but when you're home and it's feeding and changing nappies all day and all night it suddenly hits you.

The intensive study also revealed that a child's return has the effect of instituting a review of the new family order and the reverberations can be felt in all aspects of family life. For children this review was particularly important and extended to the physical qualities of the home. For five of the twenty returning children the reunion with relatives took place in a completely new home and 13 children had new adults to get to know.

For children, the smallest changes can have a marked effect and apparently insignificant aspects of the home become symbols of inner anxiety. For example, one adolescent comparing his own home with the foster home he had left, commented:

> I'd only been home five minutes and I went to the loo and I
> looked at the bath. It had brown stains all below the taps and it
> was all old fashioned and dingy. At (the foster home) it was all
> pine and they had a shower. I suppose it was then, really, I was
> just thinking how hard it was really going to be.

Noticing change is not confined to young people. Very small children become upset because of small changes, even new wallpaper. Indeed, the re-decorating of one child's bedroom as a treat to mark the return nearly led to another separation. It is noteworthy that child psycho-therapists emphasise that the treatment room must remain identically organised for each session.

The review instituted by the return often involved all family members and, in many cases, was positive. Marriages improved and in four families, parents felt their sexual relationships had changed for the better following the child's return. Relatives absent while the child was looked after suddenly re-appeared and suspicious neighbours became more friendly. Return can have the most unexpected effects.

Return involves separation; for the child there is a divorce with substitute carers and for the host family there is a break with a previous way of life. These changes in participants' lives may have positive as well as negative effects. It is difficult to take such changes into account when planning return but it is important to acknowledge them, especially in the case of young children unable to express the source of their anxiety. This reveals once again the uncertainty surrounding return and the need for a honeymoon period, which makes up the next episode in the process.

Conclusions

This chapter has considered the point at which return has occurred. The themes which run through each of the episodes have been apparent here. Return is a process not a single event and it was difficult to decide in many cases the point at which the child could be said to be home. The moment of return was defined as the time when sufficient, that is to say not all, family members perceive that the child has come home to live. The families interviewed were always clear about the point at which this happened, indeed it was apparent in the throw-away remarks they used to describe the event.

The expressive continuities which bind the family together have underpinned many of the themes apparent in this episode, for example the emotional aspects of the reunion. Likewise, the importance of role has been explored and, as will be seen, the ability of participants to suspend accepted roles during the forthcoming honeymoon period. Territory, however, is less important during the moment of return and its immediate aftermath, as family members prefer to place great stress on the value of neutral ground.

Fewer rites of passage marked the reunion than the separation, although making the episode a more public event may have the effect of safely channelling the wave of emotion which return washes up. Indeed, it is noticeable that parents in particular do respond to cultural expectations of reunion, embracing their children for the benefit of external observers as well as to express heartfelt feelings.

Return involves a separation from something to which participants are emotionally attached; children lose their substitute carers, families a life without the absent child. In addition, past separations and reunions are brought to mind. Yet the sense of loss for the lifestyle prior to reunion and the affective dimensions produced by the actual return are seldom addressed by participants in this episode and a cauldron of unresolved and little-discussed issues slowly comes to the boil.

Despite this simmering discontent and potential for discord, the social work inputs which have featured strongly in previous episodes pale during the actual return and the days immediately afterwards. The social worker can find him or herself overtaken by events during the return and it is difficult to sustain a role once the child is back. However, this might very well be the time when the family most needs help. Clearly, this is not an easy situation for professionals and the implicit messages of withdrawal have to be assessed in the context of telling parents that return will be very difficult. Financial support and advice would also be welcomed by most of the families, since most were finding it difficult with another mouth to feed.

Once again, the analysis of family experiences in this episode has suggested factors which appear to be associated with positive return outcomes. These are that: participants have a clear perception of when return has occurred; social work return plans are tailored to meet the time-scales of family members; and, once the child is at home, the family perceives the social worker as willing to help if and when needed.

10 The child back at home

As parents, children and the wider family strive to make the reunion a success, tensions and anxieties are suppressed in a make-believe world of bonhomie and unity. But the charade cannot be maintained, pressures mount, expectations are disappointed, the cosy fantasies that helped all to survive the separation are exposed to kitchen sink reality. New roles are onerous and old territories are jealously guarded. Particularly anxious during reunion are new family members, step-parents and siblings, cohabitees and friends who feel elbowed aside by the returning child. The honeymoon period ends with a domestic row in which home truths, recriminations and the pent-up resentments of separation are aired. But the majority of families survive this convulsion and the clearing of the air after the storm helps parents and offspring to accommodate to the past, to fashion continuity and meaning from the experience of separation and to settle down.

Episode Five: The honeymoon

For each of the families which experienced reunion, return was followed by a 'honeymoon period'. This was a period in which everyone was on their best behaviour, struggling to make the reunion a success. In fact none of these reunions ended swiftly; the earliest breakdown occurred after three weeks, so family tolerance was considerable. Four distinctive behaviours characterised the honeymoon period. Initially, participants needed time to get to know one another again. Secondly, poor behaviour, particularly children's, was viewed sympathetically. Thirdly, participants were happy to assume new roles and give up existing ones. Finally, family members were happy to abandon their independence, albeit temporarily.

The days immediately following the return involve the participants getting to know one another. For most this is a re-acquaintance but for others, such as step-parents and child, it can be the first time they have lived together. As in a formal gathering at which guests do not know one another, everybody tends to be on their best behaviour immediately following return and even sibling rivalries and jealousies are repressed. Thus, one step-parent who felt frozen out of the family on the day the child came back was more optimistic when visited three days later:

> I wasn't sure at first, I'll admit that. But I thought "I'll give it a go". And it's been good. Things between me and Susan (his wife) have picked up again, in fact never better really. And Susan and Tracey (his step-child) are going OK so I've been making an effort too. And so far so good.

As in any family, certain repetitive behaviours cause irritation and children are by nature liable to upset their parents. However, in the days which followed reunion, tensions were avoided and misbehaviour dealt with lightly. Indeed, several children noted a complete *volte-face* by their parents which they found remarkable and seemed to symbolise the days following reunion. For example, an older adolescent boy explained:

> Before I went away I used to like sitting by myself and reading, not bothering nobody. And this used to drive her (his mother) mad, she couldn't stand it. Then this week, same again, I'm reading and she's sitting across the room and she says "You've got so much patience". It was embarrassing really but I was amazed; it was the first time she'd said anything nice to me.

This constant striving for neutral ground eventually palls and can become the source of tension. There is a limit to how long the problems that led to the initial separation can be avoided. Indeed, it is characteristic of the days following reunion for participants to comment 'it doesn't seem real'.

Part of this honeymoon period is the sharing of roles and the allocation of tasks for children. Previously work-shy children suddenly become eager to help with Sunday lunch or Grandad's allotment. Other roles are allocated on a strictly experimental basis, for instance trusting a delinquent daughter to go to the shops with mother's purse. The days following return allowed older children insights into their parents' social lives, joining Mum on trips to Bingo or the discotheque or Dad to the public house.

The honeymoon period was characterised by the individuals abandoning their independence and the family operating as a single, apparently cohesive, unit. As with all situations where roles are displaced or threatened, tensions eventually come to the surface. The battles for power within the family and the problems which led to the child's removal from home soon loom large, leading several of those interviewed to comment, 'I'll be glad when it's all back to normal'.

Episode Six: The row

The false consensus of the honeymoon has to disintegrate. Usually the family is convulsed by a row, triggered off by something quite minor. The row and its aftermath can be a healthy reprieve from the stresses of return and from the strain of maintaining the pretence that nothing has happened. Admittedly, this relief might be somewhat modified by the 'home truths' freely scattered on such occasions.

So, for a while, the family pot simmers gently, occasionally it spits hot water, but it eventually boils over into a row. Most participants felt the tension slowly building up and, in retrospect, were able to pin-point the source of contention. Superficially, the tension concerned role or territory but, beneath this veneer, there hovered deeper unresolved questions such as the pain of separation.

The row can occur at any time during the weeks which follow reunion. In a few cases it came after a matter of hours and, in contrast, one family dragged the honeymoon out for three months. Commonly, the dispute is between mother and child but, where the offspring is a baby, the row can involve adults and others. Step-parents, noticeably absent in the previous episode, also find themselves drawn into the *contretemps*.

The catalyst for the row was usually a dispute over family roles. Parents and children argued about who should do the washing-up, parents fought among themselves about who should stay in and look after the baby and mothers chastised their daughters about the inadequacy of grand-daughter's upbringing. Territorial disputes were also common, especially between siblings over bedrooms and toys, but also between mothers and teenage daughters over where each could store property and occupy territory.

Financial rows also feature in this episode. Children were returned to parents who had grown used to managing a reduced food bill and it could be some weeks before social security caught up with the change in family circumstances. Predictably, parental discipline was an enduring source of conflict and many rows occurred on a teenager's late return from a night out or following a toddler's refusal to do as he or she was told.

Such disputes are common within all families but among return families the row encapsulates a range of deeper tensions. One mother talked about a 'slanging match' she had with her recently reunited teenage daughter and illustrated how minor conflict rapidly leads to more hurtful issues.

> Well it started with Karen wanting to come with me to the disco, she'd been with me three times since she was back and I was beginning to hope I could go by myself for a change. We had a bit of a to-do about it then I says she can please herself. Then she said she wasn't coming 'cos I showed her up, calling me a slag trying to get off with men at the disco. And next thing I'm telling her she's a fucking bitch for making that accusation against her dad and she's saying 'you should have believed me..... why did you let me go?' and before you know we are throwing things at each other and she buggers off. I didn't see her for two days, God knows where she got to.

What is at the root of these deeper conflicts? Largely, it can be explained as part of the difficulty of closing the gap between reality and the fantasy of the perfect reunion. The emotions bubbling when somebody says 'I cannot wait to be home' are difficult to recapture several weeks after reunion. The reality of being home is facing up to many of the same problems which led to the initial separation. A parent may not have made a full recovery from illness, the spectre of neglect and abuse may hover long after reunion and delinquent boys are unlikely to become saints after a sojourn in care. Thus, suspicions lurk in everyone's mind that the past is neither dead nor buried.

There are also other difficulties. For six of the 20 families which enjoyed reunion, there was a lack of common currency of conversation, although participants had been expecting to 'never stop talking'. There were other barriers such as inadequacies in the host's competence to care, deficiencies which brought back painful memories and censure from the wider family audience. As a consequence, rather than being excited as they had been at the moment of return, many parents and children complained of disappointment and boredom as time passed. All family members were unprepared for these gaps between expectations and the reality of reunion. Indeed, for many, the disappointment came as a shock and unguarded reactions to the uncertainty contributed towards the row.

But the void was wider in some situations than in others. Many of those children who drifted back home experienced the least difficulties in settling down, provided their return was perceived as structured and progressive. Surprisingly the gap between reality and expectation was widest for the planned returns and, less remarkable, for those children who ran home precipitately. Most of the early returners found the period of separation was insufficiently long for an emotional gap between parents and children to develop and they settled back easily. However, in one case, despite a very close bond between mother and child and although the separation was short due to mother's chronic illness, neither she nor the boy could cope with the reality of return. Thus, the child quickly had to be looked after again and after two more attempts at reunion seemed destined to hover in uncertainty.

For all returning families, the honeymoon ended with a row. In two cases the dispute was so acrimonious that the children were removed from home once more. The catalysts for these disputes were issues of role, territory and financial stringency. But the row often raked over long dead embers which flared up to fuel further trouble. Discussions are often bitter and brim with home truths. The row can be explained as a response to the anxiety which occurs when there is a wide gap between participants' expectations of the reunion and the reality of living together in the days following. It reflects the tensions and reluctance of family members to abandon old roles and to learn new ones, to share territories and to accept the increased responsibility of making return a success.

But, successfully handled, the row had considerable benefits; information which all were reluctant to share prior to the reunion was aired in discussion. The reasons for and the pains of separation had to be faced and families which made progress in these areas seemed to enjoy more successful reunions than those which did not.

Parental guilt about letting their children be looked after and the pain experienced by children while away had to be aired. Parents and children were together for long periods and information each had previously shielded from the other inevitably came to the fore. Returning children swiftly learned much of what went on in their absence and, if parents were reluctant to tell, the wider family readily provided others who were anxious to spill the beans. Children, likewise, hide information from their parents often because they feel their parents are unable to help but, during the aftermath of a row, they, too, volunteer comments on the pains of separation. Indeed, children sharing unhappy experiences with relatives often compounded feelings of parental guilt which were expressed in statements such as 'I should have been there ... I could have helped' or 'Why did I let them take him away?'

Episode Seven: A new *modus vivendi*

The sentimentalised family reunion conjured up in *The Railway Children* certainly did not apply in these cases. Reconciliation was more likely to be private, gradual and fragmented. Far from resolving the tensions of generations in three gin-soaked confrontations packed into one evening, in many families the reunion took several months to complete. As one parent said,

> 'You cannot go back. You cannot turn the clock back. When I look back and see what I allowed to happen I still wince, I think 'Oh no'. But it's done and over the last six months (since the reunion) we've got over some of the problems. .... No, I wouldn't say we've talked properly but it's (the separation) come up now and then, I tell him about how things got too much for me and he tells me about how he loved the children's home or hated the foster home. It's not a cure but it certainly helps.

But re-establishing the reciprocity and warmth of a relationship after a convulsive row does not merely rely on tea and sympathy. There are family norms to re-establish. During separation, children and relatives were relieved of burdensome decisions regarding one another. They enjoyed a new-found freedom. But after the reunion and especially after the honeymoon, the routine of family life becomes apparent to the participants. Relationships exact a price. Family members become aware of changes in each other. Children notice physical alterations in their parents who are greyer, fatter and slower. Parents concerned with children's intellectual and affective development often find their offspring wanting. Hopefully, the anticipated silk purse does not swiftly become a 'sow's ear' but reality has to be faced.

For the mother of young children this means changing the nappy and feeding the baby. For older children there will be disputes about pocket-money, which is frequently less than that paid in the substitute care placement and far less reliable. For the adolescents, there are rules regarding dress, sexual behaviour and the time the young person must be in at night. Frequently there is a gap between what is expected of looked after children and what parents will tolerate once they have returned home. Accommodation and compromise have to be hammered out.

Step-parents, who melted into the background during the separation can become important as the child settles back home. If the reunion is to succeed, their role, status and rights need to be recognised. Demands on step-parents may be considerable, including sharing their partner's time with the returning child. Siblings can relate well to each other in the early stages, indeed, almost uncritically in some cases, but, in the longer term, they too have to make considerable accommodations if the family is going to see itself as a unit.

Noticeably absent, however, at this stage in the return process is the social worker. Mindful of the stigma associated with the child's separation, the negotiations just described are viewed as a private affair and parents go to some lengths to hide the disputes and realignments from outsiders. From a distance and often ill-informed, the social worker has to encourage the family to maintain the impetus towards reunion while often, at the same time, being not fully conversant with the problems the families have to face. Indeed, some parents and older adolescents felt that social workers exercised informal coercion to make the reunion last and played down the difficulties they were experiencing. This sense of 'take it or leave it' in the attitude of social workers was expressed by eight of the 20 families enjoying reunion.

Conclusions

The final episodes of the return process - the honeymoon and row - are important elements in the return process. Following such *dénouements*, either the return breaks down or the participants begin to feel that 'things are getting back to normal'. Yet, 'normal' may not be very satisfactory; it may be little different from the situation prior to separation and is very likely to be in marked contrast to the fantasy fashioned in the days leading up to reunion. Nonetheless, clearing the air comes as a great relief to all concerned and begins a protracted period of negotiations during which deep-seated issues come to the fore.

Several months after relatives and child first parted, the conflicts, anxieties and problems within the family remain alive. The need to give meaning to the upheaval remains pressing for children and parents alike. Families seek a revised *modus vivendi* and discussions explore the reasons for the initial separation and the meaning of the experience for the family. The anger engendered in parents and children by their failures to live up to their own expectations has to be expressed. Parents and children have to find a new role in the family and to accept, even forgive, the role taken by others. Territories have to be established and adaptations must be made to the new set of circumstances. In addition, completely new social networks may need to be constructed, for instance at work and in school.

The new arrangement usually also involves some agreement about the issues involved in previous episodes: the hurt of separation, the feelings of loss and despair in the days that follow, the hopes and expectations prior to reunion are all explored. Such exploration does not solve much, except to evaporate some of the confusion in children's minds over the initial crisis. Often sensitive issues are still concealed within the family but such catharsis does provide an opportunity for good counselling skills and work on reconciliation, a chance which sadly often passes unrecognised by professionals.

What are the elements of success for families who managed to stay together after reunion and were happy to be together? Two of the 20 families welcomed home babes in arms and negotiations were relatively simple, involving only the parents, step-parents or wider family members. Other families welcomed home older children. Here, success was associated with giving each other freedom to pursue their own lives whilst at the same time making some efforts to gain *rapprochement* and repair the damage.

However stressful the reunion, the majority of families came to see themselves as 'a family' and this shared perspective helped the returner belong and settle back. Unfortunately, when older children have developed an identity based upon life outside the home then difficulties follow.

Finally, this episode has re-emphasised the importance of understanding continuities in understanding return and the need to give meaning to the upheaval for parents and children alike. Several factors are important in determining success at this stage in the return process. Along with the other indices already discussed they suggest that a successful reunion is more likely when the family is prepared for the anxiety generated by return and the disputes which are likely to occur and when family members are prepared to discuss with each other the pains of separation and their role in the rift.

11 Long-term outcomes

What happened to the 31 children in the intensive study? All had been expected to return home in the near future. In spite of social work optimism, however, a third of the children for whom return seemed imminent did not go back. This chapter explores the reasons for these disappointments and, conversely, the outcomes for those who managed *rapprochement* with their families.

The intensive study charted the return situations of 31 children from 24 families. Social workers expected all these children to go home; hence their inclusion in this part of the research. Some of the 31 children, however, were included on the basis that they would probably not be returned easily or would face problems once back at home. In the event, 11 children did not go home at all and 11 of the 20 who did return subsequently left, four of them in less than satisfactory circumstances.

This chapter assesses the situation of all 31 children at the end of an 18 month follow-up scrutiny. It considers first the 11 children whose returns never materialised, since their failure to go back home illuminates much about return processes. It then reviews the long-term outcomes of the 20 children who were reunited, to stress that the restoration process continues long after the child first comes home.

Children who did not return

The intensive study was deliberately designed to include children likely to experience return problems. Overall, a third (35%) of the cases nominated by social workers as highly likely to return did not get back:

a figure higher than expected. Clearly, although a considerable proportion of professionals' time is devoted to the reunion of children with their families, not all efforts are successful.

Visions for a swift reunion for all 31 children were undoubtedly over ambitious but in five of the non-returning cases, the social work plan was still for rehabilitation 18 months after return had first become an issue. Delays had been caused by difficulties of rehousing, the need for the child to complete an educational course and by vacillation among participants. In all five, the slowness of the reunion was not seen by social workers as detrimental and, thus, reunion remained the case plan.

Two cases typify the return problems of such families. In the first, an eleven year old girl and her mother continually changed their minds; when one wanted restoration the other chose prolonged separation and *vice versa*. Social workers accommodated the wishes of the family and so were also accused of dithering. In the second case, involving two teenage boys who had been in and out of substitute care over several years, the older brother went home not to mother, as planned, but to his father. The younger child was not ready to make this adjustment but the father's renewed interest had the effect of reducing the mother's desire to have her son home. He, consequently, stayed with foster parents. Social workers maintained high levels of access between all family members and, at the end of the follow-up, the aim was still eventual reunion.

For six children, however, return was not only postponed but abandoned. In one case, involving two children aged two and four, the physical and mental health of the children's mother deteriorated unexpectedly. Heavy drinking and possible substance abuse compounded her diabetes, leading to several emergency hospitalisations and generally poor health. She was persuaded that her daughters should remain looked after until she fully recovered and frequent access between them was encouraged. However, the children's foster home was quickly changed to one with long-term possibilities. Despite the inclusive nature of the social work plan, the mother realised her ability to parent was becoming increasingly impaired and, at the time the research was completed, was urging that her children be adopted.

In a second case, there was a similar unforeseen change, but this time in the home situation. It resulted from an acrimonious breakdown in a mother's marital relationship and from the financial and housing difficulties that swiftly ensued. As there was little prospect of any immediate improvement, the infant, who had originally been looked after in a family crisis, was seen as likely to remain there because of the mother's continual ambivalence and frequent family visits to Ireland. In addition, contact between mother and child, which had always been fitful, became very intermittent indeed, even when she came back to the child's immediate vicinity. Furthermore, the natural father shunned any parenting responsibility. Both parents showed no interest in the foster home and justified their coolness by maintaining that their child was better off away. Needless to say, all was not satisfactory in the placement; the foster parents were angry at being the victims of such whimsical behaviour and hardly encouraged shared care.

In a third case, a deterioration in the young person's behaviour scuppered return plans. Leroy's aggression increased to such an extent that he had to be separated from his sister who was not in the study group. She remained happily in the foster home and went back to the natural family three months later. Leroy, aged nine, had been stopped from going home at weekends because his parents could not cope with his tantrums. They said he was 'impossible to satisfy'. When he realised his sister was at home and he was not, his aggression increased. Soon, the foster parents could not cope either and he was moved to an assessment unit, then to a residential school 30 miles away. All this was done with the full consent of his parents. This pattern by which siblings are separated because of the increasingly disturbed behaviour of one of them has been noted in child-care literature. However, it is important to add that, for the child involved, it not only leads to a placement change but also to a delayed return, often in contrast to the experience of the other sibling.

In the final two cases, child-abuse came unexpectedly into the picture between the initiation and execution of return plans. In the first case, a 14 year old girl, who had been looked after because of being 'at risk' in the community, was visiting her mother and sisters in preparation for return but less regularly than the social worker wished. There seemed to be some reluctance on the girl's part, with minor excuses and procrastination; nevertheless, she was expected to be living back at home within six months.

However, plans took a complete *volte-face* when social workers found out that the mother had formed a new friendship with a raffish, scheduled sex offender. As a result, access was carefully controlled and conditions concerning the cohabitee's presence in the family home were specified. When the mother allowed her boyfriend to move into her house, plans for reunion were abandoned.

In the final instance, both social workers and researchers were taken by surprise. The situation involved a seven year old boy in the care of a single father. The boy's mother had walked out of the family home after a torrid affair with her brother-in-law. Voluntary arrangements to look after the child and support the father, who desperately wanted to resume parenting and engineer his son's return, were effected. Social services were very sympathetic to the father's needs and fostered the boy locally, encouraging access to Dad and grandparents at weekends and public holidays. However, social workers were uneasy at the lack of a female carer. Nevertheless, eventual reunion was planned and, after six months in care, going home was imminent.

This situation continued for longer than expected because of uncertainty about the parental relationship. More than once, the child's mother unexpectedly turned up to re-assume her position in the family home. Moreover, while father's continued unemployment gave him time to look after his son, his financial situation deteriorated. The boy lived in three different temporary foster homes during this period but this aroused little anxiety as his wishes were clearly to be back with dad and the father-son relationship seemed strong. Return was always the plan, even though it seldom seemed near to fruition.

Suddenly, the foster parents became aware that certain comments made by Steven could indicate abuse. They informed social services as a precaution. When questioned by social workers, Steven described consistent sexual abuse by his father on weekend visits. Father, too, admitted everything when challenged. Needless to say, there is now no access; Steven is still living in a temporary foster placement, is utterly bewildered and is reputedly becoming difficult. Father is on bail awaiting a Crown Court appearance. Social workers and researchers who had visited the father and son while at home together had never had an inkling of what was going on. All were understandably concerned that despite following procedures, they failed to protect the boy. Naturally, return plans have been abandoned and, even if ever revived, there is a probability that Steven will have nothing to return to.

His mother is now missing completely and father's tenancy will almost certainly be surrendered when, as seems likely, he goes to prison.

The significance of non-returners

How are these non-returning cases relevant to the study of children's return experiences? Firstly, it is significant that a third (35%) of the children who were expected by social workers to return home failed to do so in the time expected and for half of these return plans were abandoned altogether. While, because of the nature of the sample, this figure cannot be generalised to the whole looked after population, it does indicate the difficulties that reunion poses for children and families and the complicating factors that can intervene.

These cases also highlight the cultural barriers and expectations associated with return. For example, social workers were reluctant to return Steven to a lone father. Vicky, the adolescent girl, reluctantly went along with social work plans, pretending to enjoy her home visits when she was actually shattered by her mother's preference for a known sex offender. These two cases also show how the possibility of the child's return from care or accommodation puts the family under extra scrutiny and how the new information this generates can block return plans. All the children interviewed were clearly confused by the failure of their returns to materialise and the tendency for plans to blow hot and cold. Social workers clearly have a skilled and daunting task in helping children understand why their hopes have been dashed, particularly if they are under the impression that their care placement is temporary.

It is equally clear from the evidence that return strategies must accommodate possible changes in children's family situations. An inflexible approach that relies totally on a stable family structure with predictable patterns of relationships is likely to be confounded. Steven's return, for example, was contingent upon his mother being off the scene while the restoration of the baby, whose mother disappeared, depended on her having a place to live. In neither case were these requirements met.

These conclusions suggest one answer to the important question posed by Farmer and Parker (1991). In noting that social workers have few sanctions, limited powers and little contact with the children, the authors asked, 'who is on trial?' The study would suggest that the decision to return is being tested just as much as the children or parents.

The children who returned

The preceding chapters described the reunion of 20 children. One of the advantages of adopting an intensive scrutiny is that it facilitates a careful assessment of the success of each return and the extension of the evaluative criteria beyond the question of whether or not the placement endured. Of the 20 children going home during the 18 month follow-up, 11 moved on, while the remaining nine stayed throughout with relatives. What did an enduring return mean for these nine children?

In reviewing children's return situations, it is necessary to consider a variety of perspectives: not only those of social workers but of parents and the children themselves. Comparisons were made between the child's situation 18 months after return and several key moments highlighted in the episodes; for example, the circumstances surrounding separation, the separation itself and the point at which return became an issue. An assessment was made of family and social relationships, the child's social and anti-social behaviour, his or her physical and psychological health and, where appropriate, educational progress and employment.

Applying these wider outcome criteria, five of the nine cases could be adjudged completely successful. Three of these cases were *early returners* going home in a relatively uncomplicated fashion after the mother's recovery from illness. The fourth case involved an adolescent girl estranged from her Irish mother and Afro-Caribbean father but who settled well with paternal grandparents. The final successful reunion involved a 17 year old boy who had been long looked after. He settled well at home, began working with his step-father and got engaged to a local girl. Previous delinquent behaviour was not repeated.

For another three children who stayed at home after reunion, intensive scrutiny led to some reservations. In two cases, one sibling had stayed at home while the other took a different course. The stability of the children, whether at home or being looked after, was adversely affected and the rows and negotiations described in the previous chapter were never resolved. In the third case, a 16 year old adolescent girl went back to live with her mother and step-father after a long separation. Unfortunately, the girl's accusation of emotional rejection continued to plague the relationship between mother and daughter and a breakdown always seemed imminent.

Finally, one eight year old boy probably could have benefited from a further period of respite care. This boy had been a victim of physical abuse but had been able to return following the removal of his father. Once back, however, his behaviour became difficult and disturbed. While there was no suggestion of further abuse, it was clear that his mother was straining to cope. Nonetheless, neither she nor the social worker were prepared to let the child go back to foster parents and, anxious to escape close professional scrutiny, mother requested that the care order be discharged.

So much for the nine children who went home and stayed. What happened to the 11 children who were restored to relatives but subsequently moved to live elsewhere? Just as not all those staying at home are successful, not all those moving on after return can be deemed unsuccessful. Three children from the same family went back to foster parents two months after the reunion when their mother once again found herself unable to cope. However, on going home second time around, there were no such complications and so the children could be categorised as short-term breakdowns as described earlier.

Another boy, however, was less fortunate. He went home on three occasions during the follow-up without ever achieving stability, and typified the circumstances of children who oscillate. At the end of the intensive study, two days before his sixth birthday, he was living in his fourth foster home and long-term plans were far from clear.

Four adolescents, on the other hand, continued to enjoy good relationships with their parents after departing the family home, although leaving home after getting into further trouble with the police. Two other *long-term returners* went back without any problems, re-established healthy relationships with their parents and used this as a platform from which to seek independence.

Finally, a boy in one of the participating families exemplified the ambivalence of return. His return could only be classified as 'mixed'. Here, a 17 year old boy was restored to his Asian parents after a three year separation in a CHE for serious offending. Relationships at home were difficult in that there were language problems (the boy could not speak Urdu and his mother could not speak English) and the parents were dismayed at the delinquent identity in which their son revelled. The reunion never seemed likely to endure. However, six months after reunion, there was a sudden change in events when the boy moved to relatives in India. Whether this was a voluntary decision for him to cast off his delinquent past and fully reintegrate into the cultural norms of the family or whether his parents had imposed their will was not clear. At the end of the study, this boy remained abroad.

This evidence on the 20 children who returned during the intensive study shows the variety of long-term outcomes. It is summarised below.

Table 11.1: The long-term outcome for the 20 children who returned by the type of return case

| | Type of case | | | |
Outcome	Early return	Intermediate return	Long-term return	TOTAL
1) Child returned & stayed at home				
Outcome satisfactory	3	1	1	5
Concerns persist	-	2	1	3
Further separation needed	-	1	-	1
Sub-total	3	4	2	9
2) Children returned and subsequently moved				
Short-term breakdown	3	-	-	3
Oscillator	1	-	-	1
Satisfactory outcome but difficult move	2	1	1	4
Child seeks independence	-	-	2	2
Child moves to India	-	-	1	1
Sub-total	6	1	4	11
TOTAL	9	5	6	20

From this analysis of the progress made by the 20 children who returned from care or accommodation to live with relatives, what general conclusions can been drawn?

The process does not end

A period of separation is unlikely to cure family problems. The poverty and disadvantage of children looked after, their vulnerability to abuse and neglect and their propensity to emotional and conduct disorders all endure. None of these problems can be made to vanish with the magic wand of a substitute care placement. Nor does a partial resolution of the emotional upheaval witnessed in previous pages reduce the likelihood of further difficulties.

Furthermore, even when the problems which led to separation have subsided, new difficulties are likely to emerge. The five children who returned satisfactorily and stayed at home continued to cause anxiety on several fronts. The baby who was reunited with parents after a fortnight's separation subsequently developed medical problems which captured the attention of health agencies. The adolescents all had problems at school and tested their parents' patience with recalcitrant behaviour.

Of course, such difficulties can afflict all children but for those returning they can assume a special significance. The study emphasises the importance of positive continuities in children's lives. Where disconnection has occurred or where a sense of loss has not been resolved, the likelihood of post-return problems is increased. This can be illustrated by two contrasting quotations from mothers.

> I am at the end of my tether. If he does anything else I'll go mad. Every time you think you're getting on top of one thing another comes up. It's all since he went away, I don't know when we'll get sorted out.

> He's been OK really. I haven't noticed that anything's the matter. We've just been getting on with things. I suppose I should pay more attention and keep an eye on things but it's hard really. Since he got back it's really up to him.

Of these two cases, it was the first who returned successfully for, although the mother was at the end of her tether, she was concerned and was doing everything in her power to make things work. In the second case, apparently satisfactory progress concealed the mother's ambivalence towards her son following his return home. Unfortunately, continuity cannot be imposed once it has been lost and, although they parted on reasonable terms, mother and child drifted apart during the child's absence.

Previous chapters have charted the process of return for children looked after. This begins with the separation for, even at this moment, participants may be thinking of being back together. Events have been tracked through to the physical restoration which usually follows. Even where the child is physically at home, doubts may remain that she or he has been *returned*. In addition to the physical aspects of a reunion, there are also spiritual dimensions when parents, children, wider family members and professionals feel the child is 'at home'.

When does this happen? It took at least nine months for any of the nine families in which the child's reunion endured to be able to see the separation and return in the context of the new *modus vivendi*. Even for these families, certain stresses remained. Indeed, in three families the level of anxiety was so high even 18 months after the restoration that none of the participants felt the child was an integral part of the family.

How can professionals identify the moment at which the child is no longer returning and has 'returned'? Four aspects of the family situation are important. Firstly, the child must have a place in one of the homes of the family to which he or she has returned. The child may not live in this place; for example, one adolescent boy felt he had achieved a full reunion with home whilst living away with his girlfriend. Nonetheless, he had a room there and all the participants agreed that its occupancy was his right should he want it.

Secondly, there has to be the sense of belonging referred to in previous chapters. Most important is for the family to consider that the child is home to stay and for each to feel secure in the knowledge that there will not be a rapid turn-about; such feelings can waver during the honeymoon, the row and the early negotiations.

The third dimension to the child's full return is the professionals' view of the situation. Social workers must feel confident that the child is properly placed at home and agree, at least in broad terms, with decisions made on the child's behalf. Where there is social work anxiety, nobody feels fully secure that further separation will not follow. Finally, a sense of family identity is an important component in the child's full reunion. The family should perceive themselves as a single unit.

Arriving at this point can be long and painful. Yet, in retrospect, most family members in this situation could see the function and benefits of the difficult negotiations that had taken place. One mother summed the situation up thus,

> Well, I wouldn't like to go through all that again and it was hell at the time. I'd even go as far as saying it was worse than the day he went away. You saw what was happening to us, all the rows and things. But, I can see that there was a point to it all. We cleared a lot of stuff out of the way, we know where we stand

> with each other and I know it will never be the same again but
> we know at least, and I think Mrs. Jarman (the social worker)
> agrees, that we all belong together, back here together.

This mother's comment that the situation on return is not the same as that prior to the separation was mirrored by all of those participating in the study. During the return process there were many changes in family membership and even in the houses in which the child lived. Nonetheless, even for those returning to the *status quo ante*, there were affective changes in family relationships. In the past, this probably reflected the increased maturity of both adults and children common to all families but it is also consequent upon the lingering pain and guilt which follows separation and the sense of triumph over adversity experienced by those who had soldiered on to the end of the return path.

Conclusions

The intensive study has charted the various steps in the return process as well as the hiccoughs, false alarms and changes in plan which can occur. This chapter has looked at the children's situation 18 months after return first became an issue, an analysis which re-emphasises the complexity of reunion and its many possible outcomes. The most satisfactory definition of when return can be said to have been achieved emphasises the importance of the spiritual aspects of the process.

12 Children's return to contexts outside the family

Pre-occupation with return to the family should not obscure the wider context of return. Many children rejoining their families have to enter new schools, older adolescents will seek employment or join training schemes and all have to fashion friendships and social relationships in the local community. Sometimes the stigma and insecurities of the past make these negotiations difficult for the young person, particularly if compounded by unease and tensions within the family.

The focus so far has been the return of looked after children to their families and home communities. The many and various adaptations required have been described and different aspects of return, such as the negotiations over role and territory, explained. This chapter explores children's re-integration into contexts outside the family. Returns may have to be made to several contexts; to school, and for older children to employment or to vocational training. In addition, young people may have to rebuild their social and leisure networks. Unfortunately, some of these areas such as entry to employment or re-negotiating school networks deserve study in their own right and the difficulties can only be glimpsed occasionally from what children and adults say.

Children's return to school

A particularly important experience for many children is return to school. For both short and long-term looked after cases, school can provide one element of stability, continuity and belonging in an otherwise disrupted life. It is also clear that the way schools are organised can militate against a child's easy and successful return home. There are a number of ways in which schools can assist a child who returns after a considerable absence. For example, it is helpful if the child is prepared for entry. Although the child's situation may already be known to teachers, peers will be inquisitive and their teasing may be distressing. As an adolescent commented:

> Everyone just asked questions. Because you'd been in a children's home they thought you were criminal, they asked "what did you do?", "how much did you nick?", "did you try to kill someone?"

The recognition of the problems facing such children and the benefits of an induction programme have been highlighted by Fleeman (1984) and Pickup (1987). They emphasise the need for a particular teacher to be available for informal counselling and for senior staff to work in close liaison with social services. They also stress the benefits of close contact between the school and the pupils' families whenever possible.

Most looked after children fall into the category later called *organised* leavers. They have usually been separated because their parent has been admitted to hospital or is unable to look after them. For such children, there should be no detrimental effects on the child, provided the return from care or accommodation and entry to school are properly organised.

The importance of school for children looked after had not, until recently, received much attention in social work literature. Parker (1966) found that foster home transfers were less successful when they were accompanied by changes of school. Kahan's (1979) exploration of ten children looked after showed clearly how their attitude to school reflected their living situations. Few realised how important education would be to their future life chances.

These studies were among a handful which drew attention to the significance of the school experiences of children looked after. More recently, however, possibly following the emphasis placed on the issue by the Short Committee, more has become known. Jackson (1988), Heath, Colton and Aldgate (1989) and Fletcher-Campbell and Hall (1991) have since undertaken specific studies of the educational experiences of looked after children and it is to be hoped that social work planning now gives greater emphasis to education. It is a component of the *Looking After Children* materials widely used to monitor the progress of separated children. Berridge's (1985) example of the girl who missed her GCSE exam because she was not woken by residential staff and the indifference that some social workers can display towards the school experience of children looked after that this exemplifies are less likely to occur today. But in the intensive study of families and children experiencing reunion, return to school rarely coincided with the beginning of term and some older adolescents seemed to be left virtually to themselves to negotiate re-entry to the education system.

Social work plans increasingly consider the child's educational welfare and in five of the intensively studied cases care placements had been chosen for their proximity to the child's school, so facilitating a stable educational career. This strategy was particularly common for children attending special day schools. In addition, a number of the older children remained away until they had taken their exams. These efforts to help children attain and gain more from school seem sensible but, despite their significance for children's welfare, when reunion became an issue, few social workers looked beyond the child's family for factors which might influence the adjustment of the returning child. Yet, interviews emphasise that for adolescents, peer relations are a major preoccupation and one would hypothesise that feeling settled at school would be a contributory factor to a child's successful return.

Younger children find return to school easier than adolescents. Primary schools are more child-centred than secondary schools, in that one teacher is responsible for most of the day's activities and learning. There is less streaming by ability, more expressive and group activities, more play, music and drama, all of which encourage in children a sense of membership and group participation. The teaching and nurturing of children is largely the responsibility of one adult, thus the child who is not fitting in, is isolated or is having difficulty stands out much more. In urban areas the schools are more local in intake and likely to be more sensitive to the deprivations and difficulties that accompany childhood in their catchment area. Teachers will be familiar with the child protection register, with the clothing problems and poor nutrition of young children, they will know whose meals are subsidised and so on. The peer group which the child joins on return is less worldly wise and those coming back to school from foster homes or residential care are less likely to be considered delinquent or deviant. In the same way, the prodigal and his or her family situation and wider social structures are likely to be less of a pre-occupation with young children than with adolescents.

But return to the secondary school is more difficult. In organisation the school is subject centred rather than child-centred and, although some teachers have responsibility for age groups and others are delegated to pastoral or special needs responsibilities, the child's experience is not one of closeness to a particular adult but of numerous contacts with a wide variety of teachers. However, children's ability to seek out supportive and sympathetic adults should not be underestimated. As a boy commented,

> I hated the place, the big kids bullied you, they pinched everything you'd got and the teachers didn't care much about you at all, except Mrs. Johnson, she taught geography and made it interesting with videos and letters from kids abroad, I really liked it, you could talk to her about anything. She wasn't like a teacher at all. She seemed really pleased to see you when you came through the door.

Indeed, with regard to the issue of settling back, the contribution made to the returning child by some sympathetic person within the school cannot be overestimated. A teacher or even older pupils, aspiring apprentices for the caring professions, can ease the adjustment of new arrivals.

The school's experience of returning children

The educational disadvantage of children looked after have been commented on by many. For example, Heath, Colton and Aldgate (1991) found that as many as 91% of foster children obtained a standardised score below average for one or more of the three measures of attainment used, although the performance of another group of 'at risk' children known to social services was equally low. The authors also found a strong relationship between permanence in foster home placements and in children's attainments; the longer the duration of the placement, the better children seemed to perform at school. They comment:

The strength of the relationship between educational attainment and permanence deserves emphasis. It suggests that a sense of stability may be an important facilitating factor in allowing children to make progress at school and the longer this stability exists, the more it reinforces chances of success.

Unfortunately, for many children looked after, stability and permanence in a placement are still uncommon. This is serious because the effects of movement are not restricted to school progress. Berridge and Cleaver (1987) showed that children in foster homes, whether short or long-term, who also changed school were twice as likely to experience a placement breakdown.

This study was able to look at the ways in which schools cope with those pupils who return after a considerable absence. Children coming back from care and accommodation are only one group of mobile children needing help. Schools find returning children fall into three main categories. For the first group, both departure and return are more predictable. These are children who have to spend time in hospital, including those who experience several disruptions because of their treatment. In these cases, staff and friends from school are encouraged to visit and frequently do, parents and hospital are given a school work plan and the child's eventual re-entry is carefully organised. Once back, such children usually find school tiring but their absence need not have a detrimental effect on their work. In a school of 1,600 pupils visited during the study, in the space of a year only two such children returned after a prolonged illness. This category of returners is small and, because the absence is usually well managed and the children quickly re-adjust, the return poses relatively few problems.

The second category of returners common in schools involves pregnant girls. They have greater problems of re-adjustment to school life and the younger they are the more difficult the return. This is because girls' peer groups can be censorious in such situations and the child sometimes enjoys considerable notoriety. As one deputy head told us,

> 'The girl can become an outcast. However sympathetic we try to be, children can be cruel to one another and, once the girl returns to school, her friends can ostracise her sometimes with disastrous effects on her academic attainment'.

However, it should be emphasised that even in this inner city comprehensive, few girls actually returned after a pregnancy but, as with any exceptional child, whether those with disabilities, severe family problems or even those with unusual gifts, schools find it difficult to accommodate their needs.

The final group of children who return to school encounter far greater difficulties. This group can be described as highly mobile cases. They usually disappear due to sudden change in family situations, divorce or moonlight flits to avoid debt and other aggravations. They frequently move to live with another member of their family or are looked after by social services. Children who disappear in this way have usually been irregular attenders and have often been ostracised by peers beforehand, being seen as odd, sad, dirty or poorly dressed. Their academic performance is usually lack-lustre and they are often disruptive or withdrawn in class. Other children shrink from them and their departure can be a relief to all concerned.

Thus, the return of these highly mobile children to school presents problems all round. They come back, often unannounced and try to slot into routines without much preparation. They are made to feel unwelcome, acute problems of re-adjustment can arise and they can soon become disruptive. Their meagre attainments sink rapidly. However, it is interesting to discover that the number of children leaving and returning in this way was still low, about ten per year in the largest of the inner city schools visited.

Unfortunately, children who have been looked after for over a year fall mostly into this last group of highly mobile cases. Parents often felt they could not care for the child or cope with his or her behaviour and children's school attendance and attainments were poor. Offending and abuse were often additional complications. Thus, home and school problems, more often than not, were mutually reinforcing. Yet, when the return plans for these children were scrutinised, in nearly every case, return to school was not a considered part of the return strategy and, when included, was only a minor item.

The organisation of schools

The organisation of schools also has a role to play in helping vulnerable young people transfer successfully. A variety of approaches to the problem are possible, either within a particular school or among a group of schools, including further education, within a particular geographical area.

Naturally, one issue of school organisation has long haunted the welfare of children, namely the gulf that exists at all levels between education and social services. While both have the welfare of the child at heart, each tends to view those who return from different perspectives, with consequent problems of communication and lack of understanding.

It was surprising while talking to children's teachers to discover that they find it difficult to conceptualise return to school as an issue. Often there is little notion of the child having a 'social' career or that problems in one area could compound problems in another. For instance, following one boy's return to school, integration was seen as best promoted by a psychometric assessment of the child's ability and allocation to appropriate sets; the child's social network remained unconsidered and movement within the school aggravated his settlement problems.

Similarly, few attempts were made to build on the child's experiences while away. Thus, not only were subject choices dealt with perfunctorily but achievements in sport and art, which had often been used to boost the child's self-confidence, were also ignored and, overall, little attempt at continuity was made. One of the children in the intensive study had to cope with a move from one school where he was a 'star' athlete to another where sports were not seriously pursued. Indeed, the decline in significance of many non-core subjects in schools, the diminishing of extra-mural activities and sport have disadvantaged many children, not only those who return. Those who seek a role outside the classroom find that the spotlights have been turned off and the stage has gone.

Further limitations on the way schools approach the issue of return to school arise from recent educational changes. As many schools now control their own budgets, governors and senior staff have more power in deciding which pupils to accept and what resources should be allocated to special needs. Policies, therefore, can vary considerably between schools as well as among education authorities. For example, in a school of 1,200 pupils, there was a large special needs unit with nine staff, all of whom were also subject teachers. The school is a model in its approach to children with learning and social difficulties, among whom cluster several children on supervision and some recently returned from being looked after. However, there now exists considerable insecurity because the cost of this provision is considerable and there is parental pressure to allocate money elsewhere and to ensure that the school comes out well on published assessments. Understandably, the parents of children 'in need' do not form a vociferous or influential group within the school.

The GMS (grant maintained status) has also had implications for the social careers of children who have to spend time away in care. GMS means that the exclusion of children is the governors' decision and can only be rescinded after negotiation with parents. Disruptive young people become the responsibility of the Local Education Authority and the pupil may have to move schools again, thus producing further instability. Children from deprived families are at a disadvantage in such situations as they have limited legal power, few people pursuing their cause, parents who are poor negotiators and are likely to have had minimal home tuition.

An added problem for children who change schools is generated by the structure of the National Curriculum. In secondary schools there are two key stages, three and four, which are assessed by S.A.T.S. (Standard Attainment Test for Schools) at 14 and GCSE at 16. The National Curriculum runs in yearly blocks. In years seven, eight and nine, although the same subject areas are covered in every school, the way each year is organised in each subject could be different creating problems when compulsory testing occurs at the end of each unit.

It is easier, therefore, for a child to enter a new secondary school at the beginning of either the first or the fourth year. As one head teacher said,

> Recent changes have reduced our flexibility. I used to be able to tuck these children under the wing of Mr. Jameson in design and technology. He was marvellous with them but now he's not only too tied up to bother but also worried about the effects of such kids on his appraisal.

Unfortunately, the moment of return from a separation in care or accommodation is seldom influenced by these considerations.

At the level of immediate responsibility for the child, the contact between teachers and carers can most charitably be described as variable, although improving in local authorities that have faced the problem. Indeed, teachers and social workers can hold quite contrasting views on the importance of education for children looked after. As children are likely to move around while away, teachers tend to emphasise the stability offered by schooling while social workers feel that other issues, such as who should care for the child, are more important.

Generally, whatever their professional ideologies, there is still a tendency for teachers and social workers to have low academic expectations of children looked after. It is believed that such children will attain little and, as young adults, experience unemployment or, at best, take unskilled jobs. Some of the social workers interviewed happily viewed regular school attendance as sufficient and communications with teachers more often than not concerned children's behaviour rather than their educational progress or vocational preferences.

Yet several conscious efforts to counteract the negative effects of being looked after were encountered. Several of the residential units studied had a policy of keeping the children at their original school whenever possible. This was partly a necessity due to the fact that local schools were reluctant to accept children from community homes but, nevertheless, the policy was costly as the minibus journey to schools took an hour. It was felt that the benefits of maintaining continuity in education outweighed the disadvantages of distance. It also provided some security and sense of belonging for children experiencing considerable upheaval at home. Similarly, several local authorities have special arrangements by which resources follow the child, so overcoming the barriers to educational opportunity.

Missing from the discussion so far is the child's experience of going back to school. In the intensive study of the 20 children who actually returned home, 11 went to full-time schooling and a special study of their experiences showed that most children found the transition easier than their previously expressed anxieties would suggest. Nevertheless, children were still terrified of 'getting it wrong'. The smallest things worry children and not knowing what to do or feeling unable to trust others exacerbate these difficulties.

Indeed, theoretical perspectives on return were brought down to earth when children were interviewed about their new schools. Children's immediate anxieties over return were not the same as professionals'. Instead, they expressed surprise at things such as size, buildings, racial composition and unfamiliar routine. 'I didn't think we'd have to take our shoes off before going in the gym' was typical. But such worries should not be underestimated by teachers; they need to appreciate that these trivial anxieties are often the expression of wider and inexpressible unease. Indeed, the smallest fears can have considerable effects. One lad, for example, refused to eat school dinners simply because he was afraid that, in public view, he would not be able to operate the tap on the water urn correctly.

Many apparently routine things fill children with high anxiety when they are unaware of the required behaviours. Insecure children find the endless clatter, noise, and enforced bonhomie exhausting and disorienting. As a head-teacher told us 20 years ago,

> they trek along endless corridors, dropping precious pencils, to alien faces in distant rooms. Such an experience is even worse if you don't know which way the corridor leads and, as the last familiar companion disappears behind the sagging Nissen hut, you realise that you are not late but lost.

The newcomer, as she or he enters the school gate is an object of considerable interest, something bright on an otherwise sepia landscape. Everything they do is public, scrutinised by an audience of peers anxious for a laugh, particularly at someone else's expense. There is competition and jostling for position besides which scholastic achievement takes second place. Thus, taking off one's clothes for gym, the chilly trip to the swimming bath, grabbing a seat at lunchtime, waiting for the bus, all anxiously loom in the child's mind long before the bell rings, like a morning on the Somme, a trill that signifies you are going over the top, alone and without a comforting swig of rum.

It was noted earlier that any return involves negotiations over role and territory and that features which were once familiar to young people present new challenges. The successful establishment of a role takes time and diverts attention from anxiety but, once again, children returning to school face difficulties. Their return can follow a long separation from home and the questions of peers require a well-prepared story. Children who suddenly appear are objects of curiosity to classmates, mystery and fantasy will naturally abound. The problems of self presentation for children looked after are considerable. Even factual misunderstandings can defeat the struggling returner. As one child said,

> I came home from Shrewsbury. It had been the centre of my life but no one had the remotest idea where it was.

Several studies have stressed the importance of influential peer cultures in schools (Coleman, 1961; Hargreaves, 1967; Ball, 1981; Corrigan, 1979; Willis, 1977). Even the most astute staff were not always familiar with the dynamics of the pupil world. The use of the wrong slang, for example, immediately indicates to others that the newcomer is 'different'. While being 'different' may not worry young adults, at least in some areas such as leisure and taste, it is very important for younger children and adolescents to feel part of the group and to be the same. Coming from a strange background, being a welfare case and struggling to find a niche in the leading crowd were all significant to the children interviewed. The use of sympathetic peers to ease entry seems to be helpful and children seemed happier when there was a specific teacher in whom they could confide. Positive staff attitudes also seemed to help parents to overcome their depressed situation.

A child's entry to school is only one of several transitions that have to be made when a child returns from being looked after. Older children, in particular, have to fashion peer group relationships, find employment and cope with the vagaries of accommodation and social security.

Return to peer groups

On returning from being looked after, young people head straight for familiar bits of their social network, usually to situations where they feel people have some obligation to them. These may involve family and friends and two very isolated children in the study found fulfilling relationships via their siblings' or parents' social life. However, children looked after, who come mostly from poor working-class backgrounds, are at a disadvantage here because few such people are likely to exist and obligations may have been unmet in the past. Indeed, the Québec study previously discussed (Simard, Vachon and Moisan, 1991) stressed that difficulties in peer relations contribute significantly to young people's return difficulties.

But culture and class can also have benefits. For example, there was little of the middle-class guilt about not having kept in touch among the children interviewed and instant peer interaction with few social skill demands seemed normal. Thus, children leaving care and accommodation feel they have a right to behave in certain ways and need little preparation to help meet peers. When they do founder, however, it is because they are often unprepared for the changes that have occurred in their absence, namely the fact that familiar contemporaries have married, left the area or had children. Thus, the main defect in promoting peer relationships is the lack of 'currency' that arises during prolonged absences, a pattern described earlier.

For the older adolescents in the study, there was frequently some oscillation between family and friends. When situations got difficult in the family home, the young people drifted to situations where people had some obligation to them but where they also perceived minimal control. This was particularly the case following rows with parents and siblings. Thus, as was found in the follow-up studies of leavers from long stay secure treatment centres, there was a lot of to-ing and fro-ing from parents to other relatives and friends. Sometimes people such as distant aunts, scarcely known to the young people, were chosen simply because there was sufficient obligation to command entry to their home without the controls and detailed knowledge available to the immediate family. On some occasions, the young people went off to seek out friends they had known while away.

The situation of the young people in the study who found themselves homeless is also interesting in this respect. While the tragedy of their plight should not be understimated, they seemed able to find a peer group of similar people, suggesting that the same sense of obligation is shared among vulnerable people in times of greatest need. This was certainly functional in reducing the anxieties over accommodation that would riddle most of us. A similar situation arose with the young offenders in the study. As Little (1990) has found, while there was clearly considerable stigma in being a convict, the fact that everyone knew them, including the police, seemed to generate camaraderie and strengthen identity.

Achieving independence after return

When older teenagers return home from care or accommodation, it is naturally hoped that they will successfully achieve independence, fulfilling their personal ambitions and playing a full part in society. For all young people, this transition is a complex process and independence is achieved at different rates in different areas. Indeed, few ever become emotionally fully independent from their families. These changes require finding employment, being economically viable, getting accommodation and developing social and personal relationships. Again, these are inter-linked in that success in one transition can aid progress in others, findings echoed in the work of Stein and colleagues (1986, 1995).

For older adolescents returning from care and accommodation, these difficulties are often compounded. Training is theoretically available but offers little choice once key jobs are taken, normally in September and October. Leaving a job, even if it is unwanted, means a loss of benefit. Paid employment is not only hard to find but also difficult to keep. Many leave jobs after a few days. As has been previously noted, withdrawal when things go wrong is a well developed strategy among deprived adolescents and when applied to difficulties in training and employment situations, it creates immense difficulties for the young person.

Similarly, accommodation is problematic for 17 and 18-year-olds. They cannot sign on for social security and, at the time of the study, if they go to social services for help, they are usually sent to the 'council', that is the housing department, who send them back as they are not old enough to qualify for services. They usually end up clutching lists of homeless accommodation. Probation, of course, can sometimes help, but only for offenders.

Levels of homelessness among young people returning from care and accommodation are higher than they might first appear. Homelessness does not, of course, necessarily mean wandering the streets without hope of improvement but it does suggest a large number of young people living on the goodwill of others and moving around a series of interim 'shack-ups'. The follow-up would suggest that the number of homeless young people is higher than those sheltered in cardboard suburbs. The negative implications of this for a young person's identity, whether of person or place, are obvious.

While new responsibilities for vulnerable young people up to the age of 21 were introduced by the *Children Act* 1989, those who have been long looked after generally still have poor views of social services. While some of their dismissive attitudes may reflect the arrogance of youth, these unfavourable views must be considered when devising ways of attracting young adults to accept the new services envisaged. A clearer understanding of how difficulties in returns to contexts outside the family affect young people's subsequent living situations is needed. It is well established that in the period after being looked after, more boys than girls return to live with relations. These wider contexts may be influential in this, a relationship that would benefit from further research scrutiny.

Conclusions

In this chapter, children's returns from care and accommodation to contexts outside the natural family have been considered. The scope for helping children return successfully is considerable in all the areas discussed. In education, for example, it lies in administrative arrangements for schooling, in co-operation between teachers and social workers and in developing sensitivity to children's needs.

Children looked after are often cleverer and more capable than professionals like to think. They are seen as 'dim' or 'unreliable' and are rarely encouraged to apply themselves at school, in work or in the pursuit of personal relationships. As *Locking Up Children* concluded,

> because we cannot envisage the Sistine Chapel being nurtured in a secure unit, we must act accordingly.

But, innate intelligence apart, the experiences of children looked after can be defeating because of the situations they are put in. To expect children to return from a child-centred, supportive care placement to a large, structured day-school or unsupportive work situation and cope without money, accommodation and friends is a recipe for failure. The children will get things wrong and adapt accordingly, either by the well-tried strategy of withdrawal or by manipulating professionals, friends and relatives against one another.

The intensive studies revealed professionals' low educational, employment and social expectations for children returning from care and accommodation and the ways, many of them very subtle, that the experience of being looked after militated against academic and other achievements. One school report stated, 'the trouble is he's not educationally motivated.' True as this might be, the fact remained that without the sensitivity described, he was never going to become so.

This chapter re-affirms many of the points about continuities and transitions made throughout this study. A successful re-union reflects not only the child's reintegration within the family but also his or her ability to make progress in other settings, most notably school or, for older adolescents, work. Once at home, the child needs to establish a role outside of the family which does not undermine his or her role within it.

Summary points

1. Children return from care and accommodation to a variety of contexts. Apart from their families, children may have to adapt to school, peer groups, employment and moves to independence.

2. Separation and return and the placement changes experienced while away sometimes involve changes of school for the child. Provided the absence and return are properly organised, short-stay children suffer relatively little damage to their education. Long-stay cases, however, face more complex problems. Education often has low priority in their care plans and has to fit into other arrangements. Thus, educational continuities are difficult to maintain.

3. Return to primary and special schools is easier than to secondary schools because of the class-teacher structure and flexible curriculum. Changes in schools, such as Grant Maintained Status, the National Curriculum and published Standard Attainment Tests, have exacerbated the difficulties of finding schools for children returning from care or accommodation.

4. The success of children's return to school is further hindered by infrequent contacts between teachers and social workers and by conflicting professional ideologies about what constitutes the child's best interests. In addition, the timetable for care plans rarely matched school terms.

5. Entry to a new school is especially difficult for children returning from being looked after. Children are uncertain and frightened by seemingly trivial things, classmates can be cruel and making friends is not easy, especially after year eight. Teachers and social workers need to be aware of this.

6. Older children returning to peer groups, youth training, employment and moves to independence face especial difficulties and the provision in the *Children Act* 1989 to support 18-21 year olds is an important step in lessening the problems such young people face.

13 General patterns of return

The intensive study of 31 children has established some generalisations about the separation and return of looked after children. Social workers will generally seek to avoid separation if at all possible and where separation cannot be avoided, they will usually seek a swift re-union. Thus, the great majority of children who are separated from families whilst looked after by a local authority do go home. The establishment of a generalisation, however, must not divert attention from exceptions to it. Of every eight children looked after, one will not return to relatives within five years. Similarly, the fact that most of those who return home will still be there a year later should not obscure the experience of those for whom return to relatives is followed by further separation. It is time to examine in more detail patterns of separation and return for children looked after. Who goes home quickly, and who is likely to linger? For whom is a return home a farewell to foster parents or residential staff, and for whom is it more an *au revoir*?

As described in Chapter Five, these questions will be explored with relation to three sets of data. The first is a longitudinal study of 463 children and young people separated from relatives and looked after by seven local authorities during 1993. The sample is comprehensive in that it includes all children looked after over a specific period in the localities involved. As illustrated in Table 13.1 below the cohort replicated almost exactly the characteristics of children looked after nationally at the time (Department of Health, 1994) . There are thus good grounds to be confident that the children and young people in the study are representative of young people looked after generally.

A data set that comprises all new separations can by its nature provide little relevant information on children looked after for long periods. In order to examine the experience of such young people, reference will be made to three other data sets assembled by the Dartington Social Research Unit. As discussed in Chapter Five, these comprise, firstly, a scrutiny of all young people who passed through the Youth Treatment Centres and other long stay secure units (Bullock et al., 1998), secondly, a study of all leavers from a long-stay therapeutic community (Little and Kelly, 1995) and, thirdly, a five year follow-up of children admitted to care or accommodation during the early nineteen eighties (Bullock et al., 1993). It will be made clear where these studies are cited. Unless specified, the data in this chapter come from the prospective study of 463 children and young people described in the previous paragraph.

Table 13.1: The Going Home cohort compared to national figures

	Sample	DH figures 92-93
% boys	52	53
% under 1	10	10
% over 10	52	50
% S20	83	83
% initially fostered	71	70

General Return Patterns

It will be recalled that return has been defined as going home to live, though the reunion does not necessarily involve the same location or the same personnel as were present at departure. For the purposes of this chapter, a child is considered to have gone home where he or she has gone to live with relatives with the expectation that his or her period of being formally looked after has come to an end. Thus, weekend leaves and placements preliminary to the final reunion have been excluded. For younger children, whilst the process of return may extend considerably on either side, a 'moment of return' can usually be established fairly unequivocally. The greater fluidity in the careers of older adolescents presents more problems, and the interpretation of what constitutes 'going home to live' for such young people has been more generous. Clearly, there are fewer expectations of permanence in such situations, though the period of being looked after formally ceases.

How long are children looked after, on average, before they return home, or leave to independence? The answer to this question depends largely on the definition of 'average'. Measuring length of stay in weeks, the *modal*, or most common, period of separation was less than one week. The *median* separation, on the other hand, was seven weeks; that is to say that half the children separated had returned home within that time. The *mean* cannot be calculated from this sample until all the children in the prospective study have returned home, but it will be much higher than either the mode or the median. A high mean will reflect the disproportionate influence of those few separations that last decades, despite the fact that the vast majority finish within two months.

A more useful way to answer the question is illustrated in Tables 13.2 and 13.3. Table 13.2 shows that nearly a quarter of young people looked after returned home within a week and nearly two thirds had done so within six weeks. By the end of the research follow-up two years after separation, nearly three quarters (73%) had gone home. At this stage, only one in six (17%) was still looked after. The remaining 9% were in neither situation – 6% had left to independence 3% had been adopted outside the family. Far and away the most likely immediate outcome of a child's being looked after by a local authority, therefore, was a rapid return home.

Table 13.2: Outcomes of separation

Return home within a week	24%
Return home within a month	40%
Return home within 6 months	65%
Return home within a year	71%
Return home within two years	73%
Still looked after two years	17%
Left to independence within two years	6%
Adopted within two years	3%

Tables 13.2 and 13.3 also suggest that the rate at which children return home declines over time. For example, nearly a quarter went home within the first week and a quarter of those still looked after at the end of one week went home within a month. On the other hand, it

took a further eighteen months to achieve the reunion of a quarter of those still separated at six months. For every four children separated for more than six months who returned home within the following eighteen months, three ceased to be looked after for other reasons - they were either adopted or moved to independence. The finding that three quarters of children looked after have been re-united with relatives two years after separation is very similar to figures from other research, including that conducted before the implementation of the *Children Act*, 1989 (Millham et al., 1986; Packman and Hall, 1998).

What of that quarter of the original cohort who did not return to live with relatives within two years? Thirteen young people had been adopted and eighty were still looked after two years after separation. For two thirds of this latter group, social workers had expressed doubt about the prospects of reunion from the start. It is not surprising that for only two of these children was return home part of the current social work plan at the two year follow up. These patterns are laid out in the following table.

Table 13.3: Experience of the cohort over time

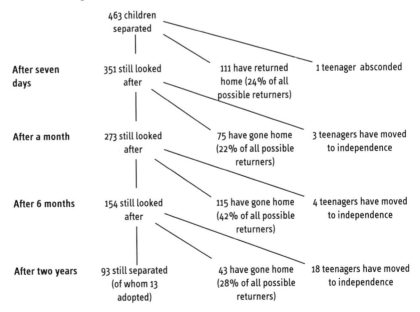

	463 children separated		1 teenager absconded
After seven days	351 still looked after	111 have returned home (24% of all possible returners)	
After a month	273 still looked after	75 have gone home (22% of all possible returners)	3 teenagers have moved to independence
After 6 months	154 still looked after	115 have gone home (42% of all possible returners)	4 teenagers have moved to independence
After two years	93 still separated (of whom 13 adopted)	43 have gone home (28% of all possible returners)	18 teenagers have moved to independence

Particularly significant for understanding the complexity of return patterns are those young people who seem unlikely to go home. The follow up evidence shows that events have a tendency to overtake such predictions. Taking the smallest group first, those adopted, Thoburn (1991) and others have assembled an extensive body of evidence to indicate that as adoption has begun to be used as an alternative to long term fostering for older children, including children with special needs, so it has begun to display some of the problems associated with long term fostering, in particular the risk of breakdown in adolescence (Berridge and Cleaver, 1987). Since a common destination following adoption breakdown is the parental home, adoption can no longer be considered a guarantee against a return home. On the other hand, the adopted children in the prospective sample could not be considered at high risk of breakdown using the factors identified by Thoburn. All the children involved were either babies or young toddlers on separation, and nine of the thirteen were less than a year old. The facts that eleven of the thirteen were adopted at the request of their mothers, all were adopted within two years of separation and none had more than two foster placements prior to their adoptive home makes return home unlikely for these particular children.

Turning to the largest group still separated after two years, those children still looked after, previous longitudinal studies at the Dartington Unit (Bullock et al., 1993) have shown that just under a third of young people separated from relatives for two years are likely to return home within the next three. Studies of specialist long stay residential establishments such as Youth Treatment Centres and therapeutic communities (Little and Kelly, 1995; Bullock et al., 1998) have also revealed that the family home is the most likely immediate destination for teenagers leaving these institutions, even for those separated from family for more than half their lives. The characteristics and experiences of these 'long term returners' are described in more detail in the next chapter: at this stage it is sufficient to note that return home from local authority care or accommodation always remains a possibility.

Neither, of course, does return home cease to be a possibility once young people leave local authority care or accommodation and move to live independently. Such transitions in late adolescence are far from an ordinary experience: only one in a hundred teenagers lives on his or her own, and only one in ten seventeen year olds have left home (Ainley, 1991; Wall and Penhale, 1989; Central Statistical Office 1996). The fact that these young people are trying to live independently at all, and are supported in their endeavours by social workers, indicates the poor prognosis entertained for a return home for this group.

Out of the 26 older adolescents who moved to independence, nine returned to live with relatives during the year they ceased to be looked after, and another two spent a considerable period in the parental homes of school-friends. Again, the characteristics and experiences of these young adults are explored in more detail in the next chapter: suffice it for now to recognise that leaving to independence certainly does not negate the possibility of a return home: indeed in many ways, it can increase it.

Table 13.4 extrapolates the findings of these various studies to predict the likely long-term experience of those in the cohort who have not returned home after two years. It is now possible to estimate the proportion of children and young people looked after who are likely to return home. Return home is most likely in the early stages of separation - nearly three quarters (73%) of the cohort having returned within two years. Return remains a possibility, however, after long separation (8% of the cohort) or following a move to independence, whether within the two year study period (3% of the cohort) or subsequently (a further 3%). Overall, this suggests that 87% of the study cohort will return home at some stage. Put another way, only 13% of children looked after - one child in every eight - will experience a permanent separation from relatives.

Table 13.4: The likely experience of the cohort (N=463) in the medium term

After two years	Eighty still looked after two years	Twenty six leave to independence within two years	Thirteen are adopted
In long term	40-50% will return home from care/accommodation in long-term	1) Half will return home whilst seeking independence 2) 10-20% will return home following a move to independence	Possibility of return home following adoption breakdown - possibly one child in this cohort

The conclusions to be drawn from this analysis are clear. For the great majority of children in care, family members are the most important resources available to social workers, as parents, grandparents, siblings and other relatives are likely to provide continuing support long after children have become adolescents, resources have dried up and social work attention has moved on elsewhere. It is certainly true that some reluctantly return to relatives because there is nowhere else for them to go. Nevertheless, whether professionals like it or not, the large majority of children looked after will eventually be restored to their family and professional perspectives and interventions need to accommodate that fact.

The success of return

What constitutes a successful return? The parable of the prodigal son offers a cultural ideal of return but the realities - the chilly nod of recognition, the grunt from behind the newspaper or the tepid supper left in the oven - may be rather different. The parable also reminds us that the perspectives of different family members will not necessarily coincide: what is a successful return for one child may spell disaster for a sibling. The question of timing is also crucial in assessing the success of return, indeed in gauging the outcome of any intervention. Success must also obviously be measured on a number of interlocking but discrete criteria - return home may, for example, safeguard a child's emotional development by maintaining continuity of parenting, whilst exposing them to the risk of neglect or abuse. By the same token, warm and loving family relationships cannot be taken as unambiguous indicators of successful social work where they are accompanied by persistent offending (Parker et al., 1991).

Deciding what constitutes a successful return in theory, moreover, does not necessarily enable either the researcher or the professional to distinguish one in practice. Indeed, there is something of a tension between the twin requirements of a definition of success, that it be valid and that it be useful. 'Hard' measures, such as whether the return endured, are easy to measure and comparatively unambiguous in meaning. On the other hand, they take no account of the subtleties and idiosyncrasies of individual lives and families. Enduring bliss and endless misery can hardly be considered to represent the same outcome. 'Soft' measures such as researcher evaluations, by contrast, are of uncertain status. Are they 'facts' or 'opinions', and what difference does it make? However objective, they inevitably involve imposing a fairly arbitrary threshold on a multi-dimensional continuum of experience. On the other hand, when dealing with large sample groups and using complex statistical procedures a simple, preferably binary, outcome measure is a necessity, and only a researcher evaluation can really meet the requirements.

In this analysis, both 'hard' and 'soft', 'objective' and 'subjective' measurements will be used. In most cases, it hardly matters which criteria are used. Around two thirds (65%) of returners were still in the same household at follow-up a year later, and around two thirds (65%) of the returns were considered by the research team to have been successful. The agreement between these two measurements was substantial, with 84% of enduring reunions being considered successful and a similar proportion of successful reunions being enduring. Other measurements tended to follow similar patterns, as illustrated in table 13.5.

Table 13.5: The success of return

	'Successful' returns	'Unsuccessful' returns
In same household at follow-up	84%	26%
Looked after again by follow-up	27%	80%
Case closed at follow-up	47%	15%
All returns	65%	35%

(a small number of returners for whom no follow-up was possible are excluded)

One item in the table - whether the child was looked after again in the year subsequent to return - must be interpreted with caution, as around a quarter of these were looked after under arrangements for a programme of regular respite care. Excluding these, it was found that a third of returners were looked after again in the year following return. The placing or removal of children's names from child protection registers must similarly be handled carefully as an outcome measure, but, again, of those whose status changed during the period from separation to follow-up nearly two thirds (62%) were de-registered and a third were added to the register. Thus whatever criteria are used, two thirds of returns can be considered to have been successful, a figure that echoes that obtained by Farmer and Parker (1991) in their study of children returning home on trial.

How do these findings compare with the success rates of substitute placements for looked after children generally? In the studies previously cited, Millham and colleagues (1986) found that only a quarter of children looked after for a year (the same length of time as the follow-up in this study) were in the same placement throughout and the rate of placement breakdown was just over a quarter (26%) even for those returning home to relatives within six months. Similarly, Rowe, Hundleby and Garnett (1989) asked whether placements could be considered to have lasted 'as long as needed' and found an overall success rate of around two thirds (62%), though this was lower for adolescents. Berridge and Cleaver (1987) found that 18% of short term and 38% of long-term foster placements broke down. Thus a success rate of around two thirds for return home is much the same as other child-care placements.

Not only is the figure of two successes to every failure consistent across a range of placements, it is also much the same irrespective of the length of separation. For anyone who has ever tried to revive a love affair after a long separation, this will be a surprising result, but the success rate for children returning home between six months and two years after separation was little different (60%) from that for those returning within the first six months. Similarly, of the nine older teenagers who returned home via a spell of independence, six were considered to have done so successfully. For those returning home after very long separation, follow-up studies of leavers from the Youth Treatment Centres and other treatment units again found that a third of those returning home, whether directly or indirectly, subsequently moved on as a result of a breakdown in relationships (Bullock, et al., 1998).

Having considered some general themes from the quantitative study, the next chapter considers the needs, problems and resources of some of the families concerned in more detail.

Summary Points

1. The sample of 463 children and young people looked after described in this chapter can be considered representative of children looked after nationally.

2. The most common period of separation was less than one week, and half the study cohort had returned home within seven weeks.

3. One child in five had not returned home within two years of separation. Some of these children will achieve stability through adoption, long term fostering, specialist residential care or independence. Some will return to relatives after long periods of being looked after, and some after a period of independent living. Overall, 85 to 90% of children looked after are likely to return home to live at some stage.

4. A successful return is difficult to define precisely. Nonetheless, whether success is defined by firm criteria such as endurance or more subjective assessments, two in every three returns are successful. Thus the chances of breakdown are much the same following return as in foster or residential care.

14 Children for whom return issues are relatively straightforward

This chapter scrutinises three groups of children for whom return issues are relatively straightforward. They are: (i) children who will not return home to live at all; (ii) children who experience a short separation followed by a successful reunion; and (iii) children experiencing respite care.

Both the likelihood of return taking place and the likelihood of its success have now been considered. Table 14.1 combines these two measurements for three groups within the study cohort whose movements between home and care or accommodation are relatively straightforward. First, there are those, comprising thirteen per cent of children looked after, who do not return home at all: for such children, the success of return is not an issue. Second, there are those who quickly return home and remain there. For a third group of children, separation and return take place as part of regular respite care. These three groups combined comprise some two in every three children looked after. Naturally, the experiences of each group will differ, but what they have in common is that their care careers are for the most part fairly predictable. When they are placed somewhere, whether it be a community home or foster care, they tend to remain there until professionals wish to move them. From the point of view of social work planning, these children and young people present comparatively few problems. Each group will now be scrutinised.

Children who do not return home

Eighty of the original 463 children were still looked after by the end of the study period. Another 13 had been adopted, and their chances of return have already been assessed as almost nil. The prospects for future happiness in their adoptive families were very good as a result of their youth, good health and stable placement history.

Table 14.1: Simple patterns of separation and return

	N (%)
Returned home within two years, not looked after again within a year of return	189 (41%)
Still looked after or adopted at two years	93 (20%)
Respite care	39 (8%)
More complex patterns of separation and return	142 (31%)

For the 80 children who remained looked after, the prospects are more equivocal. Two thirds were in foster care at the cut off period and a third in community homes. The reasons why these young people were unable to return home are analysed in more detail in the next chapter but several factors deserve mention here. Firstly, nearly half (48%) of those still separated at two years had been separated with siblings, compared with 38% of children returning home and none of those adopted. Secondly, these were children over whom social services exerted high levels of formal control. Nearly half (44%) were on care orders when initially separated, and over half (59%) were so by the end of the study. Thirdly, the long separation of these children was fairly predictable at separation: social workers had predicted the chances of return in the long term to be no better than 'medium' for five of every eight of these children, and as 'strong' for less than one in five. If the situation within the natural family was inauspicious at separation, it tended to be little better now: indeed, for the majority (56%), the family situation was seen by professionals to have deteriorated since separation. For three quarters, abuse and/or neglect had played a major role in the professional decision to look after the children.

This was a group then for whom effective planning was both necessary - given the likely duration of social work involvement and the complexity of the work involved - and comparatively straightforward, given the levels of control exercised by social workers through the courts and the expectations of professionals. Was planning much in evidence? The answer, again, is equivocal. Where the intention of the care plan was to maintain children in stable, semi-permanent placements, there was evidence of some impressive social work. For example, the majority (56%) of those separated for two years remained in the same placement throughout. As far as return to relatives was concerned, however, there was less evidence of systematic planning. Less than a third (30%) of the children experienced any significant continuities with their life prior to separation after two years, and only one in five (20%) retained territory in the home of his or her natural family by this point. Family relationships, already strained, had been allowed to be further eroded by a long period of being looked after.

Overall, around half of the children still separated at two years could be considered to have achieved some stability in substitute care. Around half of the children still looked after at two years are likely to return to relatives in the long term, whether directly or via a spell of independence. Although there may be some overlap between these two groups, it seems likely that it will not be all that great.

Children returning home and not looked after again

Early returners

Far and away the most common pattern of separation and return for the study cohort consisted of exactly that - a separation followed by a speedy and permanent return. This group also includes five children whose initial return was premature but who returned a second time soon afterwards, this time successfully. Overall, one separation and one return was the experience of just over a third (35%) of the children and young people looked after. The majority (60%) of these children had not been separated before and were looked after at a time when the stresses impinging upon their families temporarily swamped their parents' and other relatives' ability to cope. When the balance was restored, the children returned home quickly and settled back with no obvious damage to them or to the fabric of family life.

Two common scenarios summarised the immediate needs of over half of this group. Firstly, there were individuals and, more commonly, sibling groups accommodated as a result of their mother's hospitalisation. The causes of hospitalisation were varied, and included physical illnesses or accidents, mental illness and attempted suicide, births, abortions, sterilisations and admission to drying out clinics. Only one in five of the early, stable returners was living with their father at the time of separation and only a third (36%) were in any contact with him. Likewise, the majority (63%) of these children had no contact with either set of grandparents and only one in five saw or heard from aunts or uncles. These children came from very socially isolated single parent families keeping their heads above water in difficult situations but with no-one else to turn to when temporarily unable to care for their children. One of the case studies discussed later, Kelly, was fostered in such circumstances to allow her mother's second pregnancy to be terminated. Such families accounted for around a third (36%) of the early, stable returners and 13% of the study cohort overall.

A second common scenario involved a temporary rupture in relationships between parent(s) and their adolescent offspring. Nearly half (47%) of these adolescents were aged 14, and four in five (80%) were within a year either side. In such situations, a brief separation was considered the only way out of a crisis precipitated by a vicious circle of escalating misbehaviour, deteriorating relationships and violent confrontations. In a quarter of cases, this involved a serious fight between a teenage girl and her mother's new male partner. Misbehaviour ranged from merely ignoring parental curfews to serious offending - two in five (38%) of this group, mostly boys, had been cautioned or convicted for offences. On the other hand, the young people were often victims of maltreatment - child abuse and neglect were seen as contributing to the separation in nearly half (48%) of cases. Whilst recriminations flew back and forth between parents and offspring, professionals were also conscious of the other stresses - particularly unemployment, poor housing and illness - undermining family relationships. Nonetheless, the crisis that precipitated separation was invariably short-lived and in a fifth (20%) of cases it was sorted out within 48 hours. Two thirds (70%) of the young people had not been looked after before and two thirds (63%) had been known to social services for less than a year prior to being looked after. Thus these families' involvement with social services was fairly tangential.

Prior to the *Children Act*, 1989, a sizeable proportion of these adolescents might have been looked after under some form of care order. Following the introduction of the 'no order' principle, however, it is not surprising to find that nine out of ten of them were looked after under Section 20 of the Act, with the remainder comprising a mixture of remands following arrests and protection orders following assaults by parents. Informal negotiations between social services and parents were also the norm where children were looked after as a result of their mother's hospitalisation. Overall, 92% of the early, stable returners were looked after under voluntary arrangements, compared with 80% of the total cohort. The characteristics of the 'early, stable returner' group reflect the dominance of a mother's hospitalisation as a cause of separation, but otherwise are not so very different from the other children in the cohort. The details are summarised in Table 14.2.

Table 14.2: Characteristics of early, stable returners

	Early, stable returners	Total sample	p[1]
Females	53%	48%	ns
With siblings	42%	38%	ns
Living with mother only	52%	46%	ns
Looked after previously	40%	50%	<0.05
Fostered	74%	63%	<0.05
On CPR at separation	30%	42%	<0.05
Under one	5%	10%	<0.05
Separation primarily as a result of parental illness	32%	20%	<0.05

Although the sudden nature of the crises involved might necessitate an emergency placement, subsequent planning for these children once separated is generally straightforward. Unsurprisingly, continuity was a more typical experience for the early, stable returners than for the others in the cohort. For one in six, for example, separation was so short that contact during separation was not regarded as an issue, whilst

---

[1] Simple Chi-square, df=1

the remainder were in at least weekly contact with relatives. Social workers also strove to preserve other continuities, particularly in education, which often involved bussing and taxi-ing children considerable distances. Most heartening, though, was the fact that the vast majority of early, stable returners - 92% overall and 97% of under 10s - experienced only one placement whilst looked after. Thus again stability and continuity whilst separated were associated with a rapid return home, and stability and continuity once re-united.

Table 14.3: Children returning to same household (82% of total): early, stable returners

From		% of total sample
Mother and father	21	13
Mother and stepfather/ male cohab.	27	17
Mother	77	47
Father	0	0
Father and stepmother/female cohab.	2	1
Other	5	3

Return was further eased by the fact that four in five of the early, stable returners returned to the same household from which they had originally been separated, though in several cases with the addition of a new baby. Their families are summarised in Table 14.3. It is noteworthy that whilst all of the households to which the children returned contained a woman, less than two in five (37%) contained a man.

The experience of those who returned to a different household is summarised in Table 14.4 below. It can be seen that movement from a two parent household to a one parent household (9%) was twice as common as movement the other way (4%). Sometimes these changes could be sufficient on their own to precipitate return. In three cases separated parents were re-united and took over the care of the children. On the other hand, the departure of an abusive father or father-figure could make the important difference. On other occasions, it was not a change in circumstances so much as a change in social workers' perceptions of circumstances that allowed a return home; for example, when enquiries concluded that protection was a less pressing need than other family problems.

To summarise, the early, stable returners have in common a temporary breakdown of family life. The bulk of the social work effort is centred around the original admission to accommodation, but if things are managed well the children involved usually enjoy as much continuity as can humanly be expected, both during separation and subsequently. The majority (60%) of these cases were closed at follow-up and in nine out of ten cases (89%) the research team considered the reunions to have been successful.

Intermediate returners

A further 7% of the cohort - 32 children - returned successfully to relatives following a much longer separation - between six months and two years. As a six month cut off point is fairly arbitrary, the characteristics and problems of these children will overlap with those of the early, stable returners. Thus, there were no significant differences in terms of children's age, gender, legal status or initial placements. The difference lay in the length of time it took to sort out their problems. Three children, for example, experienced a long separation from their mother as a result of her extended stay in a psychiatric hospital. Another three were looked after whilst their parents served prison sentences.

Table 14.4: Children returning to different household: early, stable returners

From	To	N
Mother and father	Mother	5
	Sister	1
Mother and stepfather/ male cohab.	Mother and father	2
	Mother	5
	Grandparents	3
Mother	Mother and stepfather	3
	Mother and father	2
	Father and stepmother	1
	Other	4
Father and stepmother/ female cohab.	Mother and stepfather	1
Aunt	Mother and stepfather	1
Other	Mother alone	3

As a result of their longer separations, change and loss of continuity were far more common for these intermediate returners than for those who went home more rapidly. More than a quarter (28%) experienced at least one change of placement during separation. A comparison of tables 14.5 and 14.6 below with tables 14.3 and 14.4 above illustrates these points. Whilst four in five early returners returned to an unchanged household, this was the experience of only a third (38%) of intermediate returners.

Whilst changes in family membership are usually disruptive and damaging for children looked after, they may on occasion be a necessary and sufficient condition for a return home. Such observations take on added significance when considering those looked after for longer periods. In a third (34%) of cases, for example, the chief factor leading to return was the availability of new or additional carers to help with parenting. For a further fifth (19%), return followed swiftly on the departure of an abusive father or stepfather from the family home. Changes in family membership, however, were not the only developments that might propel children back. Three children were sent home as a result of a change of social worker and four went home when a parent was rehoused. When such major changes occur in the lives of children and parents, professionals may feel that if return is to take place ever it must happen now.

Table 14.5: Intermediate returners returning to the same household (N=32)

From	
Mother and father	1
Mother and stepfather/ male cohab.	5
Mother	4
Other	2

Several intermediate returners did not return to parents at all. Instead, as the chances of a satisfactory return to their original carers declined and the children began to drift, professionals began to sound out distant relatives and family friends. Grandparents, aunts and uncles, older sisters, even great grandparents and cousins were recruited with varying degrees of enthusiasm, as well as parents' friends, previous partners and neighbours. Another common route home, particularly for adolescents, followed the collapse of a foster placement. Social workers often held out little hope of success for such reunions, but in six cases represented here they were proved over-pessimistic.

Table 14.6: Intermediate returners returning to different household (N=20)

From	To	N
Mother and father	Mother	4
	Other	4
Mother and stepfather/ male cohab.	Mother	7
Mother	Other	1
Father and stepmother/ female cohab.	Other	1
Father	Mother	1
Grandparents	Mother and father	2

Table 14.7 below summarises the reasons the intermediate returners went home. There are clearly differences in the social work task between them and the early returners. For the early returners, the need is to provide accommodation, food and reassurance until parents recover, tempers die down or immediate problems are overcome. The scope for decisive social work intervention beyond this facilitating role is limited and the immediate outcomes of interventions are largely beyond social workers' control. Where a sibling group is looked after as a result of their mother's imminent confinement, for example, there is very little a social worker can (ethically) do to speed up the return process. Likewise, if family members swing punches every time they meet, there is probably little that can be done beyond waiting for tempers to cool. Once tempers are cooled, the problems are often found to have disappeared.

Table 14.7: Why intermediate returners went home

	Early, stable returners(%)	intermediate stables(%)	All looked after(%)
Original carer(s) able to resume parenting	51	25	38
Placement breakdown	5	19	8
New or additional carers	10	34	12 (inc. adoptions)
Abusive parent left household	5	16	5
Other	29	5	16
Did not return home	-	-	21
	100	100	100

Once a young person has been separated for several months, his or her return increasingly comes to depend less on the ups and downs of parental fortunes and more on the actions, or inactivity, of professionals. This occurs for two major reasons. Firstly, if a return is to take place it is as likely to be as a result of decisive social work as through an unaided improvement in parental circumstances. This may take the form, for example, of putting pressure upon housing departments and other public agencies. Where a child cannot be returned to his or her original carer, it will involve a great deal of hard work in the search for alternatives. The fact that effective social work can make a difference is illustrated most vividly by the three children who returned home purely as a result of a change of social worker.

Secondly, as the weeks of separation lengthen into months, so discontinuities accumulate and the risk of drift and permanent estrangement grows. Poor practice will simply allow such situations to evolve, allowing emotional bonds to weaken and roles and territories to become memories. Effective social work will seek to ensure that continuities are maintained as far as possible. As separations lengthen this will increasingly require action, especially with regard to access and contact between parents and children. Then, if and when circumstances arise to permit or perhaps oblige a return home, such as a placement breakdown or the arrival of a new carer, the chances of success are maximised.

Once a child has been looked after for six months, it is increasingly likely that only a major change will enable a return home. This often involves a return to entirely different carers or at least to a household that has lost or gained a parent-figure. Alternatively, it may come about as a result of the collapse of a placement or a change of social worker. The preservation of other continuities, however, becomes increasingly important as the passage of time threatens to loosen emotional bonds.

Respite care

The growing popularity of respite care arrangements seems at first sight to challenge one of the central themes of the current study, that return home from substitute care is a stressful and difficult experience for both children and parents. Here, after all, is a service designed apparently to maximise the number of separations and returns and yet one for which short-term outcomes are usually positive, and one generally popular with both parents and children (Aldgate and Tunstill, 1995). In the field of respite care, however, the boundaries between children looked after and children provided with services whilst still at home become somewhat blurred: it is debatable whether such children can be said to have left home in the first place. The fact that separations are not only short but highly predictable likewise constitutes a major difference. Whilst children looked after under respite care arrangements clearly are children 'looked after' in the legal and administrative senses, they must be treated for the purposes of this study as something of a special case.

'Respite care' is a term used informally by social workers to cover a variety of arrangements for the care of children away from their families. Here the term is used in the narrow sense of an arrangement covering a series of placements that are no more than three days in duration, regularly spaced and planned well in advance and with the same carers every time. The cohort included, for example, a sibling group who returned to the same foster carers every time their mother suffered a crisis of mental health, and several adolescents who attended weekly boarding schools. One of these was accommodated with different carers every weekend due to the unavailability of any more settled placement. None of these would be classed as respite care arrangements under the above definition, though they might fit the *Children Act*, 1989 definitions in Regulation 13.

According to contemporary Department of Health figures (Department of Health, 1993), two in every five new episodes of being looked after consisted of respite arrangements. The Department, however, has since changed its way of recording such separations, now preferring to regard an entire series of such placements as a single episode. This was also the methodology employed in this study, and only new arrangements have been included. Overall, some 8% of the study cohort were separated under respite care arrangements. Table 14.8 compares these children with the others in the cohort.

Table 14.8: Characteristics of children in respite care arrangements

	'Respite care'	All looked after
Male	59%	52%
Separated with siblings	54%	38%
Looked after previously	54%	38%
White European	100%	90%
Voluntary arrangements	90%	83%
Fostered (initially)	95%	73%
Abuse/neglect an issue	43%	38%
Return to single mother	72%	38%
Aged 1 to 9	84%	38%
Mother under 35	98%	71%
N =	39	463

The 'respite care' group in the study cohort were less conspicuous by the extent and severity of physical, behavioural and learning disabilities in the children, than by the difficulties faced by the parents. By far the most common scenario was that of a lone young mother with several children, predominantly boys, under the age of ten. Only one in ten of the children concerned had no siblings, whilst over two thirds (69%) had siblings under eleven. One in five (20%) had both brothers and sisters aged under 11.

Nationally, the availability of and eligibility criteria for schemes offering respite care vary considerably. Although the *Children Act,* 1989 encouraged the use of respite care for all children in need, in some local authorities it is still confined to the child with physical or learning disabilities. The characteristics noted in the current study are consequently very different from those identified in other studies of respite care (e.g. Robinson and Stalker 1993, Aldgate and Tunstill 1995), where the children tend to be significantly older and the great majority of families contain two parents. One consistent finding, however, is the under-representation of children from black and ethnic minority families (Baxter et al., 1990).

In the study, the children experiencing respite care were invariably fostered (95%) for a few days at regular intervals with carers who were occasionally available for emergencies, such as hospitalisation. A typical pattern would be separation for one weekend a month. Sometimes sibling groups were fostered together, sometimes the separations were staggered. The fact that residential facilities were not used more extensively again reflects the local authorities participating in the study, rather than the lack of such facilities nationally: in some authorities nearly all respite care is residential.

Summary points

1. Early, stable returners and children on respite care arrangements constitute the majority of children looked after. Such services represent a significant contribution by social workers to the health and happiness of large numbers of children and families, albeit one rarely acknowledged other than occasionally by the recipients. As the study moves on to discuss more complex patterns of separation and return, and more problematic situations in planning terms, this should be borne in mind.

2. There is a tendency amongst social workers to regard every new episode of being looked after as reflecting the failure of work aimed at family preservation. For most of the children discussed in this chapter, separation in the short term has proved to be an effective means of keeping the family together in the long term. Clearly, any attempt to pitch separation and family preservation as somehow in opposition is misguided.

3. A fifth of those looked after have not returned home within two years of separation. Some of these have achieved a degree of stability away from the family. In particular, a small number of pre-school children have been adopted and a small number of post-school teenagers have managed to keep their heads above water in flats and bedsits. Social work achievements such as these should not go unrecognised; neither, in the latter case anyway, should the achievements of the young people themselves.

4. The majority of those who have not returned after two years remain in long term foster or occasionally in residential care. As the years go on, their numbers dwindle. Some will return home after long separation and a small number will leave care or accommodation as a result of an administrative move elsewhere, perhaps through

adoption or into custody. The others will gradually attain school-leaving age and begin to seek independence.

15 Children for whom issues of return are more complex

This chapter scrutinises five groups of children for whom return issues are complex. They are: **long-term returners, short-term breakdowns, oscillators, adolescents seeking independence** and **homeless, skill-less adolescents**.

For the majority of children, patterns of separation and return are relatively straightforward and good practice should produce good outcomes. For others, movement between family, substitute care and (in some cases) independence is more complex. The distinction between simple and more complex patterns of movement is important for several reasons. Firstly, as a general rule, simplicity implies stability and continuity, both central to most care-planning. Continuity has long been recognised as a protective factor, and its converse - turbulence, unpredictability, uncertainty and movement - as risk factors in child development. In most circumstances, stability and continuity would be regarded as important components of any measure of outcomes.

Complex patterns of movement and frequent separations and return are not necessarily, of course, a sign of instability. After all, most parents and children will be separated several times during the course of an ordinary school-day. Frequent separations and returns at longer intervals are part and parcel of many successful respite arrangements. As described in Chapter Four, large numbers of other young people, particularly adolescents, make regular journeys between one parent and another, or between parents and other relatives, boarding schools, university halls of residence, hospitals and so forth, without suffering any apparent ill-effects. In addition, a degree of rootlessness becomes almost the norm as older teenagers begin to seek to establish themselves in independence. Regularity and predictabilities of movement, however, offer continuity in ways that erratic, unplanned movement does not. Planned and predictable movement, as in respite care, must be distinguished from movement as a means of crisis management.

Given this important rider, it is generally the case that complex and/or irregular movement between a number of different locations and carers, and the discontinuities associated with such a lifestyle, are something that most children find disturbing and that most parents seek to avoid. However, frequent erratic movement, at least in the short term, cannot in itself be regarded as a poor outcome whether for youngsters from intact and affluent families or for those looked after. The longer this rootlessness continues, however, the more worrying it becomes.

The second reason for dividing the cohort into simple and complex patterns is that such a division reflects a fundamental polarity in social work planning. Whilst good planning and effective intervention remain ideals within social work, and ideals which administrative procedures are apt to pretend is the reality, the social work task is as frequently typified by crisis management, emergency placements and picking up the pieces. Whilst reliability and predictability of movement may be good news for children, they are no less welcome to social workers. Without some predictability of address and carers, any other social work goals, whether in terms of effecting changes in behaviour or simply ensuring regular visits to the dentist, are unlikely to stand much chance of success. Thus, complex patterns of separation and return present problems to social workers in a way that simpler patterns do not. The division between simple and complex patterns is likely to be important from the point of view of the professional as well as the child and family.

Five groups of young people for whom the return process is complex will now be discussed. The first comprises those who go home after a separation of more than two years.

Long term returners

The following discussion of long term returners concerns young people returning home more than two years after separation. The evidence comes not from the main data set used in Chapters 11 and 12, but from three other recent studies; a long term follow-up of children looked after in the 1980s (Bullock et al., 1993), an evaluation of the Caldecott Community (Little and Kelly, 1995) and a study of the Youth Treatment Centres and other long stay secure units (Bullock et al., 1998). The findings of each are generally consistent. Although there are three distinct routes by which young people return home after long separation, the types of children and families involved are similar in all three.

A scrutiny of the characteristics of long-term returners shows first that they are predominantly male. In Bullock and colleagues' (1993) follow-up of children in care in the 1980s, for example, three quarters of those returning home between two and five years after separation were boys. Table 15.1 likewise shows that whilst a return to the parental home became less likely the longer a child remained at the Caldecott Community, this applied far more to the girls than to the boys. The majority of the boys, but only a third of the girls, returned to live at the parental home for at least some part of the two years after leaving. Gender was also a powerful indicator of the likelihood of return home following a stay in a secure treatment unit.

Table 15.1: Destination of Caldecott leavers by gender

	Boys	Girls
Returned to parental home on leaving	45%	29%
Returned to parental home within two years of leaving	55%	35%
Returned to parental home within two years of leaving, having been at the community less than four years	60%	60%
Returned to parental home within two years of leaving having been at the community more than seven years	38%	0%

Secondly, rather than any particular issue dominating their care careers, long term returners impress by the sheer variety and complexity of the needs that lead to separation. Commonly, poverty and family dislocation, abuse, neglect and behavioural difficulties, including offending, are combined to the extent that it is hard to disentangle quite who is being protected from whom by separation. Of those returning home between two and five years after separation in Bullock and colleagues' (1993) study, two thirds had been cautioned or convicted for offences, but neglect or abuse was a contributory factor at separation for nearly two fifths (37%). Those leaving the secure units had likewise often been placed there, rather than in Prison Department facilities, because their harrowing backgrounds aroused guilt sufficient to make punitive disposals difficult. A similar combination of disadvantage, abuse and disruptive behaviour was evident in many of those returning home from Caldecott after long separation, particularly those placed there by social services.

Thirdly, the chances of return after long separation peak between 14 and 18 years of age. Nearly two thirds of the long-term returners in the original retrospective study cohort were aged twelve or over at separation, and two thirds (65%) of those returning from Caldecott to parents after an absence of four years or more were aged between 14 and 16. The mean age of leavers from the long-stay secure units was 17. There are a number of reasons why long term return should be most likely around this age. The mid-teens are a peak age for offending and for disruptive behaviour generally, and those in their mid-teens may thus become increasingly hard to place anywhere other than back at home. The mid-teens are also an age where the responsibilities of different agencies become confused and there is greater scope for passing responsibility. Education agencies may consider their responsibilities to end at 16, for example, or social services and social security argue over who pays the rent of a 17 year old. Social workers, police and courts negotiate an uneasy balance between welfare and punitive disposals for offenders. All in all, the seams in the seamless web of the welfare state are never more visible than in a young person's mid teens.

A fourth factor shared by most long-term returners is the failure of placements outside the family to provide 'not just ...a place to stay until he or she reaches adulthood but a family for life' (Parker, 1991). The turbulent placement histories of those arriving at the YTCs and the Caldecott community are well-documented. Many at the YTCs have simply exhausted the range of available placements; there is nowhere else for them to go on departure. Amongst long term returners from care, a third had experienced both foster and residential care.

The career routes of long term returners reflect the features of the children and families concerned. Firstly, some young people return in a planned way, largely as a result of fairly dogged social work. These are young people for whom return has always been on the cards but the complexity of their problems has made it a long, drawn-out process. Of those returning between two and five years after separation in the retrospective study, for example, social workers had entertained strong hopes for restoration within two years for over four fifths (86%) and regular contact with relatives was maintained for a similar proportion. The experience of these long term returners will overlap with that of the intermediate returners described in the previous chapter and Table 15.2 illustrates the changes in household composition that affected nearly half (47%) of them. It is noticeable that only one of these 22 children returned to a household that contained their natural father. By this stage the role of 'male parent' is far more likely to be played by a step-father, grandfather or uncle, if at all.

Table 15.2: The patterns of movement of 22 long-term returners going back to a changed household

Child separated from	Child returning to
Natural mother (6)	Mother and step-father (4)
	Other relatives (2)
Father alone	Other relatives
Mother and father (3)	Mother
	Other relatives (2)
Mother and step-father (7)	Mother (5)
	Mother and different step-father
	Mother and father
Father and step-mother	Step-mother
Other (4)	Mother (2)
	Mother and stepfather
	Other relatives

A second route home after long term separation reflects rather less creditably on agencies. This is when the supply of placements simply dries up and young people return home either against their own wishes or to the despair of professionals because there is simply nowhere else for them to go. This was a common experience for those children excluded from the Caldecott Community at fourteen or fifteen, for example, but it may also occur following the breakdown of a long-term foster or adoptive placement. The closure of long-stay residential institutions, for example, usually results in residents being sent home. Where young people return home in such circumstances, the outcomes are usually depressing.

A third route, even longer and more convoluted, involves reunion following a move to independence. It has been seen that about two in five of the study cohort who left to independence nonetheless spent some part of the subsequent period living with relatives. If the definition of relatives is extended to include family friends and the parents of school-friends, the proportion is even higher. Studies of leavers from the long-stay secure units show that although only a quarter of graduates left the centres directly for home, two thirds spent some part of the following two years living with relatives. What to do with the disaffected teenage boy long separated from his natural family, too awkward to live comfortably in anyone else's, too young to start his own? In the past, a number of options were available, such as the armed forces, emigration, residential employment, migratory labouring. In the late twentieth century, the most likely solution is a return home.

Short term breakdowns

A second group for whom separation and return are marked by ambivalence and uncertainty are those younger children whose return home is a temporary and unsatisfactory affair, and who are soon back in care or accommodation. There were 28 such children in the study cohort. Although they represent only a small proportion of the total, these children are likely to occupy a disproportionate amount of professional attention in the months and years to come. Table 15.3 compares their characteristics with those of the early, stable returners. Certain types of child, for example, those under two and boys, are clearly more susceptible to breakdown following return than others, and the existence of a care order is an obvious barometer of social work unease. In other respects, however, the differences between those enjoying an enduring return and those for whom return is likely to prove more temporary are less striking.

Table 15.3: Short-term breakdowns (N=26) compared to early stable returners

	Early stables	Short term breakdowns
Male	45%	70%
Separated with sibs	53%	36%
Looked after before	43%	46%
On care order	1%	18%
History of abuse/neglect	56%	64%
Under 2	11%	30%
Living with mother	91%	85%

Further illumination is gained from consideration of the circumstances of return, rather than its participants. Table 15.4 lists the reasons for the original return of the 28 children who became short term breakdowns. Clearly, where return occurs as a result of consensus between the family and professionals, on a time-scale that suits family and child, it is more likely to be more successful than where it is hurried or acrimonious. A return to relatives other than those from whom the child was originally separated also carries an increased risk of breakdown.

Table 15.4: Reasons for short-term breakdowns' (N=26) original return home

	N
Carer's original problems reduced	6
Parents withdrew child against SW wishes	4
Child went to new carers	5
Time-limited placement	5
Child miserable in placement	1
Abuser left original household	5

Such considerations are also apparent in social workers' prognoses for the reunion at the time. Half (48%) the reunions in this group were seen as likely to be unsuccessful, compared with less than a third (29%) of reunions overall. In fact many of these reunions probably would not have taken place at all had social workers had their way unopposed. In only half (48%) of cases, for example, did professionals consider voluntary arrangements with the family to be entirely satisfactory and in only a third (36%) of cases were child and family considered adequately prepared for re-union. For a third of the children, even visiting the family was problematic. Following an informal separation and a messy and unsuccessful return, social workers frequently sought to formalise their concerns. The majority (54%) of the short term breakdowns had their names on the child protection register by follow-up, compared with less than in one in five (18%) of the cohort overall.

Return home followed by rapid breakdown, further separation and long term care or accommodation thus occurs in at least two very distinct situations, with two very different sets of causes. In one scenario a young child is returned with the agreement of all parties concerned, and with a reasonable expectation of success, but professional optimism is confounded by subsequent events. Such cases often involve mothers in their early twenties with problems of mental health or substance abuse. A second scenario involves return and breakdown as part of a tug of war between parents and professionals, in which the advantage swings first one way then the other, and each believes they are safeguarding the welfare of the children. In such cases the courts invariably end up arbitrating between the two, and usually support the professionals' opinion. In addition, short term breakdown can take place as part of the career of an adolescent seeking independence, discussed later.

Oscillators

Of the 463 children in the study cohort, 41, nearly 9%, were 'oscillators'. The word is used to describe children who move back and forth between parental and state care. Sometimes other relatives, such as grandparents, and other agencies, particularly education, may also be involved. Of all the groups described in this chapter, oscillators probably generate the most anxiety and dissatisfaction amongst social services professionals, the entire experience of the children being one of insecurity and constant movement. On the other hand, there are many analogies between such oscillation and respite care, which is generally regarded as a positive experience, and there is also considerable overlap between the two where the characteristics of the children are concerned. Table 15.5 compares the characteristics of oscillators and those experiencing respite care in the study cohort.

Table 15.5: Characteristics of children receiving respite care compared with oscillators

	Oscillators	Respite care
Single parent family	58%	74%
Male	58%	59%
Brothers living at home	58%	59%
Sisters living at home	58%	62%
Under care orders	12%	10%
Aged under 2	20%	18%
Name on CPR at follow-up	22%	36%
Aged 10 or over	37%	3%
N=	41	39

One way of interpreting this data is that movement in and out of substitute care is a means by which children and families under stress give themselves a degree of respite from each other in the absence of any service specifically designed to do so. Oscillators and children on respite care programmes look very similar, except that respite care is rationed to the very needy, such as those whose names are on protection registers, the disabled and those from one-parent families. Older children, and those from intact families, are obliged to rely on more *ad hoc* arrangements, usually organised in crisis.

Another situation in which oscillation is likely to occur is when the carers' health is unstable, or when carers indulge in periodic bouts of heavy drinking or drug abuse. For a third (36%) of oscillators, being looked after was a regular consequence of a parent's periodic hospitalisation. Whilst the exact timing of these events is not predictable, that they will occur at some point is more or less inevitable. That oscillation irritates social workers is beyond doubt but it can also be seen as a form of shared care, similar to respite care. The replacement of a long-stay by an episodic model of intervention, however, is a trend noticeable not only for children looked after but in other child-care contexts, such as the replacement of regular out-patient attendance for long-term hospitalisation and the growth of weekly as opposed to termly boarding in both state and private, ordinary and special schools (Gooch, 1996). This development is partly driven by concern for children's welfare and partly by budgetary and administrative pressures. Oscillation has been assumed to be bad for children in some contexts, but not in others, whilst there has been little evidence either way.

Adolescents seeking independence

The fourth group of young people for whom return raises complex issues comprises adolescents seeking independence. These are young people for whom the process of leaving home and setting up in independence becomes suddenly urgent in their early or mid teens, long before it becomes an issue for most of their peers. Girls are twice as common as boys in this category. For a variety of reasons, these young people are unable to live at home: sometimes following conflict with parents, sometimes following the collapse of the family home as a result of divorce, illness or accident.

Whilst these young people's problems defy generalisation, their subsequent needs and careers are more predictable. Given their age, it was no surprise that getting these young people established in independence took several attempts and a great deal of time. Professionals were always quietly confident, however, about the outcome. Despite the difficulties they faced, these young people had a wide variety of resources on which to call. Firstly, whilst the parental home was not an option in the long-term, the relationships and obligations involved were usually sufficiently strong to allow the young people to use it as a base for forays into independence. Where initial attempts at independence failed, as they frequently did, this group was usually able to return home briefly, before trying again. Secondly, the young people often possessed considerable inner resources of their own, in terms of social and living skills or academic or vocational qualifications to assist in the search for a job or training course. Whilst it was unusual to find both of these protective factors in operation, it was unusual not to find at least one. Thirdly, problems were generally confined to the family and rarely spilled over into school or the local community.

Despite their age, these young people experienced foster care as often as residential care. If they did return to relatives, it was rarely with the expectation that such arrangements would be long term. Only half of those who went back returned to the same relatives from whom they had originally been separated. The extended family often featured extensively in these young people's pathways to independence, particularly older sisters, aunts and uncles and occasionally honorary relations such as the parents of school-friends. One young woman, both of whose own parents were dead, lived for a time with the paternal grandmother of her baby. None of these placements lasted very long; of those who returned to relatives, for example, less than one in three (31%) remained in the same household a year after follow-up. Nonetheless, movement tended to forestall rather than follow conflict with the result that it was better planned, and there was more evidence of slow progress being made towards independence rather than just the most recent crisis having been averted.

Sally encapsulates many of the features of this group. She was fourteen when she requested the local authority to rescue her from life in an out-of season sea-side caravan park with both parents and several younger siblings. Her father, downwardly socially mobile as a result of a series of business failures, was a bitter and, according to Sally, violent-tempered man, and her mother too exhausted and disillusioned to put up much resistance. Sally spent several difficult years away from her family, firstly in foster care and then in a boarding school, where she passed her GCSEs. Whilst contact with her family was infrequent at first, it soon became re-established once the pressures of cohabitation were removed. As Sally left school, two flats became vacant in the nearby town, a large one and a smaller, on adjacent floors of the same building. Social services bagged both, putting Sally in the small one and her family in the larger.

This pattern of a temporary return as a prelude to a permanent but more amicable separation is typical of the group: it is almost as if they return to say their goodbyes properly. The process of establishing these young people in independence may take many years and meetings to accomplish but these are not the sorts of cases that cause social workers sleepless nights.

Homeless, skill-less adolescents

The most complex patterns of movement encountered in the study were those of the final group who face serious return difficulties; homeless, skill-less adolescents. This category could be further subdivided into a group returning home after long separation and a group of 'no fixed abode'. An example of the former is the small group of adolescent boys on care orders excluded from long-term foster and residential care as a result of their escalating misbehaviour. To the despair of social workers, they returned to the families from which they had been previously separated for their own welfare. There was nowhere else for them to go, and most ended up drifting or in some form of secure accommodation. Thus whilst it was estimated that 45 young people, or about eight per cent of the cohort, could be classified as homeless skill-less adolescents by the end of the study, the numbers could swell were the follow-up to be longer.

The problems posed by the other sub-group were of more recent standing, but apparently no more tractable. These were young people whose rapid rake's progress through the system soon exhausted the placements available to professionals. Nearly one in three (31%), for example, experienced three or more placements during their initial separation, even though the periods of accommodation were generally shorter than for other groups. Planning for such children represented the triumph of obligatory professional optimism over experience in most cases, and social workers were generally reduced to keeping track of their clients' movements retrospectively. One consequence of the rapid exhaustion of alternatives was that it was those least able to survive independently who were most likely to leave care or accommodation for independence, rather than returning directly to families. Of the twenty six young people in the study who left for destinations other than the home of a relative (natural or adoptive), twelve were classified as homeless, skill-less adolescents.

The initial destination of these young people on leaving care and accommodation, however, was a poor predictor of where he or she would be in a year's time. Of the twelve, six were known to have returned to live with relatives for a significant period of the following year. The majority of those who had left in order to return to relatives, meanwhile, had flown the family nest by the time they were followed up a year later. Since half (49%) of this group were re-united with families as a direct result of a placement breakdown, these results were hardly surprising.

Whether long-term returners who fail to find a niche back at home or teenagers beyond the control of parents, schools and social services, the careers of homeless, skill-less adolescents are thus typified by regular, almost constant movement. Half of those who leave to independence spend some part of the next year living at home, and most of those who go home soon move out. What is distinctive is not any particular pattern in the detail of these young people's ins and outs, but the sheer volume of movement. Movement between foster care, residential care, independence and relatives occurs in any and all directions with more or less equal frequency, and there is a depressing sense that only custody or prostitution are likely to put a more permanent roof over these young people's heads. Whilst it should always be borne in mind that such young people represent a small minority of leavers from care and accommodation, they highlight the inadequacies of the services designed to divert them from such careers.

Conclusions

Both more simple and more complex patterns of separation and return have now been examined. What do these figures imply, in terms of needs and numbers, at a national level? Every year, just under 30,000 children and young people commence a new episode of being looked after. Of these, some 2,500 will be beginning a programme of respite care, short breaks at regular intervals with familiar carers. A high proportion of these children will have disabilities, commonly a mixture of learning, physical and behavioural disabilities. Such provision is unevenly spread around the country. Respite care arrangements sometimes collapse and lead to longer separations, and respite care may be part of a package of services that allows a return home for a child long looked after. On the whole though, respite care operates as a distinct and distinctive sector of services for children looked after.

For around 9,000 children every year, a much larger number of children than of families, contact with the looked after system will be brief and comparatively uneventful. Being looked after will generally involve a few days or weeks in a foster placement, very possibly with siblings, until parents are able to resume their roles.

For a further 2,500 children separation will be considerably longer, measured in months rather than weeks, but the outcomes will be much the same. For most of the time, though under stress, such families rely upon their own resources: when they are temporarily unable to, the looked after system operates as a safety net, and in most cases a highly effective one. The family is held together through crisis, bounces back and is never seen again.

Some 4,000 separated children each year will remain looked after for several years and will not return to relatives in the medium term, if at all. These tend to be either older children who do not want to return home or younger ones whom professionals do not feel are safe there. In the latter case, social services departments may strengthen their hand by recourse to the courts. To these should be added a further 2,500 for whom a return home will represent a brief interruption to an extended separation. Of these 6,500 children, some six or seven hundred will be formally adopted and perhaps twice as many will find stability in the form of a long-term foster placement or, less commonly, in a children's home or therapeutic community. Return home remains a possibility for such children, particularly in mid-adolescence, but the immediate focus will shift from the natural family to consolidation of the alternative placement. For every child who achieves such stability, however, there will be another two children every year for whom separation from relatives is merely the first in a series of farewells. For such children, every breakdown will increase the likelihood of further disruption, until they end up, in the words of one young person 'forgetting how to feel anything'.

Around one in five children looked after, some 6,000 young people every year, will be older adolescents for whom a period in a children's home, or increasingly a foster home, will be part of the process of leaving home. Around half of these will manage the transition successfully although this is not to say that independence will be achieved at the first attempt or that it will not require several years of social work oversight and support. The group referred to as 'adolescents seeking independence' demonstrate that there is nothing inevitable about moving from care and accommodation to homelessness and hopelessness, although this is the experience of homeless, skill-less adolescents every year.

Finally, 3,000 children every year will have come to regard being looked after as something of a home from home. These are oscillators who have been looked after before, and will almost certainly be looked after again following return. Periodic crises associated with mental or physical illness, drug or alcohol dependence or volatile relationships ensure that, for these children, the planning questions are concerned with when substitute care is required again, rather than if. Very little is known about the effects of such repeated separations and returns. Although it is assumed that such frequent dislocation will prove damaging to children in state care, there is apparently less concern about its effects on pupils in boarding public schools or children who oscillate between one parent and the other following divorce.

Were the follow-up to be extended, some leakage between the categories described would certainly be found. Some children long looked after, for example, will become homeless, skill-less adolescents; closed cases will be re-opened and past crises will rekindle. On the other hand, the prognosis for some children will undoubtedly improve, perhaps due to an exceptional placement or a new step-parent who provides a child with a degree of stability previously lacking. Naturally, research is better able to answer questions about what has already happened to these children than about what will happen in the future. Professionals, on the other hand, are planning ahead. It is one thing to be wise after the event and quite another to be wise before it. Predicting return outcomes before they occur is the theme of the next chapter.

Summary points

1. Return home remains a possibility even after long separation, particularly as alienated, rootless boys reach mid-adolescence and exhaust other options.

2. Some factors distinguishing short term breakdowns from children returning successfully can be identified, but the differences between

success and failure are as likely to reflect the timing and mode of return as the participants.

3. Where parents' ability to care is interrupted periodically by illness or substance abuse, children may become oscillators. Oscillation is generally assumed to represent a worrying state of affairs, but it has parallels with other forms of shared care, such as boarding and respite care, that excite less concern.

4. Despite the stereotypes, as many young people make a successful transition to independence from care or accommodation every year as become homeless, skill-less adolescents. Even when young people are unable to live at home, the move to independence is made much easier where families are supportive and prepared to shelter young people in emergencies.

16 Predicting return outcomes

The previous chapters have identified common scenarios where rapid return is extremely likely and others, much rarer, in which return is likely to require a great deal of work, possibly in vain. Groups of children vulnerable to problems after return have also been described. This chapter takes this analysis a step forward and identifies those factors which best predict return outcomes. Two sets of outcome measurements are considered: whether or not children will go home and whether or not the reunion is likely to be successful. The factors to be taken into account when planning for children looked after and issues helpful in understanding outcomes for particular groups of children are identified.

Findings from the retrospective study

The process by which the results presented in this chapter were obtained was described in Chapter Five. Technical details are also covered in Appendix A and in Bullock and colleagues (1993). To recap, the histories of 875 children entering and/or leaving care during the 1980s were analysed retrospectively to identify those factors that, in combination, best predicted return outcomes. The process of analysis involved the identification and removal of very exceptional cases, known as 'outliers', in the data (Sneath and Langham 1989), followed by a multivariate analysis using logistic regression techniques.

The retrospective study identified three areas as determining the overall chances of a child's reunion. Firstly, there were the problems and stresses affecting the family. Bebbington and Miles (1989) identify a number of chronic stress factors, particularly poverty, single parenting and overcrowding, much more common amongst the families of children looked after than in the population generally. These chronic stressors considerably reduce families' abilities to cope with acute stressors such as illness, unemployment or family conflict, and hence increase the chances of family disintegration at these times. Quinton and Rutter (1988), for example, concluded that environmental stresses such as poor housing and social isolation lay at the root of parenting breakdown amongst parents who had themselves been in care, rather than any putative psycho-social mechanisms. Poverty, single parenting and insecure housing have similarly been shown to be linked to professional concerns over child abuse and neglect (Steinberg et al., 1981; Packman et al., 1986; Gibbons et al., 1995) and 'families overwhelmed and depressed by social problems form the greatest proportion of those assessed and supported by child protection agencies' (Department of Health, 1995).

Whilst there were thus good reasons to assume that the stress factors within the family home might influence the chances of return, it was less easy to demonstrate any independent effect for such variables. This was particularly true for the younger child. Whilst the range and variety of stress factors acting upon the family were important predictors of the chances of separation, they were less useful as predictors of return. Since children looked after tend to share a background of multiple disadvantage, the presence or absence of particular stress factors could not be used to distinguish likely returners from non-returners. Factors such as poverty, parental ill-health, and family reconstitution were no barrier to return - at least, not in the context of children looked after.

The quality of relationships between parent(s) and separated offspring, on the other hand, was found to have a major influence on the likelihood of reunification. Conflict, even to the extent of physical violence, is a common feature of family life, particularly for adolescents (Smith et al., 1995; Noller and Callan, 1991). Occasionally, relationships may sour to the point where 'time out' is required. Whether the separation then turns out to be more permanent will depend to a large extent on how much individual family members ultimately want to be together. Whilst abuse and/or neglect on the part of parents or delinquency on the part of youngsters may jeopardise the affective ties that bind families together, they are rarely sufficient to break them altogether. A method to assess the quality of family relationships is provided in Appendix B.

Finally, there were factors reflecting the professional input. Keeping the family involved, keeping siblings together wherever possible and in regular contact with each other where it was not, and encouraging relatives to visit, phone and write to their absent offspring were all associated with rapid reunion. By contrast, a social work approach that excluded parents from the decision-making process and prized formal power over informal negotiation severely jeopardised young people's chances of return. Sometimes, as in some cases of very severe abuse, the prevention of return was the very basis of care planning. At other times, obstacles to return arose almost by default and seemed to reflect the convenience of professionals rather than the best interests of children (Millham et al., 1986). Even where a confrontational strategy is intentional, however, it is a high risk approach: youngsters removed in childhood may choose, or be obliged, to return to parents in adolescence despite the efforts of professionals (Millham et al., 1989, Little and Kelly, 1995).

Predicting the likelihood of return

The retrospective quantitative study and the prospective qualitative study were combined to produce a series of checklists predicting the likelihood of return at various points in a child's care career - at separation, soon after separation, six months after separation and two years after separation. Each checklist contained between six and 15 factors which in combination best distinguished returners from non-returners. These checklists were then tested prospectively on a cohort of 463 children and young people separated from family during 1993 and followed up for two years. The results of this prospective study are presented here.

Both the original checklists and the statistical techniques and calculations by which they were validated are elaborated in Appendix A. The statistical techniques used are common in medical research and a commercial necessity for insurance companies seeking to assess risk. Their use in meeting the needs of deprived children is less developed.

Statistical models such as those presented here are simplifications of reality and that is both their strength and their weakness. On the negative side, no model can achieve 100% predictive power. It would be highly irresponsible blithely to send a child home assuming that all will be well on the basis of a few indicators highlighted by research. The models describe what does happen, not what should happen.

Secondly, the more variables are to be considered as possible causes, the more statistical analysis tends to rely upon blunt, unequivocal measurements of effect. The evidence presented in this chapter has relied on clear, objective outcomes such as the endurance of a reunion, whilst acknowledging that these may conceal rather than identify difficulty. The fact that it has endured is no guarantee that a marriage has been happy and likewise a child stuck at home may envy the footloose adolescent. Taking alternative perspectives and using different measures, the factors in the predictive models might well change.

Nonetheless, what is likely to happen to a child in the future must be an important consideration for any professional making decisions about separation and return. The aim is not to de-skill the management of family re-unification or to reduce professional judgement to the level of a checklist, but to provide guidelines to be taken into account, alongside other influences, when making decisions about returning children to their families.

The checklists tested prospectively

Generally, the findings of the retrospective study were confirmed when tested prospectively. In particular, the stress factors impacting upon families at the time of separation were once again shown to be of much less importance in predicting the likelihood of return than the quality of relationships between parent(s) and child, and between parent(s) and professionals. Of the six factors identified retrospectively as independent predictors of return at the point of separation, two stood out in the prospective study:

1. that the child's separation was by voluntary arrangement

2. that relationships within the family were reasonably good.

Where both these factors applied, the chances of return were very high - nine out of ten children (90%) were home within two years. Where neither applied, less than half (42%) were reunited within that time.

Early returners

It will be recalled that early returners were defined as those returning to family within six months of separation. Given that most returners are back home within the first six months of separation, it was not surprising that the factors predicting early return were similar to those predicting return at any point. The retrospective study revealed three factors as being particularly influential in ensuring an early return:

1. that the child enjoyed regular contact with family members during his/her absence from home

2. that the social worker encouraged family links with the absent child

3. that the child's separation was arranged on a voluntary basis.

It was thus clear that the likelihood of return could be influenced for better or for worse by social work action even prior to separation. It was findings such as these, buttressed by a wealth of other evidence, that led to the stress within the *Children Act,* 1989 upon negotiation and consensus as a basis for social work intervention, upon regular contact during separation and upon the use of care orders and access restrictions only as a last resort. One consequence of these legislative changes was that nearly all children in the prospective study - undertaken after the implementation of the *Children Act* - were in regular contact with parents, at least during the early weeks of separation. Ironically, where there was little or no contact for younger children this was often because the separation was planned to be so short that contact was not considered necessary, practicable or useful. Such considerations often applied in programmes of respite care, for example, or where a mother went into hospital to give birth. Some adolescents did not wish to see their relatives during the early days of separation, though this did not stop them returning home when the dust had settled. As a result, regular contact no longer distinguished early returners from non-returners in the prospective study. This is not to say that regular contact, and the encouragement of that contact by professionals, are not important: merely that (like poverty) they are too much the norm for children looked after in the 1990s to have much predictive power.

Separation under voluntary arrangements has already been shown to be associated with return home. Five other factors identified in the retrospective study were also confirmed in multivariate analysis as important predictors of early return in the prospective study;

1. that the problems that made separation necessary had been eased or resolved

2. that the family considered itself to be a family

3. that the child had retained a role within the family

4. that the child had territory in the family home

5. that the social work plan was 'inclusive'

6. Of these, statistically the most important were issues of role and territory. Of children with both a role and territory within the family, nearly nine in ten (85%) returned to it within six months of separation. Children with neither had, in many ways, rather less to return to, and only a quarter (23%) did so within six months.

Intermediate returners

Many of those children who do not return within the first six months will nonetheless do so within the next eighteen. Three variables shown to be associated with intermediate return in the retrospective analysis were

1. that there was no history of abuse and/or serious neglect at the time of the separation

2. that the child was not currently (i.e. six months after separation) placed with siblings

3. that relatives of the child, especially parents, participated in decisions about looking after the child.

These findings were not, however, confirmed by the prospective study. Only two factors were found to be associated with intermediate return to a statistically significant level even using simple Chi-square tests.

1. that the family and child(ren) felt that their problems had been resolved or much diminished

2. that relationships within the family were reasonably good.

Following multivariate analysis, the first was shown to achieve its predictive power largely through its association with the second, and for children looked after six months or more the quality of relationships emerged as the key to predicting the likelihood of return. Nearly half of those whose family relationships were assessed as reasonably good at six months returned home before two years, compared to less than a quarter where this was not the case. The quality of family relationships alone was almost as good a predictor as much more complex and sophisticated models.

The 'quality of family relationships' variable also interacted in complex ways with other variables. In the retrospective study, for example, sibling groups still looked after together at six months emerged as less likely to return than single children. In the prospective study, this association was not found at all in univariate analysis. Where family relationships were comparatively good in the prospective study, however, children in sibling groups were found to be more than twice as likely (69% compared to 26%) to return as singles. Where family relationships were poor, however, the prognoses for sibling groups and singles were much the same.

Long term returners

Although those still looked after two years after separation in the retrospective study were marked by diversity, three variables were found to predict strongly return direct from care or accommodation within the next three years. These were:

1. that the child's mother was the main provider of emotional support at the time of separation

2. that the child was male

3. that the family received state financial benefits.

Where all these factors applied, the chances of return between two and five years after separation were nearly five times as great as where none applied. Eight other factors were also important but were less influential than the three listed.

Some adolescents also return to family after an intervening period of independence. Two factors proved good predictors as to whether those who moved to independence would subsequently be reunited with relatives. First, there was the question of where the young person referred to as 'home'. If it were the family home, the chances of return were greater than if it were a foster placement or children's home. Second, was the quality of family relationships. Members of inadequate, chaotic, abusing and delinquent families often mean much more to each other than is immediately apparent.

It will naturally take several years yet before these findings concerning long term returners can be confirmed prospectively. The numbers of leavers in the prospective study are as yet too small to allow adequate multivariate analysis and two years is a short separation by the standards of older teenagers leaving care or accommodation. The prospective study can, however, offer some estimates concerning teenagers who moved to independence within two years of being looked after. Of these, nearly half (45%) subsequently returned to live with relatives. Return to family from independence was more likely in certain scenarios than in others, particularly where the child was a boy and where there was no father in the family home. Return to family was also more likely from more supervised semi-independence placements such as supported lodgings than from more independent ones, such as flats and bedsits. Such findings tend to support the findings for long term returners previously discussed.

Predicting the success of return

The retrospective study identified 20 factors that best predicted successful returns. To gauge the success of each reunion, each case was scrutinised to see whether the return endured, what it provided for the child, what were the perceptions of the participants, whether agreements were upheld and stresses mitigated and, finally, the consequences for social services and other agencies, such as whether the child was looked after again, the problems that arose and how effectively agencies co-operated in their resolution.

When tested prospectively using the same success criteria, all the factors remained useful indicators of a successful return. They applied to all children returning home, irrespective of the reasons for the original separation. Following multivariate analysis, however, three factors emerged as particularly important. These were:

1. that the family was prepared for the anxiety generated by return and the disputes which were likely to occur

2. that the family relationships were of a fairly high quality

3. that the child was not an offender

These factors applied independently and cumulatively. For example, in situations where the underlying family relationships were sound, the timing and mode of return made a significant contribution to its chances of success and even the closest of families could not always withstand the tensions brought about by a young person's offending. On the other hand, unpromising scenarios could change for the better if family members cared enough to make the effort.

Although legislative change has abolished the 'home on trial' category central to Farmer and Parker's study, it was nonetheless important to see whether the influence of factors varied for different groups, as they had found. One obvious question was whether different factors applied for adolescents compared with younger children. Whilst the three factors described above were good predictors for both age groups, a fourth factor was found to apply particularly to adolescents:

4a. that the young person established a role outside the family that was complementary to those within the home, a process discussed at length in Chapter Twelve.

As far as younger children were concerned, the central role of child-care professionals was highlighted once again. In addition to the factors applying to both groups, two others predicted a successful return for younger children (under 11). These were:

4b. that there was evidence of highly competent social work

5. that professionals were satisfied with voluntary arrangements, or were considering discharging a care order, if one was in force.

Effective social work can clearly make the difference between success and failure for all young children returning home, not just victims of abuse and neglect.

Summary points

1. Groups of variables that predict return outcomes can be used by social workers in making decisions about children. Such variables have been identified in a retrospective study and tested prospectively. Some very robust markers have been presented.

2. Regardless of the length of separation, the quality of family relationships is more important in determining the likelihood of return than the stresses on the family. Any social work action that tends to undermine family relationships - particularly by restricting contact - is likely to reduce the chances of return. Barriers to return erected by social workers have become less of an issue for children looked after since the implementation of the *Children Act*, 1989.

3. Different factors predict the likely success of return for different ages, though there is some overlap. Gender has also emerged as an important issue in some contexts. No doubt it will be possible in the future to identify factors particularly pertinent when other possible sub-groups are considered, such as children from minority ethnic groups or rural as opposed to urban children. Family re-unification is a complex issue; the aim in this chapter, however, has been to keep things simple.

4. The variety of factors ensure that research-based checklists, as well as being potentially good servants to social workers, are likely to provide robust indicators that inform predictions; however they are unlikely to be a substitute for professional judgement.

17 The revised checklists

> In this chapter the revised checklists described in Chapter 16 are summarised. These checklists are then applied to two case studies from the retrospective study to predict likely outcomes. The predictions are then compared with what actually happened.

Chapter Sixteen and Appendix A analyse the factors that best predict return, and that best predict a successful return. These factors are summarised here in the form of checklists before being applied to two case studies. It should be emphasised that the checklists presented were originally derived from a retrospective study, and have subsequently been validated prospectively. They can thus be considered extremely robust. The case study material is introduced not to show the effectiveness of the checklists, but to illustrate how the factors identified help to explain observed differences in outcome. Indeed, the two case studies have been selected precisely because their outcomes are complex and ambivalent. In the first, two girls from a family of four returned home whilst their sisters remained in foster care, whilst in the second a toddler returned home successfully on one occasion but was not so lucky on the second.

The checklists

The first checklist, predicting the likelihood of return at any point, consists of just two factors, and is illustrated in Figure 17.1.

Checklist One: Predicting return at any stage

Separation by voluntary arrangement	
Relationships within the family reasonably good	

It will be recalled from Chapter Thirteen that where both these factors applied nine out of ten children (90%) were home within two years, compared to less than half (42%) the children for whom neither applied.

Whilst these two factors distinguished returners from non-returners, a second set of five factors distinguished early returners from those likely to experience a longer separation - Checklist Two below.

Checklist Two: Predicting an early return

The problems that led to separation have been eased or resolved	
The family considers itself a family	
The child has retained a role within family	
The child has territory in family home	
The social work plan is inclusive	

Again, nearly nine in ten (85%) children with both a role and territory in the family home returned to it within six months of separation, compared to only a quarter (23%) of children with neither.

For 'intermediate' returners, those children separated for more than six months, only one factor consistently and independently distinguished returners from non-returners - the quality of family relationships. Some additional predictive power was added when the family and child(ren) felt that their problems had been resolved or had much diminished.

Checklist Three: Children looked after at six months: Factors predicting a return in the following 18 months

Relationships in the family are reasonably good	
The family and child(ren) feel that their problems have been resolved or much diminished	

For children still looked after at two years, prospective testing of factors was not possible because of the time needed to follow up the study group. The best predictors available of the child's return in the following three years are those obtained from the retrospective study of looked after children described in Chapter Five. The list will probably be reduced when tested against prospective data. They are:

Checklist Four: Children looked after at two years: Predicting a return in the following three years

The child's mother is the main provider of emotional support at the time of separation	
The child is male	
The family receives state financial benefits	

In considering the likely success of return, multivariate analysis suggested that slightly different factors applied to younger children - Checklist Five A - compared with adolescents - Checklist Five B.

Checklist Five (a): Predicting the success of return for a child under 11

The family are prepared for the anxiety generated by return and the disputes likely to occur	
Family relationships are of a fairly high quality	
The child is not an offender	
There is evidence of highly competent social work	
Professionals are entirely satisfied by voluntary arrangements with the family	

Checklist Five (b): Predicting the success of return for a young person over 11

The family are prepared for the anxiety generated by return and the disputes likely to occur	
Family relationships are of a fairly high quality	
The child is not an offender	
The young person will establish a role outside the family that is complementary to those within the home	

Where all five factors in Checklist Five A applied to a younger child, nine in ten (92%) returned successfully, compared to just over half (57%) where none applied. Where all four factors in Checklist Five B applied to an older child, four in five (81%) returned successfully, compared to only a quarter (25%) where none applied.

The checklists applied to two case studies

Melanie and Michelle, Karen and Kim

Melanie and Michelle were abandoned as toddlers by their mother, exhausted by years of making do and rows, with Gary, her shattered, listless husband. Gary was as disorganised and unreliable as the mobile fish and chip van he occasionally drove. Indeed, both Gary and the van were well known in the local community for their immobility. With the departure of his wife, and with two children to look after, Gary pressed himself into action. The 'fryer' was wondrously re-assembled from its parts once scattered between bedroom, bathroom and garden. With the help of a neighbour, the tyres were inflated and, phantom-like, the van lifted from the pile of bricks on which it had rested. It emerged resplendent from the garage; 'Gary's Grill and Fry-up' was back in business.

Trade, at first slow, soon picked up. While there were undoubtedly times when Melanie and Michelle were left to cope alone, neighbours and grand-parents rallied to help. As Gary slipped back into the routine of regular work, he sought a baby-sitter. One cold night, as the pubs closed, he got talking to Alison who, anxious to share more than the salt and vinegar, swiftly volunteered to help. Soon, Alison's care of Melanie and Michelle became continuous. The girls awoke to find her preparing breakfast, she was there when they came out of play-school and, as time passed, she was there more often than Gary. The house brightened up, spare parts for the van were evacuated to the home of paternal grandparents and Gary all but disappeared. Not that Alison and the girls were ever lonely, for they were joined first by half-sister Karen and, soon afterwards, by half-sister Kim.

For nearly four years all seemed well and a domestic bliss based upon Gary's inadequacy and regular absence from home prevailed. But the parental relationship coughed and spluttered to the tune of the mobile van. With time it died altogether and Gary withdrew to his parents who welcomed him back sympathetically. However, left alone and largely unsupported, with four children and no relief, Alison, too, fell into periodic depressions. She began to neglect the children and on two occasions social services were called after neighbours complained that they had been left alone while Alison went down to the pub. On a cold November night Michelle was picked up by the police after being found, somewhat ironically, asking passers-by for money to buy fish and chips. She was dressed only in her dirty frock.

The pressures mounted on Alison, the gas was cut off, albeit temporarily, and she took an overdose of anti-depressants. Melanie was eight at this time, Michelle two years younger. Gary, on the days he could function, was wholly preoccupied with building a re-conditioned engine for the chip van, once more consigned to its brick stilts in the garage. Alison finally agreed to let all the children be accommodated by social services for a while, something she had resisted despite her ever-worsening situation. How likely was it, according to the checklists, that the children would be quickly home, or home at all?

Figure 17.1: Checklist One applied to Melanie and Michelle

Checklist 1 - predicting return at any stage	
Separation by voluntary arrangement	Yes
Relationships within the family reasonably good	?

Checklist One, suggested that the underlying quality of family relationships would determine whether or not the children returned, rather than the more immediate questions of neglect, unpaid gas-bills and attempted suicide. At this stage, however, the crisis was such that the quality of these family relationships was difficult to assess. The four sisters stayed together, first in a temporary placement then, when Alison's situation failed to improve, in a long-term foster home. The social worker, delighted to find a place which would take all four girls, put a lot of effort into keeping things going but links with home became tenuous. Alison, overwhelmed by her health problems and anxiety over the children, was evicted from her home for non-payment of rent. She was understandably preoccupied and largely uninvolved in decisions about the children. Her visits became infrequent.

Checklist Two suggested that the chances of a rapid return home were rapidly diminishing, and indeed the next six months saw little improvement. The girls' natural mother had completely disappeared, and their one-time step-mother Alison appeared to care little. It was all Gary could do to leave it all to social services. The girls' family contacts came to consist of uneventful, routine visits organised without reward by a long-suffering social worker who waited with the grand-parents while the girls and Gary sat in the gloom of the immobile chippy in a cold, oily garage. Nonetheless, the social worker was determined that the sense of belonging that Gary and the girls obviously shared should not be allowed entirely to wither. It was largely her doggedness that ensured that even one checklist factor applied; despite an extended separation, the family did still consider themselves to belong together.

Fig 17.2: Checklist Two applied to Melanie and Michelle

Checklist 2 - predicting an early return	
Problems have been eased or resolved	No
Family considers itself a family	Yes
Child has retained a role within family	No
Child has territory in family home	No
Social work plan is inclusive	No

A year after the children were first looked after, the foster parents asked for a major review of the situation and intimated that they had put up with enough. Melanie, in particular, was behaving badly and her younger half-sister, Kim, was enuretic. Two weeks before the review requested by the foster home, Gary's parents, who had put him up since his precipitate eviction, decided to move into sheltered accommodation. They were eager to hand over their three bedroomed council house to their son and to head for something more manageable. Thus, Gary found himself with a house and furniture and the wherewithal to keep it going. His depression lifted and he was persuaded by his erstwhile rival, Brian, to merge businesses. Between them they cobbled together a mobile chippy that moved. When the girls failed to appear for their bi-monthly access, Gary, once more on the road, decided on a surprise visit to the foster parents, blissfully unaware that it was Melanie's birthday.

And so it was that, as the social worker hurried down the foster parents' garden path, eagerly clutching Melanie's card and present, around the corner sped the mobile chippy. It was instantly recognisable to the social worker, for whom hunger suddenly became more of a driving force than the need to keep professional distance. Soon father and social worker found *rapprochement* over cod and chips and a cuppa. They talked about the impending review of the children's situation and, when asked whether he would like to come along and see how things were going, Gary mumbled consent. It was only at the review that he understood how difficult the girls had become to manage. On their rare visits they were always on their best behaviour and the social worker, as worried for the father as she was for his offspring, felt it was wrong to spoil the occasion with her concerns. Somewhat to his surprise, Gary felt guilty; completely out of the blue, he blurted out that he would take the girls home with him, if everybody thought that it would be all right. Nobody had any better ideas. A family *aide* and a volunteer were arranged to support the sisters at home and six weeks later the father and elder daughters were re-united.

Thus the story of Melanie and Michelle illustrates several themes from the checklists.

Firstly, the rapid deterioration of both their stepmother and their home after their departure, and with it all their familiar roles and territories, ensured that the girls' separation was always likely to be a long one. Secondly, however, despite a bleak prognosis, the social worker involved went to great lengths to ensure that the family's sense of belonging was maintained during the months of separation. Thirdly, Gary did feel a sense of responsibility towards his daughters, and though he was happy to pass this on to others if possible, he was aware that the buck stopped with him. When the elder girls found themselves short of options, he was there for them, and better than nothing.

Thus, whilst the younger two remained with the foster parents, the older two returned home. What were the chances they would still be there six months later? No doubt spurred on by the fact that return was to a lone man, the social worker provided a family *aide* and volunteer, visited daily in the days leading up to the reunion and encouraged the grand-parents to be very supportive, albeit from a distance. Gary, anxious to overcome his guilt for previous failings, was only too glad to seek help and advice. Checklist Five, below, suggests that the outlook was perhaps better than might otherwise have been expected.

Figure 17.3: Checklist Five applied to Melanie and Michelle

Checklist 5a: predicting the success of return for a child under 11	
The family is prepared for the anxiety generated by return and the disputes likely to occur	Yes
Family relationships of a fairly high quality	Yes
Child not an offender	Yes
Evidence of highly competent social work	Yes
Professionals satisfied with voluntary arrangements	Yes

Did they all live happily ever after? After the reunion, Gary was married again, this time to Eva, a widow ten years his senior. With just the two girls, now in their teens, to manage, they got by. Their younger half-sisters Karen and Kim similarly remained with foster parents, and visited every other month. Whilst life for Melanie and Michelle is never likely to be champagne and roses, the children were, nonetheless, 'at home'. It would surely be churlish to deny that Melanie and Michelle's reunion with Gary and Eva should be adjudged a 'successful return'.

Kelly

Kelly's maternal grandparents arrived in England from the West Indies in the 1960s. Her mother Madelaine was the youngest of their seven children and perhaps somewhat too well adjusted to city life for a religious and authoritarian household. During adolescence she spent increasing periods away from home. She smoked 'ganjah', was cautioned several times by the police for shop-lifting and, by her own account, she 'slept around'. Her parents, worn out by their large family, retreated into the gospel hall.

Discovering herself pregnant, Madelaine set herself up in a small flat and looked forward to the life of a single mother. Although the health visitor had constant concerns about the cold and damp in the flat, Madelaine proved herself a fairly competent mother. It was clear, however, that she missed the bright lights, those few left in her run-down neighbourhood. Social services kept a watchful eye. Discovering that she was again pregnant, Madelaine asked social services to look after Kelly for a few weeks. Somewhat relieved, the social worker placed the baby with Afro-Caribbean foster parents, whilst her mother was admitted to hospital for an abortion, a decision that outraged Kelly's religious grandparents.

Figure 17.4: Checklist One applied to Kelly

Checklist 1 - predicting return at any stage	
Separation by voluntary arrangement	Yes
Relationships within the family reasonably good	Yes

Fig 17.5: Checklist Two applied to Kelly

Checklist 2 - predicting an early return	
Problems have been eased or resolved	Yes
Family considers itself a family	Yes
Child has retained a role within family	Yes
Child has territory in family home	Yes
Social work plan is inclusive	Yes

What were the chances of an early return? Checklists One and Two above did not suggest any likely difficulties. As it turned out, the separation was even shorter than planned: two days before the planned date of return, Madelaine, feeling lonely, decided to remove the baby from the foster parents. Using Checklist Five, Figure 14.9 below, Kelly's reunion would be predicted to prove successful. In particular, there was no doubting that mother and child wanted to be together. The social work had been highly competent, extra supports had been arranged and Madelaine was well prepared, even anxious, for her daughter's return. The baby had never before been separated from her mother, which was a good sign, and there was no hint of compulsion or constraint in social work plans.

Figure 17.6: Checklist Five applied to Kelly

Checklist 5a: predicting the success of return for a child under 11	
Family prepared for the anxiety generated by return and the disputes likely to occur	No
Family relationships of a fairly high quality	Yes
Child not an offender	Yes
Evidence of highly competent social work	Yes
Professionals satisfied with voluntary arrangements	No

Nonetheless, the precipitate removal of her child from foster parents intimated that Madelaine did not always agree with the social workers' diagnosis of what was good for her, and that her own needs took a higher priority than professionals might have wished. Eight months later, when Madelaine again fell pregnant, Kelly was looked after once more. Though this separation was similarly planned for only a few days, this time it was to accommodate a birth rather than a termination.

Whilst both factors in Checklist One still applied, suggesting that return was very likely at some stage, the arrival of a new baby cast a very different light on Checklist Two (Figure 17.10 below).

Fig 17.7: Checklist Two applied to Kelly (second separation)

Checklist 2 - predicting an early return	
Problems have been eased or resolved	No
Family considers itself a family	No
Child has retained a role within family	No
Child has territory in family home	Yes
Social work plan is inclusive	Yes

Preoccupied with the new arrival, Madelaine repeatedly delayed Kelly's restoration until finally requesting her adoption. Uneasily, the social worker sought a foster placement with a view to this end. Eighteen months later this broke down, prompting renewed efforts to achieve reunion. What were the chances of this second reunion enduring? Checklist Five, Figure 17.11 below, would suggest that the chances were no better than evens, and so it proved. A home placement was arranged, but despite a promising start, Madelaine once more asked for Kelly to be returned to care.

Figure 17.8: Checklist Five applied to Kelly (second separation)

Checklist 5a: predicting the success of return for a child under 11	
Family prepared for the anxiety generated by return and the disputes likely to occur	No
Family relationships of a fairly high quality	No
Child not an offender	Yes
Evidence of highly competent social work	No
Professionals satisfied with voluntary arrangements	Yes

Kelly's story illustrates the importance of family roles and territories. Although her social worker made gallant efforts to achieve rehabilitation not once but twice, the arrival of a new baby deprived Kelly of a role within her family. She found her place taken by another.

Conclusions

Melanie and Michelle returned to their father, and Kelly to her mother the second time, as a consequence of fostering breakdowns. In both cases, the circumstances of return were far from ideal and the decision to return the children was taken in the absence of any realistic alternative. One return was successful, the other not. How can these outcomes be explained?

It will be remembered, firstly, that the retrospective study identified three areas as important in determining the likelihood of return - the stress factors impinging upon the family, the quality of relationships within the family and the nature of the professional intervention. Consideration of each in turn shows again that the external stresses on the family - poverty, poor housing and so forth - are more likely to affect the timing of return than its overall likelihood. It was Gary's parents' decision to vacate their house, for example, that made the girls' return a possibility.

Secondly, both stories illustrate the importance of a family's sense of belonging together. Although he had given little such indication previously, Gary ultimately felt a sense of responsibility towards his daughters in a way in which Madelaine did not. Madelaine was committed to a set of roles - that of mother and baby - more than to the specific actors who played those roles. When Kelly lost her role, she also lost her place in the family, and her chance of return.

Thirdly, the social work approach to the two families differed considerably. Melanie and Michelle's social worker fought hard to preserve some affective continuities in the children's lives, even when the prospects of return seemed slight; Kelly's social worker pursued a plan for adoption. Given Kelly's mother's lack of interest, there was probably little else her social worker could do, and there is certainly no intention here to allocate blame with hindsight. Social workers can obviously only facilitate family contact to the extent that family members want to be together. Nonetheless, the story of Melanie and Michelle illustrates the importance of not squandering such affective ties as do exist.

Summary points

1. The stories of Melanie and Michelle and of Kelly illustrate that family relationships are far better predictors of the likelihood of successful return than the stress factors impinging upon the family. Except in extreme cases, stress factors are more likely to affect the timing of return than its overall likelihood.

2. Even the best social work interventions cannot realistically hope to build firm relationships where there is no foundation for them. But where return remains a possibility, however remote, and in the absence of any compelling reasons to the contrary, social work interventions can at least aim to avoid jeopardising such affective ties as do exist.

3. The case stories illustrate again that the longer a child is separated from family, the more likely it is that only a major change in his or her circumstances is likely to permit return. Whilst the timing of such events is unpredictable, that they will occur at some point is highly likely. That events are unpredictable does not mean that they cannot be incorporated into care planning.

18 Conclusions

The nineteenth century and early years of the twentieth witnessed a concerted attempt to disrupt supposed cycles of immorality and deprivation through education and religious exhortation. One of the main strategies employed was the 'rescue' of children from parents unable or unwilling to rear them satisfactorily. It was firmly believed that the only hope for such young people was a completely new start, away from contaminating neighbourhoods and corrupting families. These beliefs reflected a potent cocktail of compassion, evangelism and self-interest on the part of the middle-classes who paid the taxes and subscriptions to finance the Industrial Schools and children's homes that were to provide this break with the past.

Such values are no longer in keeping with the spirit of the times, but the rejection of 'child rescue' has also reflected accumulating evidence of the failure of children's homes and foster parents to meet the emotional needs of children or of reformatory settings to check delinquency. Doubts over the adequacy of provision for children 'deprived of a normal home life' were being raised even before the upheavals of the Second World War. Then, in 1939 and 1940 the evacuation of large numbers of working-class urban children highlighted both the poverty of many families and the inadequacy of much child health and welfare provision. As the threat of Nazi invasion receded, so the war against Beveridge's four great evils took on ever greater salience. The *Children Act* 1989 represents yet another scene in a drama upon which the curtain was first raised by the Curtis Report of 1946.

Research in recent years has suggested that improving standards for children looked after away from home have all too often failed to keep up with rising living standards and expectations. Too often isolation, drift and anomie have been identified as the experience of looked after children and studies of leavers have highlighted the poor social and vocational skills and disappointing educational attainments of those who stay long in children's homes and foster care. Whilst separated children may be no more deficient in skills than those of their peers who remain at home, the looked after experience hardly seems to enhance life chances.

This study is a reminder that the majority of children and adolescents separated from home do return to parents or the wider family once they leave care or accommodation. These reunions occur no matter what the reasons for being looked after or the length of time away. Even young adults convicted of grave offences and long separated from home are likely to come to rest in the bosom of their families once professionals have ceased their ministrations. As statutory agencies abandon the task, it is usually the family, frequently identified as damaging or deficient, which takes up the role of main supporter of children and young adolescents. Young people may not stay long at home, using the parental home as a springboard to and bolt-hole from outside excitements. They may return home swiftly because all else fails or because they exhaust the tolerance of other benefactors. But whatever the context, parents and the wider family, however deficient on whatever criteria, are a crucial resource, and one which could frequently be enhanced by social work support and encouragement. Involving parents and sharing care with the family in all but the most extreme cases is now recognised as a statutory social work responsibility.

This study has addressed specifically the problems surrounding reunion. It was undertaken to fill an identified gap in knowledge. The research literature concerning family separation rarely looks at the same children's experiences as they go home. In most studies, interest in reunion is incidental to other concerns. Nevertheless, the evidence presented here suggests that return is as fraught and as stressful an experience as separation, that the management of reunion is far from simple and that, while the majority of reconciliations are successful, those that fail can carry with them serious long-term implications for the rejected child.

Not only do most children go home, the majority enjoy a very swift reunion with parents. It can be calculated that nearly nine in every ten -

87% - children looked after by a local authority away from home will return to live with relatives within five years. Indeed, nearly three-fifths of children looked after will be home within six weeks and one in five will go back in the first week. The swift return of the majority of separated children is a largely unsung social work contribution to family welfare. It also undermines the popular myth that would see the social work task as deciding whether to do too much or not enough. Separation is not 'all or nothing': it can involve a thousand subtle gradations.

Happy reunions for the majority should not, however, obscure the problems of those few who linger. Indeed, the problems of reunion for those long-separated from home, usually adolescents, have excited particular concern in these pages. Nor can reunion be regarded as the end of the story. Some groups of children have more appealing prospects than others. For example, some older children do not necessarily stay long at home after reunion and a small number are prone to precipitate breakdown in family relationships.

Useful classification must be the first step of any analysis, and dividing children according to their length of separation helps shed light on the processes involved. *Early returners* are usually children whose families have been temporarily unable to cope. Made vulnerable by illness, by marital instability, by social isolation, poverty and poor housing, and sometimes by violence and alcohol or drug abuse, families have had to surrender their children to social services to cope with an immediate crisis. While the families to which they return may not be as turbulent as those of long-stay children, they nevertheless remain vulnerable. Whilst long-term family difficulties undoubtedly remain, the immediate problems leading to the separation of *early returners* tend quickly to resolve themselves. Parents return from hospital, family rows blow over, depressions lift, abusive family members leave.

For *intermediate returners* on the other hand, more radical change is often required before reunion can be envisaged. About one in 14 of the study cohort, 32 children in total, returned to relatives between six months and two years after separation. The characteristics and problems of these children overlapped considerably with those of the early returners. The differences were to be found in the length of time their problems took to sort out. As a result of their longer separations, however, change and loss of continuity were far more common for these *intermediate returners* than for those who returned earlier. More than a quarter (28%) experienced at least one chance of placement during separation, for example, and only a third (38%) of intermediate returners returned to an unchanged household. Changes in family membership might involve the arrival of new or additional carers, usually step-parents but often grandparents, to help with parenting, or the departure of family members whose contributions to family life were less welcome. For intermediate returners, discontinuity and disruption were not so much obstacles to return as the very thing that enabled it to take place at all.

Where return did not follow a change in family circumstances, it often followed a change in the aims of the care plan. As children drifted in substitute care, professionals began to seek around for other, more distant relatives as well as adults to whom the child was not related, but with whom he or she was very familiar. Another common route home, particularly for adolescents, followed the collapse of a foster placement.

Long-term returners – those returning home after a separation longer than two years – are difficult to identify in a prospective study but retrospective evidence from a number of sources tells a similar story. Most are boys returning home to families in their mid-teens. Many have been separated from their families whilst still at primary school as a result of a combination of child-protection and child-behaviour concerns.

Unlike those children whose separations are short and where social workers negotiate almost all aspects of the reunion, in long-stay cases return is frequently informally negotiated between relatives and offspring. Sometimes these negotiations are in defiance of social work decisions and some adolescents actually vote with their feet. There were high levels of family change during the children's separation from home. Nearly half of them returned to families with different key family members.

But the passage of time is not entirely detrimental as it allows for reflection and self-examination. Some adolescents repaired long-damaged relationships, became more tolerant of home circumstances and more sympathetic to hard-pressed parents. In addition, many parents were more benign about the antics of their offspring and welcomed the prospect of their having a job and eventually achieving some independence.

How successful were these reunions and what were the consequences for children and families of a stressful return that finally ended in breakdown? As has been seen, the outcomes of reunion are difficult to assess. Even if a child lingers under the parental roof, there is no guarantee that happiness and fulfilment attend the stay. The need to re-negotiate family roles, to compromise and to share territories, often with new adults and rival children, made return stressful for some young people. The passage of time, however, encourages many to settle.

It is encouraging to note that the majority of children who go home stay put and that social workers' assessments of the reunion suggest it is tranquil and unremarkable. For example, some 70% of those who went home stayed, apparently in satisfactory circumstances. As might be expected, those whose separations were short tended to settle more readily than those who were long looked after, particularly if they stayed longer than two years away from home. On return, adolescents were more footloose than younger children but many, even those in their late teens, achieved a *modus vivendi* with their families. Naturally, the older the young person, the more movement around the family occurred and the more common were forays into independent living followed by retreats to the asylum offered by home. However, it is important to note that a considerable proportion of long-stay children go home and remain with their families without any noticeable disadvantage.

Nevertheless, this study has identified groups of children who are particularly vulnerable to return problems. A number of children whose separations are short fail to settle on their return home and about a quarter of those going back within six months have to be looked after again. A small number continue to oscillate for a considerable period. Some adolescents cause similar problems on return. Although the majority settle back at home, a small number of skill-less adolescents drift rapidly into the ranks of the homeless. Unremarkable other than by their poor looked after experience and withering links with home, these casualties of the welfare system are difficult to spot early on. This makes special strategies of reunion for these children particularly difficult to mount.

This study has also demonstrated that a number of variables are associated with return outcomes. Multivariate analysis has highlighted those factors which predict the likelihood of a child's return and of its success. As these variables were originally derived from a retrospective study and have now been tested prospectively, they are extremely robust and have been used to compile check-lists. Some of the predictive factors are unlikely to cause surprise, such as the significance of close family links while the child is away and the importance of an accepting warm relationship between mother and absent child. Others are less obvious and could only be established by careful research.

The use of such predictive factors in assessing the outcomes of interventions is less common in child-care than in medicine or delinquency studies. Unfortunately, such predictions cannot be fool-proof. The check-lists are intended to aid professionals making decisions about return, not to replace the need for careful evaluation of each case as it arises. However, whatever the limitations of the study, several messages helpful to social workers faced with return decisions have emerged. Initially, and perhaps most importantly, is the need to recognise that most children looked after by local authorities return home. If this one fact is kept firmly in mind at the point of separation, then key decisions about the child's future should reflect this likely outcome.

A positive attitude to the child's family needs to be encouraged, and allowed to seep into all decision-making, particularly that concerned with adolescents. The check-lists will highlight youngsters who 'drift' and for whom return plans could be accelerated. As so often in child-care, even the darkest prospects can brighten.

The discovery that so many short-term outcomes are positive should bring comfort to social workers. It might also be stressed that the situation in the long-term is often more satisfactory than imagined, especially for abused and neglected children. Indeed, these acute cases arouse much less anxiety several years on than the quiescent, skill-less, drifting adolescents, boys as well as girls, who become bereft of support and seem unable to seek succour.

For them, and for all children in need, the *Children Act* 1989 stresses partnership between social services and families. However, 'shared care' should not be interpreted as a crude division, for instance allowing the child to spend four days in a foster home and the remainder of the week with parents. Such a rigid plan would seldom work. Repeated returns are not easy for participants to manage and, when the pattern does endure, it can encourage the child in later years to choose flight as a strategy to cope with stress.

Consequently, the value of keeping parents on the scene, making separation and return part of a package and the fostering of parental responsibility need to be emphasised. The attitude and involvement of all participants are more important to the child's future than administrative arrangements such as who lives where.

Indeed, there is often a mismatch between the management of the looked after experience and the perceptions of family members. For the parents and children studied, life's course is marked by a series of episodes, hence the approach in the intensive study. If professionals are to take good practice on board they will have to work to the timescales of parents and children and remember that in a care career the situation at one moment in time is very much fashioned by preceding events.

Are more resources needed to ease children's returns? Faced with limited resources, one way forward is to work most intensively with those families requiring greatest help. Increasingly, research is producing a variety of indices which identify vulnerable children and the factors described in this study can also be used to pinpoint the most worrying cases. There is plentiful information on not only who is long looked after and faces difficulties in getting home but also who will need extra support after reunion.

This study has also highlighted children's and families' needs for a sense of continuity and meaning in the face of disruption, separation and random difficulty. Return is a process and by looking at key moments as the drama enfolds, it becomes clear how reunion is coloured by what has gone before. The recognition that return means a re-negotiation of cherished roles and the sharing or surrendering of territory and possessions is also very important. These fraught negotiations particularly affect step-parents and newcomers, cohabitees and their children. Above all, unease, friction and argument do not signify a breakdown of return but seem to be a common feature of all families experiencing reunion, not only those haunted by poverty, illness and re-constitution. Thus, stress does not always lead to a poor outcome, indeed the reverse might almost be suggested.

As such, the solution for the child and family of these inevitable disputes lies not in flight or withdrawal but in negotiating, with social work support, a *modus vivendi*. Particularly important is for the social worker and other supports to be available in the days that follow the restoration. Many respondents felt that the resolution of disputes during these early days provided a valuable opportunity for children and parents to understand better the reasons behind the separation.

Working with the family after return will be eased if, during separation, social workers have nurtured continuities, however tenuous these may be. Moreover, while temporal continuities may wither naturally, they should not be severed abruptly. So, just as one strives to keep the family involved during the child's absence, one should similarly try after return to keep the looked after experience alive. Maintaining links with foster parents or a residential centre and the surrounding environment can have a considerable pay-off, especially for those youngsters who oscillate between social services and parents.

Above all, this study amply illustrates what previous social work has often implied, preoccupied as it has been with other child-care concerns: *viz*, reunion is quite as stressful as separation for both children and parents. Reconciliation involves facing up to one's personal responsibilities and failures because the fantasies which maintain every-day life have to be examined in the cold light of day and because inexorable change reminds all that the past cannot be undone. It thus needs all of the preparation of a foster or adoptive placement.

But it greatly helps to know that reunion does not mean taking up, once more, abruptly and without support, the duties so precipitately thrown down on separation. It also helps to realise that preparation, counselling and support are not wasted efforts as return takes place. Just as a shoulder to cry on is important in managing separation so a go-between to yell at on return, someone who can catch the flying plates and interpret what is happening, is particularly important. Thus, as the social worker hurries back down the garden path, clasping a check-list and brimming with sensitivity to the pains of reunion, even the errant chip van as it rounds the corner might offer wondrous insights and opportunities!

Appendix A: The statistical analysis used to predict return outcomes

The findings of two extensive studies of over 1,000 children looked after were discussed in Chapters Ten to Fourteen. A retrospective study of 875 children produced factors predicting the likelihood of return within certain time periods and the chances of success of the restoration. These findings were then tested prospectively. To arrive at these indicators, a rigorous statistical procedure was designed to identify amongst the many variables associated with a particular outcome those with the most *independent* predictive power.

What is meant by 'independent'? Variables may predict particular outcomes not due to any direct link between the two but as a result of their mutual association with a third factor. For example, since incomes generally increase with age, so anything else that necessarily tends to increase with age, such as dental decay, can be used to predict one's income, with some success. Multivariate analysis reduces the chances of making the sort of mistake that would be involved in concluding from this association that not brushing one's teeth might be a good career move. It is unlikely that dental decay has any independent predictive power once the effects of age have been controlled for. To take a more serious example, while there were over 50 variables significantly associated with a child's return within six months of separation in univariate analysis, it was possible to distil these down to three that, in combination, best predicted this particular outcome.

What exactly was process? Firstly, by using a range of statistical tests, the 15 most statistically and consequently significant variables were selected for consideration. A second stage was the construction of a correlation matrix using Goodman and Kruskal's *gamma* to measure the association between the dependent variables. Thirdly, the data were checked for *outliers,* individual cases that defy predictions but whose idiosyncrasy is explicable in terms of particular events or situations. Here an approach applied in the field of bacteriology by Sneath and Langham (1989) proved useful. A fourth step was to use a special type of multivariate analysis, a loglinear approach known as logit, to select two, three or, at most, four factors which, in combination, best predicted the outcome under study. It was then possible to estimate the odds of a particular outcome, given specified conditions. Fifthly, having established the best set of factors, the logit procedure was repeated but excluding the *outlier* cases. This gave a better indication of the true predictive power of the statistical model.

The strengths and weaknesses of this approach have been discussed at length in Chapter Five. Given the data set and computing power available at the time of the initial analysis (1992), the approach described was the best available at the time. Finally, the procedure was repeated using a new data-set, gathered prospectively. This procedure was undertaken four times, once for each of the outcomes being predicted. The original analysis of the retrospective study, which produced the factors to be tested prospectively, is described elsewhere (Bullock et al., 1993) - this appendix concentrates on the findings of the *prospective* study.

Return within six months

The eight variables selected by retrospective analysis are laid out in table A1. Of 463 children in the prospective cohort, 103 were excluded from the analysis because the answer to at least one of the eight questions was 'not applicable'. These were nearly all children separated for very short periods, many on regular programmes of respite care, for whom questions of contact during separation did not arise. Ten further cases were excluded from the analysis, having been identified as 'outliers'. The cases suggested as statistical outliers were, without exception, cases in which no, or very few, of the eight factors were said to apply. In such cases it was necessary to consult the original case records to determine whether no boxes were ticked because no factors applied, in which case the data was retained in the analysis, or whether the social worker had misunderstood or ignored instructions, in which case the data was rejected.

Table A1: The relationship between variables associated with return home to relatives within six months of separation

	a	b	c	d	e	f	g	h	j
a		5	5	5	7	6	4	2	4
b			8	8	8	7	7	4	7
c				8	8	8	7	5	8
d					9	7	6	6	5
e						8	6	5	8
f							8	5	8
g								4	7
h									3

Keys represent variables: a = regular contact during separation b = problems eased or resolved c = family considers itself a family d = continuities in the child's life e= child has retained a role in family f = child has territory in the family home g = social work plan inclusive h = intended plans not affected by any new information j = return within six months of separation

Numbers represent power of relationship i.e. 6 = gamma g+0.550 to +0.649

Whilst all the eight variables identified retrospectively were thus shown to predict return prospectively, logistic regression removed three factors that were seen to derive their predictive power from other variables. These were a (regular contact during separation), d (continuities in the child's life) and h (no new information arising during separation). Table A2 summarises the model achieved using the five remaining criteria. Summing the co-efficents in the 'ExpB' column gives odds of around thirteen to one if all five criteria are met: that is, of fourteen children who met all five criteria it could be expected that all but one would return home within six months. That the coefficients are of more or less the same size suggests that no one factor dominates the analysis.

Table A3 provides the percentages of children returning home within six months according to the number of criteria they met. Nearly half (48%) of the sample met at least four of the five criteria predicting an early return. To summarise, a child who retains a role and territory within his or her family, where the family considers itself a family, the social work plan is inclusive and the problems that led to separation subsequently ease, has a very high probability (.93) of rapid return. Since most children meet most of these criteria, most return quickly.

Table A2: Logistic regression of factors associated with return within six months

	Sig.	ExpB
Problems eased or resolved	.008	2.4
Family considers itself a family	.018	2.1
Child has retained a role	.002	2.6
Child has retained territory	.001	2.9
Social work plan inclusive	.010	2.6
Constant	000	
Odds of return given all five factors about 13 to 1		
Chisquare=140 df=5 p<0.00005		

Table A3: Return within six months by number of factors applying

Number of Factors Applying	Number returned within six months	Number not returned within six months	Percentage returned within six months
None	5	33	13
1	11	44	20
2	19	31	38
3	17	23	43
4	75	18	81
5	69	5	93
Total	196	154	56

Return between 6 and 24 months

A high proportion of children return to relatives soon after entering care. What of those who fail to get back home quickly? Whilst the data was again searched for outliers, none were found, and no data was removed at this stage of the analysis other than, obviously, those children who were no longer looked after. Return between six and 24 months after separation proved - unsurprisingly - much harder to predict prospectively than early return. Table A4 shows that variables were associated with each other far more than they were associated with return. Not surprisingly, then, of the nine factors suggested in the retrospective analysis as predicting intermediate return and listed in the table, only two - d (that problems were felt to be eased or resolved) and i (that relationships within the family were reasonably good) - proved of any significant predictive value at all, even in univariate analysis.

Table A4: The relationship between variables associated with return home to relatives between 6 and 24 months after separation

	a	b	c	d	e	f	g	h	i
b	6								
c	0	0							
d	5	1	8						
e	1	0	4	6					
f	-4	-2	1	2	1				
g	5	4	3	6	5	5			
h	2	1	5	4	4	6	7		
i	3	3	8	8	6	3	6	5	
j	-1	-2	0	4	1	1	2	2	5

Key letters represent variables a = abuse/neglect not an issue b = not placed with siblings at 6 mths c = relatives participate in care decisions d= family feel that problems eased e= continuities f= child retains territory g = stress factors not overwhelming h = social work plan inclusive i = family relationships reasonably good j = return 6 - 24 mths after separation

Numbers represent power of relationship i.e. 6 = gamma g+0.550 to +0.649

Multivariate analysis, moreover, suggested that problems invariably did ease during separation, providing that family relationships were not themselves the problem. (Since separation tends to come in response to crisis, it is hardly surprising that things tend to improve subsequently). Other factors, such as inclusive social work and the retention of territory, tended to reflect the quality of family relationships, rather than acting independently to increase the chances of return. Thus, only one factor was shown to be of consistent value in predicting return outcomes after six months - the quality of family relationships. Table A5 below shows that of the 149 children still looked after at six months, 41, or 28%, returned home within the next 18 months. Where family relations were reasonably good, however, the proportion rose to 44%. In seeking to predict who would go home, no other combination of variables would be more useful than this one on its own.

Table A5: Return between 6 and 24 mths by the quality of family relationships at 6m

	Relations reasonably good at 6m	Relations not so good
Returned home within next 18m	17	24
No return	22	86

Pearson chisquare=6.8 df=1 p<0.01

Probability of return if relations reasonably good = 0.44

Return between 25 and 60 months

It is not possible to provide any prospective evidence concerning late returners, and the analysis is restricted to the retrospective study. Table A6 shows that the three variables identified as, in combination, best predicting return between 24 and 60 mths were: c (whether the child's natural mother was the main provider of emotional support at the time of separation), e (whether the household was dependent on supplementary benefit) and a (whether the child was a boy). Return was more likely where boys were separated from mothers than in other combinations, and this was particularly so where poverty contributed to the original need for separation. In five of every six cases where each of these three criteria were met, the boy returned home within five years.

Table A6: The relationship between variables associated with return home to relatives between 24 and 60 months after separation

	a	b	c	d	e
return	-4	3	-5	-4	-4
a		-3	1	+0	-1
b			-0	1	4
c				9	1
d					4

Key letters represent variables return = return 25- 60 mths a= gender b = breakdown in parental care c= natural mother main provider of emotional support d = primary female in child's life is natural mother e= household on state benefits.

Numbers represent power of relationship i.e. 6 = gamma g0.6000001 to 0.6000009.

Predicting the success of return

The 'success' of return is defined in Chapter Ten. All 318 children who returned to live with natural family members within two years of

Table A7: The relationship between variables associated with successful return home to relatives within 24 mths of separation

	a	b	c	d	e	f	g	h	i	j	k	l	m	n	o	p	q	r	s	t
b	3																			
c	2	-4																		
d	7	3	3																	
e	8	2	2	7																
f	4	1	3	5	6															
g	6	2	2	7	6	9														
h	4	2	4	6	5	10	9													
i	7	5	2	7	5	6	5	6												
j	8	6	-1	7	7	6	8	7	8											
k	6	9	-2	5	5	5	5	6	8	8										
l	6	0	0	5	6	3	5	3	5	6	3									
m	7	4	2	8	7	6	7	7	7	7	7	7								
n	7	2	3	8	7	5	7	6	6	8	6	5	8							
o	6	4	3	8	7	7	6	7	7	6	6	4	7	8						
p	6	3	-2	7	6	6	6	6	7	6	6	3	7	8	8					
q	5	4	1	6	5	6	6	6	8	7	6	5	6	6	6	6				
r	6	3	1	8	7	7	8	8	8	8	6	5	7	8	7	6	9			
s	4	-1	-1	3	5	5	4	4	1	5	1	5	6	5	5	6	3	6		
t	1	2	3	5	4	5	2	6	7	10	3	0	3	7	4	5	5	7	7	
u	5	3	2	5	3	6	6	5	3	4	4	4	2	7	4	3	5	5	3	3

Key letters represent variables: a = successful social work; b = returning to same house; c = no previous returns; d = voluntary arrangements satisfactory; e = plans tailored to family timescale; f = family prepared for return; g = family will discuss separation; h = family see value in tensions associated with return; i = continuities in the child's life; j = child retains a role; k = child retains territory; l = non-offender; m = inclusive social work; n = family relationships fairly good; o = visiting family will be straightforward; p = family will call for help if needed; q = child will establish complementary role outside home; r = clear perception of when return has occurred; s = special efforts made to ease transition; t = return brings change for better in family relationships; u = successful return.

Numbers represent power of relationship i.e. 6 = gamma g+0.550 to +0.649

separation, no matter how brief the separation, were included in the analysis of the success of return. The search for outliers revealed such a range of return situations and participants that it seemed arbitrary to exclude any. Nonetheless, a number of children no longer looked after two years after separation were excluded, such as children who were adopted, those who left to independence and a handful of young men in custody. Table A7 shows the associations within the 20 variables identified retrospectively as predicting the success of return, in the new prospective dataset.

Again, whilst most of these variables were clearly associated with a successful return home, many of them appeared to be measuring the same thing in a number of different ways. Table A8 provides the result of a logistic regression analysis, showing that of nine non-offenders returning to families prepared for the tensions surrounding return but in which the underlying relationships are sound, eight are likely to succeed.

Table A8: Logistic regression of factors associated with return within six months

Factor	Sig.	Exp (B)
Family prepared for the anxiety generated by return	.001	2.5
Child not an offender	.073	1.7
Family relationships of a fairly high quality	.000	3.5
Odds of successful return if all three met about 8 to 1		
Pearson chisquare= 58 df=3 p< 0.005		

Finally, Table A9 shows the numbers and percentages of successful returns according to the numbers of factors met. Again, two of every three (66%) returning children meet at least two of the criteria. At the risk of tautology, most returns are successful because most children meet most of the criteria for a successful return.

Table A9: Success of return by number of criteria met

Number of Factors	Successful returns	Unsuccessful returns	% returns successful
0	13	24	35
1	28	43	40
2	73	33	69
3	90	14	87
Total	204	114	64

Conclusion

This concludes the summary of the analysis used to test prospectively a large number of factors found retrospectively to be associated with various return outcomes. Most factors were found to stand up well to prospective testing, though others were possibly statistical accidents. A few were probably specific to the legislative and practice climate of the early 1980s. Several factors were shown to be particularly strong independent predictors of good return outcomes, and these can now be regarded as extremely robust indicators. Such factors tended to revolve around family relationships, roles and territories rather than the specific problems that led to separation. The social work strategies that were most effective in ensuring return were those that did not jeopardise existing relationships - encouraging regular contact, for example, and avoiding confrontation through the courts. Such an approach could only facilitate return, however, not ensure it. Nonetheless, the great majority of children looked after did tend to retain viable family relationships, roles and territories, and thus achieved an early and successful return from substitute care.

Appendix B: Making assessments of the quality of relationships between the members of the families of children in care

In the extensive study, the quality of family relationships is important in understanding return outcomes. Like social workers, researchers working intensively with families can get a 'feel' for the quality of relationships between members, but on what are such assessments based?

Initially, it should be stressed that any assessment is relative to the particular experience of the families of children looked after by social services. They are often deprived and, in such contexts, there is little to be gained from making assessments used to gauge the situation of middle-class families. When visiting the families of children looked after, who tend by nature to be more reticent, there are few obvious positive attributes which indicate a high quality of relationships and there is a tendency to note the absence of negative features, for example, relatively little conflict between siblings.

But even in middle-class contexts, there is a danger of judging children's positive experiences, for example 'doing well at violin class', as indicative of a happy family life. A clever use of verbal skills can be an effective strategy to conceal troubled family relationships. It is quite possible to be very unhappy in a conflict-torn or rejecting home and still be described by a subject teacher as 'doing well'.

Similarly, in deprived families, all may not be what it seems. There may be a united capacity to offer their children 'good enough parenting', in terms of meeting needs for warm and caring, affectionate support. The assessment of this 'quality' of relationships is made more difficult when, in consequence of past experience, either in their own families or with other 'authority figures', family members are reticent, mistrustful and defensive.

There are other difficulties to overcome. There is always a danger of misinterpreting the signs given by family members. A dominant relationship in which a parent overwhelms a child or one sibling eclipses another is not necessarily a deep relationship. There is a need to look beyond superficial indicators and to accept that some aspects of the relationship between family members may be ritualistic, for instance visiting absent children to keep up appearances.

There are many dimensions to the assessment. The age of the child must be taken into account. The interaction appropriate to a mother and her four year old may be totally inappropriate when the child is older. The position of children in families is also important; children in the middle of a large group may get less attention than a new baby or the first born. Different measures are required for scrutiny of mother-offspring dynamics than for inter-sibling relationships. The role of wider family members, such as grand-parents, aunts and uncles, also needs to be kept in mind as well as their impact, if any, on family relationships, both overt and covert.

It is useful to consider the quality of family relationships from a range of perspectives. Obviously important is the societal view, such as that applied by social workers when they consider a child's restoration. There are, however, sub-cultural norms. Does the local community accept or even value the way family members interact with each other? More important still are the perceptions of family members and of the child him or herself. Often, socially unacceptable practices are viewed as acceptable or even normal within a particular family group. Parker and colleagues (1991) have stressed that situations such as poor health or neglect are widely accepted as being negative features, while positive criteria for children's progress are often culturally specific, as, for example, with regard to obedience, success at school or observance of religious rules and practices.

But what aspects of the family relationship are being assessed? Three dimensions are important. Firstly, there is a spiritual, expressive component to family relationships. This report has consistently stressed the importance of caring relationships and of asking the question 'Is there a sense of belonging between parents and children? Are they partisan? Do they love each other?'

Secondly, as in any relationship, there is a functional dimension to family dynamics. Does the family meet the needs of the child, his or her care and protection or emotional, educational and health requirements? Just as important, does the child meet the needs of the family, for instance by enhancing parental identity or simple self-interest such as financial well-being?

Finally, the structural and material requirements of a family must be addressed. Is it a viable unit? There may be a high quality of relationships between members but this does not mean that parents and children can live together. Particularly important is the family's ability to provide accommodation, especially a bed for the child, to have a membership which is compatible with the child's needs and wishes and to offer a reasonably stable environment for the child's upbringing.

From this basis, judgements can be made about the quality of relationships between the family members of children looked after. However, in many cases, this assessment will have to be made during the child's absence from home and any views about the way in which, for example, mother and child interacted when they were living together will be clouded by the problems which led to the separation.

How can the quality of relationships between a family and an absent member be measured? Morris's (1965) work on prisoners' families, Shaw's (1987) work on prisoners' wives, West and Farrington's (1977) research on the family life of delinquents, Quinton and Rutter's (1988) studies of adolescents' family lives, Parker and colleagues' (1991) work on child care outcomes and previous work at Dartington on the families of children looked after by social services have all been useful in seeking an answer to this question.

An initial starting point might be *contact*. Parental contact, however, can be misleading. Frequent visiting may reflect loyalty rather than love or be a collusion against authority. Nonetheless, looking at contact in its broadest sense, that is to include visits, telephone calls, letters and the exchange and cherishing of photographs can be helpful, especially if observations include the range of perspectives described above.

Assessing how dependent children are upon their families and *vice-versa* is also helpful. The reciprocity of relationships between relatives and absent child is another important dimension to this problem. This means looking at the quality and continuity of communications between family members, the ability of the parent to provide emotional security for the child, the ability of parent and child to help solve each other's problems, the consistency of support provided and the stability of relationships in the face of adverse circumstances.

The following set of questions is designed to explore these various themes. As in the other parts of this study, no attempt is made to provide a definitive scale as this would be unduly optimistic given the complexity of situations under scrutiny. Rather, the intention is to provide an instrument which, in combination with other information, helps social workers make effective decisions on the return of children from care. The aim of the exercise is to assess whether the relationships within the home are good. Thus, the general picture may be encouraging even when relationships between individual members are rocky and the answers to some of the following questions are negative.

A) Spiritual/expressive

1. Does the social worker perceive a sense of belonging between family members? (n.b. exchange and cherishing of photographs, remarks defensive of each other)

2. Does the child share one-to-one tasks with other family members? (eg. shopping, sporting/leisure activity)

3. Do the family see themselves as one unit? (ie. is there a family identity?) Are there any emotional outlets for tensions within the family?

4. Does the child want to go home? Is the child wanted by sufficient family members to offset those who are ambivalent about the return? When asked, 'where would you most like to live?' does the child answer 'at home'? When you ask the child to list his/her favourite people, are family members mentioned?

B) Functional

1. From the social worker's perspective, does the family meet the child's needs? (n.b. emotional, educational, physical, health)

2. Will the neighbourhood in which the family live relieve or exacerbate family stresses? (n.b. are there strategies for strengthening local networks for this family?)

3. Does the family perceive the child to have special needs? Is the family strong enough to overcome the anxieties of return? (n.b. are they prepared for this?) Is there anybody, including wider family members, who will spend time with the child and will focus on his/her specific needs? (n.b. importance of siblings)

4. Is the child able to get his/her view across about what s/he wants?

C) Structural

1. Is there a mutually accepted dependency between family members? Does the child have a home, a bed, toys and belongings at home? Is the parents' health of sufficient quality to sustain meaningful relationships over time?

2. Is the family structure and identity acceptable to the local community? (n.b. Is there anything we can do to improve neighbours' views of this family?)

3. Do family members have strategies for offsetting structural weaknesses within the family (eg. overcrowding, poverty)? Are tensions within the family acknowledged by members (eg. step-parents and children)?

4. How does the child feel about structural weaknesses within the family? (n.b. problems of moving from substitute care placement which is relatively well off)

Appendix C The old and revised checklists compared

The prospective study of children returning home after being looked after has produced five checklists to be applied at different points during the child's separation. The aim of this Appendix is to compare the new checklists with those obtained from the earlier retrospective follow up. Checklist 1 indicates two factors shown by both studies to best predict a child's return at any point. These are: that the child's separation is by voluntary arrangement and that relationships within the family are reasonably good.

Checklist 2 can be used for all children who are looked after. It contains those factors which in the retrospective study predicted the likelihood of children going home to parents or other relatives within the following six months. Those confirmed in the prospective study are starred in the right hand column. Indicators known at the point of separation are distinguished from those which only become apparent at the point at which return becomes an issue.

CHECKLIST 2: Factors associated with a child's return within six months of separation

a) Variables known at the point of separation		
	Especially significant in the retrospective study	SIGNIFICANT IN THE PROSPECTIVE STUDY
1. That the child's separation is arranged on a voluntary basis	*	*
2. Family and children perceive the problems necessitating the original separation to have been resolved or to have been much assisted by the child's being looked after	-	-

3.	Participants' perspectives of the return are realistic and there are no wide gaps between fantasy and reality in their perceptions	-	-
4.	There are relatively few stress factors within the family (in the context of looked after children)	-	-
5.	The family relationships as assessed (using the factors described in Appendix B) are of a relatively high quality	-	*
b)	Variables known at the point return becomes an issue		
1.	That the child had enjoyed regular contact with family members during his or her absence from home	*	-
2.	That the social worker encourages family links with the absent child	*	-
3.	The problems necessitating the original separation are perceived as having been partially resolved at the point at which return becomes an issue	-	*
4.	The family perceives itself as a 'family'	-	*
5.	There are continuities in the child's life (including family relationships, education, cultural identity and social networks)	-	-
6.	The child retains a role within the family at each stage in the return process	-	*
7.	The child retains territory in the return home either by having a room, a bed or by the leaving of toys and other personal possessions or by the retention of keepsakes	-	*
8.	The social work plan is 'inclusive' (i.e. that the family have maintained a caring role and have been involved in decisions)	-	*

All these factors are 'protective' in that their presence is associated with a swift reunion. There are, however, 'risk' situations which can delay the return of children in care. These have to be balanced against the preceding indicators.

c)	Risk factors which can delay a child's return		
1.	There is a history of abuse and/or serious neglect at the time of the child's separation	-	-
2.	After return becomes an issue, intended return plans are affected by new information emerging concerning risks to the child, e.g. child abuse	-	-

The third checklist can be applied to those children who have already been looked after for six months. The factors, which are divided into those known at the six months point and those on which information emerges once return becomes an issue, predict the likelihood of the child's return within the following 18 months, that is between six and 24 months after coming into care or being accommodated.

CHECKLIST 3: Children looked after at six months: factors associated with the child's return in the following 18 months

a) Variables known at six months after separation		
	Especially significant in the retrospective study	SIGNIFICANT IN THE PROSPECTIVE STUDY
1. There is no history of abuse and/or serious neglect at the time of the child's separation	★	-
2. The child has no siblings or, if there are siblings, they are separated from one another during the child's absence from home	★	-
3. Relatives of the child (especially parents) participate in care decisions	★	-
4. Family and children perceive the problems necessitating the original separation to have been resolved or to have been much assisted by the child's admission to care or accommodation	-	-
5. There are continuities in the child's life (including family relationships, education, cultural identity and social networks)	-	-
6. The child retains territory in the return home either by having a room, a bed or by the leaving of toys and other personal possessions or by the retention of keepsakes	-	-
7. There are relatively few stress factors within the family (in the context of children looked after)	-	-
8. The social work plan is 'inclusive' (i.e. the family have maintained a caring role and have been involved in decisions)	-	-
9. The family relationships as assessed (using the factors described in Appendix B) are of a relatively high quality	-	★
b) Variables known at the point return becomes an issue		
1. After the point at which return becomes an issue, there are no unforeseen changes in parents' health, family relationships or household membership	-	-
2. Social workers find little difficulty in visiting the family or gaining accurate information	-	-
3. Participants' perspectives of the return are realistic and there are no wide gaps between fantasy and	-	-

	reality in their perceptions		
4.	The problems necessitating the original separation are perceived as having been partially resolved at the point at which return becomes an issue	-	*
5.	The family perceives itself as a 'family'	-	-
6.	The child retains a role within the family at each stage in the return process	-	-

The fourth checklist concerns long-stay cases, that is children who have been separated for two years. If a child long in care or accommodation meets the criteria in the forthcoming list, the chances of his or her reunion with parents or relatives in the following three years, that is between 25 and 60 months after separation, are greatly increased. It was not possible to test this prospectively because of the lengthy time some children are looked after.

CHECKLIST 4: Children away at two years: Factors associated with the child's return in the following three years

		Especially significant in the retrospective study
1.	Mother is the main provider of the child's emotional support	*
2.	The child is a boy	*
3.	The family receives financial support from the Department of Social Security	*
4.	Family and children perceive the problems necessitating the original separation to have been resolved or to have been much assisted by the child's being looked after	-
5.	No radically new information about family problems emerges during the separation	-
6.	Social workers find little difficulty in visiting the family or gaining accurate information	-
7.	Participants' perspectives of the return are realistic and there are no wide gaps between fantasy and reality in their perceptions	-
8.	The problems necessitating the original separation are perceived as having been partially resolved at the point at which return becomes an issue	-
9.	There are continuities in the child's life (including family relationships, cultural identity and social networks)	-
10.	The child retains a role within the family at each stage in the return process	-
11.	The child retains territory in the return home either by having a room, a bed or by the leaving of toys and other personal possessions or by the	-

	retention of keepsakes	
12.	There are relatively few stress factors within the family (in the context of children looked after)	-
13.	The social work plan is 'inclusive' (i.e. the family have maintained a caring role and have been involved in decisions)	-
14.	The family relationships as assessed (using the factors described in Appendix B)	-

Finally, the fifth checklist contains factors which best predict the success of a child's reunion. For these, indicators that are known at the point the child goes home are separated from those that can only be known after he or she is back. In the prospective study, the factors found to be significant for children under the age of 12 were different from those that applied to adolescents.

CHECKLIST 5: Factors associated with the success of children's returns

a)	Variables known at the point of return	CONFIRMED IN PROSPECTIVE STUDY FOR CHILDREN AGED:	
		0-11	12+
1.	There is evidence of highly competent social work (i.e. that options are considered, a plan is created and social workers are highly committed to its implementation)	★	-
2.	The child has never previously been returned after being looked after by social services	-	-
3.	The social worker is sufficiently confident about the situation to consider discharging the care order or is entirely satisfied with the voluntary arrangements	★	-
4.	Social work return plans are tailored to meet the time-scales of family members	-	-
5.	The family is prepared for the anxiety generated by return and the disputes that are likely to occur	★	★
6.	Family members are prepared to discuss with each other the pains of separation and their role in the rift	-	-
7.	Family members are able to see value in the tensions associated with return	-	-
8.	There are continuities in the child's life (including family relationships, education, cultural identity and social networks)	-	-
9.	The child retains a role within the family at each stage in the return process	-	-
10.	The child retains territory in the return home either by having a room, a bed or by the leaving of toys and other personal possessions and by the retention of keepsakes	-	-
11.	The child is not an offender	★	★
12.	The social work plan is 'inclusive' (i.e. the family have maintained a caring role and have been involved in decisions)	-	-

13.	The family relationships as assessed (using the factors described in Appendix B) are of a relatively high quality	★	★
b)	Variables known after return		
1.	The social worker does not experience difficulty in gaining access to the child or family	-	-
2.	Once the child is at home, the family perceives the social worker as willing to help if and when needed	-	-
3.	Once at home, the child establishes a role outside of the family which does not undermine his or her role within it	-	★
4.	Participants have a clear perception of when return has occurred	-	-

In making assessments about the likely success of children's returns, special cases have to be taken into account. For example, in both the extensive and intensive studies, it was found that persistent offenders seldom settle back at home although their departure does not necessarily indicate an unsuccessful reunion. Deep-seated offending patterns are difficult to break and repeated court appearances and sojourns in custody frequently separate persistent delinquents from their parents. This risk factor can overwhelm the protective indicators described above.

There are also some children who fail to match the criteria in checklist 5 but who nonetheless succeed back at home. As was explained, there were two protective factors which can make an apparently bleak scenario more optimistic. These are:

		CONFIRMED IN PROSPECTIVE STUDY FOR CHILDREN AGED:	
c)	Variables which can protect a child vulnerable to difficulties after return		
		0-11	12+
1.	The placement prior to the child's return makes especial efforts to ease the transition home	-	-
2.	The return brings about a radical change for the better in family relationships	-	-

References

Ainley, P. (1991) *Young People Leaving Home*, London, Cassell.

Aldgate, J. and Tunstill, J. (1995) *Making Sense of Section 17, Implementing Services for Children in Need Within the 1989 Children Act*, London, HMSO.

Anderson, E. and Morgan, A. (1987) *Provision for Children in Need of Boarding/Residential Education*, Boarding Schools Association.

Audit Commission (1993) *Children First: a Study of Hospital Services*, London, HMSO.

Bailey, S., Thornton, L. and Weaver, A. (1994) 'The first 100 admissions to an adolescent secure unit', *Journal of Adolescence*, XVII, 207-21.

Balbernie, R. (1966) *Residential Work with Children*, Brighton, Human Context Books.

Ball, S. (1981) *Beachside Comprehensive*, London, Cambridge University Press.

Barth, R. and Berry, M. (1987) 'Outcomes of child welfare services under permanency planning', *Social Service Review*, LXI, 71-90.

Barth, R., Snowden, L., Ten Broek, E., Clancy, T., Jordan, C. and Barush, A. (1986) 'Contributors to reunification or permanent out of home care for physically abused children', *Journal of Social Service Research*, IX, 31-45.

Baxter, C., Poonia, K., Ward, L. and Nadirshaw, Z. (1990) *Double Discrimination: issues and services for people with learning difficulties from black and ethnic minority families*, London, The King's Fund/Campaign for Racial Equality.

Bebbington, A. and Miles, J. (1989) 'The background of children who enter local authority care', *British Journal of Social Work*, XIX, 349-68.

Becker, H. (1958) 'Problems of inference and proof in participant observation', *American Sociological Review*, XXIII, 652-59.

Becker, H. and Geer, B. (1960) 'Participant observation: the analysis of qualitative field data' in Adams, R. and Preiss, J. (eds.), *Human Organisation Research: Field Relations and Techniques*, Illinois, Davsey Press.

Berridge, D. (1985) *Children's Homes*, Oxford, Blackwell.

Berridge, D. and Cleaver, H. (1987) *Foster Home Breakdown*, Oxford, Blackwell.

Biehal, N., Clayden, J., Stein, M. and Wade, J. (1995*) Moving On: Young People and Leaving Care Schemes*, London, HMSO.

Bonnerjea, L. (1990) *Leaving Care in London*, London Boroughs Children's Regional Planning Committee.

Bowlby, J. (1952) *Maternal Care and Mental Health*, Geneva, WHO.

Brearley, P., Black, J., Gutridge, P., Roberts, G. and Tarran, E. (1982) *Leaving Residential Care*, London, Tavistock.

Bridgeland, M, (1971) *Pioneer Work with Maladjusted Children*, London, Staples Press.

Bullock, R., Little, M. and Millham, S. (1992) 'The relationships between quantitative and qualitative approaches in social policy research' in Brannen, J. (ed.) *Mixing Methods: Qualitative and Quantitative Research*, Aldershot, Avebury, 81-100.

Bullock, R., Little, M. and Millham, S. (1993*) Going Home: The Return of Children Separated from their Families* (first edition) Aldershot, Dartmouth.

Bullock, R., Little, M. and Millham, S. (1998) *The Care Careers of Young People in Long-stay Secure Treatment Units*, Aldershot, Ashgate.

Burford, G., Pennell, J., MacCleod, S., Campbell, S. and Lyall, G. (1996) 'Reunification as an extended family matter', *Community Alternatives*, VIII, 33-55.

Cawson, P. (1988) 'Children in exile', *Insight*, Sept., 12-15.

Central Statistical Office (CSO) (1996) *Social Trends 26*, London, Central Statistical Office.

Coleman, J. (1961) *The Adolescent Society*, Glencoe, Free Press.

Colton, M. (1988) *Dimensions of Substitute Care*, Aldershot, Avebury.

Cooper, P. (1992) 'Exploring pupils' perceptions of the effects of a residential schooling on children with emotional and behavioural difficulties', *Therapeutic Care and Education*, X, 22-37.

Cooper, P. (1993) *Effective Schools for Disaffected Students*, London, Routledge.

Copley, C. (1981) *Aspects of the Effects of the Penal Environment on Familial Relationships*, unpublished report, London, Prison Department.

Corrigan, P. (1979) *Schooling the Smash Street Kids*, London, Macmillan.

Curtis, P. and McCullough, C. (1993) 'The impact of alcohol and other drugs on the child welfare system', *Child Welfare*, LXXII, 533-542.

Denzin, N. (1970) *Sociological Methods: A Sourcebook*, London, Butterworth.

Department of Education and Science (1978) *Special Educational Needs: Report of the Committee of Enquiry into the Education of Handicapped Children and Young People' (Warnock Report)* London, HMSO.

Department of Health (1991) *Patterns and Outcomes in Child Placement*, London, HMSO.

Department of Health (1995) *Child Protection: Messages from Research*, London, HMSO.

Department of Health (1997) *Children Looked After by Local Authorities 31 March 1996, England*, London, Department of Health.

Department of Health and Social Security (1985) *Social Work Decisions in Child Care*, London, HMSO.

Department of Health and Social Security (1987) *The Law on Child Care and Family Services*, CM 62, London, HMSO.

Dinnage, R. and Kellmer Pringle, M. (1967) *Residential Child Care: Facts and Fallacies*, London, Longman.

Fanshel, D. and Shinn, E. (1978) *Children in Foster Care*, New York, Columbia University Press.

Farmer, E. and Parker, R. (1991) *Trials and Tribulations*, London, HMSO.

Farrington, D. (1995) 'The development of offending and antisocial behaviour from childhood: key findings from the Cambridge Study in Delinquent Development', *Journal of Child Psychiatry and Psychology*, XXXVI, 929-64.

Fein, E., Maluccio, A., Hamilton, V. and Ward, D. (1983) 'After foster care: outcomes of permanency planning for children', *Child Welfare*, LXII, 485-558.

Fein, E. and Staff, I. (1991) 'Implementing reunification services', *Families in Society*, LXII, 335-43.

Fein, E. and Staff, I. (1993) 'Last best change: Findings from a reunification services program', *Child Welfare*, LXII, 25-40.

Fein, E. and Staff, I. (1993) 'The interaction of research and practice in family reunification' in Maluccio et al., *Together Again*, op.cit., pp.3-19.

Festinger, T. (1983) *No-one Ever Asked Us*, New York, Columbia University Press.

Festinger, T. (1994) *Returning to Care: Discharge and Reentry into Foster Care*, Washington DC, Child Welfare League of America.

Filstead, W. (1970) *Qualitative Methodology: First Hand Involvement with the Social World*, Chicago, Markham.

Fleeman, A. (1984) 'From special to secondary school for children with learning difficulties', *Special Education: Forward Trends*, XI, Research Supplement.

Fletcher-Campbell, F. and Hall, C. (1991) *Changing Schools? Changing People? The Education of Children in Care*, Slough, National Foundation for Educational Research.

Fratter, J., Rowe, J., Sapsford, D. and Thoburn, J. (1991) *Permanent Family Placement: A Decade of Experience*, British Agencies for Adoption and Fostering.

Fuchs, D. (1993) 'Study finds neighbourhood support reduces child abuse and is needed prior to return of abused children to parents', *Community Alternatives*, 5(1) 155-66.

Gardner, H. (1996) 'The concept of family: perceptions of children in family foster care', *Child Welfare*, LXXV, 161-83.

Garnett, L. (1992) *Leaving Care and After*, London, National Children's Bureau.

Gemal, B. (1993) 'Placement of children with EBD', *Therapeutic Care and Education*, II, 295-313.

Gibbons, J., Gallagher, B., Bell, C. and Gordon, D. (1995) *Development after Physical Abuse in Early Childhood: A Follow-up Study of Children on Protection Registers*, London, HMSO.

Giddens, A. (1982) *New Rules of Sociological Method*, London, Hutchinson.

Goerge, R. (1990) 'The reunification process in substitute care', *Social Services Review*, LXIV, 422-57.

Gooch, D. (1996) 'Home and away: the residential care, education and control of children in historical and political context', *Child and Family Social Work*, I, 19-32.

Griffin Francell, C., Conn, V. and Gray D. (1988) 'Families' perception of care for chronically mentally ill relatives', *Hospital and Community Psychiatry*, XII, 1296-300.

Grimshaw, R. and Berridge, D. (1994) *Educating Disruptive Children: Progress and Placement in Residential Schools for Children with Emotional and Behavioural Difficulties*, London, National Children's Bureau.

Haggerty, R., Sherrod, L., Garmezy, N. and Rutter, M. (1995) *Stress, Risk and Resilience in Children and Adolescents: Processes, Mechanisms and Interventions*, Cambridge, University Press.

Hall, P. and Stacey, M. (1979) *Beyond Separation: Further Studies of Children in Hospital*, London, Routledge and Kegan Paul.

Hammersley, M. and Atkinson, P. (1983) *Ethnography: Principles in Practice*, London, Routledge and Kegan Paul.

Hargreaves, D. (1967) *Social Relations in a Secondary School*, London, Routledge and Kegan Paul.

Heath, A., Colton, M. and Aldgate, J. (1989) 'The education of children in care', *British Journal of Social Work*, XIX, 447-60.

Hess, P. and Folaron, G. (1992) *Disrupted Reunification: 62 Families' Experiences*, Indianapolis, University School of Social Work.

Hess, P., Folaron, G. and Jefferson, A. (1992) 'Effectiveness of family reunification services: an innovative evaluative model', *Social Work*, XXXVII, 304-11.

Hess, P. and Proch, K. (1988) *Family Visiting in Out-of-Home Care: A Guide to Good Practice*, Washington DC, Child Welfare League of America.

Hess, P. and Proch, K. (1993) 'Visiting: the heart of family reunification' in Pine, B. et al., *Together Again, Op. Cit.*

HMSO (1945) *Report by Sir William Monckton on the Circumstances which led to the Boarding Out of Denis and Terence O'Neill at Bank Farm, Minsterley*, Cmnd. 6636.

HMSO (1946) *Report of the Care of Children Committee* (The Curtis Report), Cmnd 6922.

HMSO (1984) *The Second Report of the House of Commons Social Services Committee 1983-4*, HC360-1.

Hundleby, M. (1988) 'Returning children home' in Family Rights Group, *Planning for Children*, London, FRG.

Jackson, S. (1987) *The Education of Children in Care*, Bristol Papers in Applied Social Studies, University of Bristol.

Johnson, B. (ed.) (1968) *The Evacuees*, London, Gollancz.

Jolly, R. (1987) *Military Man, Family Man, Crown Property?*, London, Brassey's Defence Publishers.

Jones, G. (1995) *Leaving Home*, Milton Keynes, Open University Press.

Jones, M., Neumann, R. and Shyne, A. (1976) *A Second Chance for Families: Evaluation of a Program to Prevent Foster Care*, New York, Child Welfare League of America.

Jones, M. (1985) *A Second Chance for Families: Five Years Later: Follow-up of a Program to Prevent Foster Care*, New York, Child Welfare League of America.

Kahan, B. (1979) *Growing Up in Care*, Oxford, Blackwell.

Keegan, J. (1976) *The Face of Battle*, London, Pimlico.

Kellmer Pringle, M. (1975) *The Needs of Children*, London, Hutchinson.

Kreiger, R., Maluccio, A. and Pine, B. (1991) *Teaching Reunification: A Sourcebook*, Center for the Study of Child Welfare, University of Connecticut.

Lambert, R. and Millham, S. (1968) *The Hothouse Society*, London, Weidenfeld and Nicolson.

Lambert , R. with Bullock, R. and Millham, S. (1975*) The Chance of a Lifetime? A Study of Boarding Education*, London, Wiedenfield and Nicolson.

Laslett, R. (1995) 'Beliefs and practice in the early schools for maladjusted children', *Therapeutic Care and Education*, IV, 5-9.

Lewis, R. and Callaghan, S. (1993) 'The peer parent project: compensating foster parents to facilitate reunification of children with their biological parents', *Community Alternatives*, V, 43- 65.

Little, J. and Schueman, J. (1996) *A Synthesis of Research on Family Prevention and Family Reunification Programs*, University of Chicago, Chapin Hall Center for Children.

Little, M. (1990) *Young Men in Prison*, Aldershot, Dartmouth.

Little, M. and Kelly, S. (1995) *A Life Without Problems?: The Achievements of a Therapeutic Community*, Aldershot, Arena.

Lofland, J. and L. (1970) *Analyzing Social Settings: A Guide to Qualitative Observation and Analysis*, Belmont, Wadsworth.

Malek, M. (1993) *Passing the Buck: Institutional Responses to Controlling Children with Difficult Behaviour*, London, The Children's Society.

Maluccio, A., Fein, E. and Davis, I. (1994) 'Family reunification: research findings, issues and directions', *Child Welfare*, LXXIII, 489-504.

Maluccio, A., Fein, E. and Olmstead, K. (1986) *Permanency Planning for Children: Concepts and Methods*, London, Routledge, Chapman and Hall.

Maluccio, A. and Sinanoglu, P. (eds.) (1981) *The Challenge of Partnership: Working with Parents of Children in Foster Care*, New York, Child Welfare League of America.

Maluccio, A., Warsh, R. and Pine, B. (1993) 'Rethinking family reunion after foster care', *Community Alternatives*, V, 1-17.

Maluccio, A., Pine, B. and Warsh, R. (1994) 'Protecting children by preserving their families', *Children and Youth Services Review*, XVI, 295-307.

Maluccio, A., Warsh, R. and Pine, B. (eds.) (1993) *Together Again: Family Reunification in Foster Care*, Washington DC, Child Welfare League of America.

McCarthy, B. (1988) 'The role of relatives' in Lavender, A. and Holloway, F. (eds.) *Community Care in Practice*, London, John Wiley.

McDermott, K. and King, R. (1992) 'Prison rule 102: 'Stand by your man: the impact of penal policy on the families of prisoners' *in* Shaw, R. (ed.) *Prisoners' Children: What are the Issues?*, London, Routledge.

Millham, S., Bullock, R. and Hosie, K. (1978) *Locking Up Children*, Farnborough, Saxon House.

Millham, S., Bullock, R., Hosie, K. and Little, M. (1986) *Lost in Care*, Aldershot, Gower.

Millham, S., Bullock, R., Hosie, K. and Little, M. (1989) *Access Disputes in Child-Care*, Aldershot, Gower.

Ministry of Health (1959) *The Welfare of Children in Hospital* (The Platt Report), London, HMSO.

Morris, P. (1965) *Prisoners and their Families*, London, Allen and Unwin.

Mrazek, D. (1986) 'Childhood asthma: Two central questions for child psychiatry', *Journal of Child Psychology and Psychiatry*, 27, 1-5.

National Black Child Development Institute (NBCDI) (1993*) Parental Drug Abuse and African American Children in Foster Care: Issues and Findings,* Washington DC, NBCDI.

Noller, P. and Callan, V. (1991) *The Adolescent in the Family*, London, Routledge.

Norris, M. (1984) *Integration of Special Hospital Patients into the Community*, Aldershot, Gower.

Packman, J. and Hall, C. (1998) *From Care to Accommodation: the Implementation of Section 20 of the Children Act, 1989*, London, Stationery Office.

Packman, J., Randall, J. and Jacques, N. (1986) *Who Needs Care?*, Oxford, Blackwell.

Page, R. (1977) *Who Cares?*, London, National Children's Bureau.

Parker, R. (1966) *Decisions on Child Care*, London, Allen and Unwin.

Parker, R., (1980) *Caring for Separated Children*, London, National Children's Bureau.

Parker, R. (1988) 'Children' in Sinclair, I. (ed.*) Residential Care: The Research Reviewed*, London, NISW/HMSO, 57-124.

Parker, R. (1990) *Away from Home: A History of Child Care*, Barkingside, Barnardos.

Parker, R.., Ward, H., Jackson, S., Aldgate, J. and Wedge, P. (eds.) (1991) *Looking After Children: Assessing Outcomes in Child Care*, London, HMSO.

Pickup, M. (1987) *A Critical Study of a Research Study by A.M.F.Fleeman (1984)*, M.Ed. thesis, University of Exeter.

Pill, R. (1979) 'Status and career: a sociological approach to the study of child patients' in Hall, D. and Stacey, M. *Beyond Separation, Op.Cit.*

Pilling, S. (1991) *Rehabilitation and Community Care*, London, Routledge.

Pine, B., Warsh, R. and Maluccio, A. (eds.) (1993) *Together Again: Reunification in Foster Care*, Washington DC, Child Welfare League of America.

Pinkerton, J. (1991) *Home on Trial in Northern Ireland*, PhD. thesis, Queen's University, Belfast.

Quinton, D. and Rutter, M. (1976*) Young Children in Hospitals*, New York, Basic Books.

Quinton, D. and Rutter, M. (1988) *Parenting Breakdown: the Making and Breaking of Inter-generational Links*, Aldershot, Avebury.

Robertson, J. (1970) *Young Children in Hospital*, London, Tavistock.

Robinson, C. and Stalker, K. (1993) 'Patterns of provision in respite care', *British Journal of Social Work*, XXIII, 45-64.

Rossi, P. (1991) *Evaluating Family Preservation Programs*, New York, Edna McConnell Clark Foundation.

Rowe, J., Hundleby, M. and Garnett, L. (1989) *Child Care Now*, London, BAAF.

Rowe, J. and Lambert, L. (1973) *Children Who Wait*, Association of British Adoption Agencies.

Rutter, M. (1972) *Maternal Deprivation Reassessed*, Harmondsworth, Penguin.

Rutter, M. (1975) *Helping Troubled Children*, Harmondsworth, Penguin.

Rutter, M. (1981) 'Stress, coping and development: some issues and some questions' *Journal of Child Psychology and Psychiatry*, XXII, 323-56.

Rzepnicki, T. (1987) 'Recidivism of foster children returned to their own homes', *Social Services Review*, LXI, 56-70.

Shaw, R. (1987) *Children of Imprisoned Fathers*, London, Hodder and Stoughton.

Simard, M., Vachon, J. and Moisan, M. (1991) *La Réinsertion Familiale de l'Enfant Place: Facteurs de Succes et d'Echec*, University of Laval. Centre de Recherche sur les Services Communautaires.

Smeaton, G. (1869) *Memoir of Alexander Thomson*, London, Edmonton and Douglas.

Smith, M., Bee, P., Heverin, A. and Nobes, G. (1995*) Parental Control within the Family: the Nature and Extent of Parental Violence to Children*, London, Thomas Coram Research Unit.

Sneath, P. and Langham, C. (1989) 'Outlier: a basic program for detecting outlying members of multi-variate clusters based on presence-absence data', *Computers and Geosciences*, XV, 939-64.

Staff, I and Fein, E. (1994) 'Inside the black box: an exploration of service delivery in a family reunification program', *Child Welfare*, LXXIII, 195-211.

Stein, M. and Carey, K. *Leaving Care*, Oxford, Blackwell.

Steinberg, L., Catalano, R. and Dooley, D. (1981) 'Economic antecedents of child abuse and neglect', *Child Development*, LII, 975-85.

Sylva, K. and Stein, A. (1990) 'Effects oi hospitalisation on young children', *Newsletter of the Association for Child Psychology and Psychiatry*, XII, 3-9.

Tam, H. (1996) 'Factors influencing the prospect of children returning to their parents from out-of-home care', *Child Welfare*, LXXV, 253-68.

Tatara, T. (1989) 'Characteristics of children in foster care', *Newsletter of the American Psychological Association*, Division of Child, Youth and Family Services, XII, 16-17.

Thoburn, J. (1980) *Captive Clients*, London, Routledge and Kegan Paul.

Thoburn, J. (1990) *Success and Failure in Permanent Family Placement*, Aldershot, Gower.

Titmuss, R. (1976) *History of the Second World War*, London, HMSO.

Triseliotis, J. and Russell, J. (1984) *Hard to Place*, London, Heinemann.

Tunstall, J. (1962) *The Fishermen*, London, Routledge and Kegan Paul.

Turner, J. (1984) 'Reuniting children in foster care with their biological parents', *Social Work*, XXIX, 501-5.

Turner, J. (1993) 'Evaluating family reunification programs' in Pine, B. et al., *Together Again: family Reunification in Foster Care, Op.Cit.*, 179-98.

Triseliotis, J., Borland, M., Hill, M. and Lambert, L. (1996*) Teenagers and the Social Work Services*, London, HMSO.

Upton, G., Bundy, C. and Speed, B. (1986) 'Parent and family involvement in residential schools for the maladjusted', *Maladjustment and Therapeutic Education*, IV, 3-11.

Vernon, J. and Fruin, D. (1986) *In Care: A Study of Social Work Decision Making*, London, National Children's Bureau.

Wall, R. and Penhale, B. (1989) 'Relationships within households', *Population Trends*, LV, London, OPCS.

Walton, E., Fraser, M., Harlin, C. and Lewis, R. (1995) 'Intensive family reunification services: a conceptual framework and case example', *Family Preservation Journal*, I, 51-68.

Walton, E., Fraser, M., Lewis, R., Pecora, P. and Walton, W. (1993) 'In-home family-focused reunification: an experimental study', *Child Welfare*, 72, 473-87.

Ward, H. (1990) *The Charitable Relationship: Parents, Children and the Waifs and Strays Society*, Ph.D. thesis, University of Bristol.

Ward, H. (ed.) (1995) *Looking after Children: Research into Practice*, London, HMSO.

Warsh, R., Maluccio, A. and Pine, B. (1994) *Teaching Family Reunification: A Sourcebook*, Washington DC, Child Welfare League of America.

Warsh, R., Pine, B. and Maluccio, A. (1996) *Reconnecting Families: A Guide to Strengthening Family Reunification Services*, Washington DC, Child Welfare League of America.

Wattenberg, E. (1993) 'Children in the Minnesota child welfare system', *Community Alternatives*, V, 143-144.

Wedge, P. and Mantle, G. (1991) *Sibling Groups and Social Work*, Aldershot, Avebury.

Wendelken, C. (1981) *Children in and out of Care*, London, Heinemann.

Werbach, G. (1993) 'The family reunification role-play', *Child Welfare*, LXXII, 555-68.

West, D. and Farrington, D. (1977) *The Delinquent Way of Life*, London, Heinemann.

Whitaker, D., Archer, L. and Hicks, L. (1998) *Working in Children's Homes: Challenges and Complexities*, Chichester, Wiley.

Whitaker, D., Cook, J., Dunne, C. and Lunn-Rockliffe, S. (1986) *The Experience of Residential Care from the Perspectives of Children, Parents and Caregivers*, University of York.

Whyte, W. (1982) 'Interviewing in field research' in Burgess, R. (ed.) *Field Research: A Source Book and Field Manual*, London, Allen and Unwin.

Williams, P. (1991) *The Special Education Handbook*, Milton Keynes, Open University Press.

Willis, P. (1977) *Learning to Labour*, Farnborough, Saxon House.

Winnicott, D. (1984) *Deprivation and Delinquency*, London, Tavistock.

Woods, P. (1986) *Inside Schools: Ethnography in Education Research*, London, Routledge and Kegan Paul.

Woodward, J. (1978) *Has Your Child been in Hospital?*, London, NAWCH.

Wulczyn, F. (1991) 'Caseload dynamics and foster care re-entry', *Social Service Review*, 65, 133-56.

Young, M. and Willmott, P. (1973) *The Symmetrical Family*, London, Routledge, Kegan Paul.

Index

dartington social research series

This book is one of a series dealing with aspects of what is beginning to be known as a common language for the personal social services. The aims is to build up knowledge about different groups of children in need in a form that will be readily understood by policy makers, professionals, researchers and consumers and so make it possible to predict outcomes for such children and to design an effective agency response.

CHILDREN GOING HOME tests the results of an earlier study to predict which children looked after away from home return to live with relatives and which of them are reunited successfully. It demonstrates the strengths and weaknesses of broad-based prognoses with case studies of children who defy or conform to statistical predictions. As such, the book begins to set out the connections between evidence on what happens to large groups of children and clinical judgement about the experiences of an individual child.

The language of the personal social services is evolving. It is making use of the results from Dartington studies, of practical developments properly evaluated in a number of test sites and other findings from other groups working in the area. Comment from those making policy, managing services, working directly with children and families or receiving help from personal social service agencies is always welcome. There is a website describing the evolution of the common language at **www.dsru.co.uk** and a series of related papers is available from the Dartington Unit at Warren House, Warren Lane, Dartington, Totnes, Devon, TQ9 6EG email **unit@dsru.co.uk** and Fax +44-1803-866783.